VOICE AND JUDGMENT

The Practice of Public Politics

Robert J. Kingston

Voice and Judgment: The Practice of Public Politics is published by the Kettering Foundation Press. The interpretations and conclusions contained in this book represent the views of the author. They do not necessarily reflect the views of the Charles F. Kettering Foundation, its directors, or its officers.

This book is printed on acid-free paper.

First edition, 2012

Manufactured in the United States of America

ISBN: 978-0-923993-42-9

Library of Congress Control Number: 2012940499

"... after several decades of deliberation, some of us have come to suspect that at the core of our democracy may be less the right to vote than the opportunity to deliberate."

For

DAVID MATHEWS

and

DANIEL YANKELOVICH

without whose work, the importance
of public politics in a democracy
might not have been understood,
nor this book about it written.

CONTENTS

Introduction

AS READERS WHO ARE THEMSELVES familiar with public deliberation may know, the task of publicly talking through a national or community problem is not always easy. Nor has an answer (or an agreement) always been found—or universally shared! But what regularly does emerge, when a people deliberates, is a kind of shared understanding. At best, it is the sense of a shared public will. More important yet, such public deliberations, shot through with both reservations about and important recognition of the commonality of American experience, suggest something of what it may take to make democracy work as it should. And intriguingly, after several decades of deliberation, some of us have come to suspect that at the core of our democracy may be less the right to vote than the opportunity to deliberate.

This study of deliberation and its value is presented in six chapters, with each chapter growing from what preceded it. The first sets the stage or elaborates the purpose of what follows by describing the circumstances under which, and the intentions with which, two organizations in particular—Kettering Foundation in Dayton, Ohio, and Public Agenda in New York City—set out to learn more clearly how the public might find and exert its will in shaping its communities and directing its nation (which sometimes seems, paradoxically, more oligarchy than democracy).

Chapter 1 also introduces the vehicle then designed for this exploration of "public politics," the National Issues Forums.

Because it is sometimes easier to trace patterns of behavior—and in this case, of public thinking—by examining reactions to comparable exigencies over time, the second chapter focuses upon Americans' slowly developing sense of their role in the world, as revealed in public deliberations on that topic over the past quarter of a century. While focusing on what is often loosely referred to as foreign policy, the chapter explores half a dozen recognizably different historical moments—from the fear of nuclear annihilation in the early 1980s, through the Vietnam era, to the ending of the Soviet Union and the emergence of the Middle East as this country's more fearful horizon—each of which was encapsulated in a carefully framed discussion guide (variously also called by Kettering an "issue book" or an "issue guide") and explored nationwide by deliberative public groups. Some of these group discussions were recorded on camera and their outcomes reviewed by politicians, professionals, and the press, thereby providing for 16 years the substance of a popular, nationwide PBS television program, *A Public Voice*, on which we will often draw.

Then follow two chapters on public thinking, primarily responding, in distinctively different patterns, to three critical and controversial domestic issues that have challenged and still do challenge citizens' relations to each other and their degrees of trust in their elective government. Along with brief references to deliberations on several different issues, Chapter 3 focuses its attention primarily on the issues of "immigration" and "energy" (which is to say, what is called "the energy crisis," with its sometimes suggested implications for the economy, global warming, and international competition). Both issues remain continuing problems for the American public and its leadership, but the discussion of each reveals, in a compelling way, not merely the need for, but also the extraordinary promise of public deliberation as a means of moving tensely conflicting issues toward the kind of shared understanding from which viable public policy may grow—or to an increasingly shared understanding even of issues that, at points, have seemed to bare irreconcilable expectations! The fourth chapter, while similarly employing brief references to a range of public deliberations over the years, focuses upon the nation's health-care problems, which, after several earlier efforts, eventually became the core substance of forums in 2007 and 2008. The topic of health care in this chapter reveals with stark clarity the degree to which interests and convictions may contend irrevocably—perhaps unalterably—when democracy itself is understood as a contest between predetermined opinions wherein practiced interests are at stake. At question in modern America (and in Europe too, of course) is still whether democracy is the only ultimately acceptable response to public challenges. Public deliberation, so far, has not come to a way out of all such problems that it sees, in part because while we may share some common values, and even a few common experiences, our individual interests often remain different if not inherently at odds.

The fifth chapter therefore brings our analysis of public thinking to bear on communities themselves, as they wrestle with issues that occur nationally yet reveal their implications most clearly to those who share their destinies in a common culture and place, where they experience the implications of political decisions with some immediacy. The public school—its accomplishments, purpose, and destiny—has proved a most popular issue for discussion in communities around the nation over the past 30 years; more often than any other issue it has appealed to local groups eager to frame problems to which a community's attention needs to be addressed. That it remains an issue both popular and elusive is reason in itself for inclusion; more important, however, we begin to see in this context why the school, like the topics of other provocative and contested local issues, remains more often talked about than agreeably improved. Understandings in a community need often to be changed before opinions can be!

The public's deliberative process remains, ultimately, in itself a process of learning; and perhaps, ultimately, government itself is a hard process to learn. Thus, finally, a closing chapter looks at Americans' repeated deliberations about their own sense of their government's worth, or their reservations about it, and considers what continued deliberative judgments by the public—or at least the serious attempt to reach such judgments—might suggest for our future as a democracy. This is the central aim of the book: to show the role of public deliberation on the path toward the practice of democracy, and the challenge that faces a democratic people if it is truly bent upon self-government.

The phrase *public politics,* which this book has adopted in its title, is itself a commonly and variously used coinage of David Mathews. It suggests that the public, a community of citizens, has its own way of "doing politics." At its best, that way is deliberative: a way of weighing the likely outcomes of different courses of action, undertaken to cope collectively with shared community or national problems. "Come let us reason together!" This little volume is about citizens reasoning together, that they may live together more harmoniously and more productively, therefore.

I.

Amidst Values and Interests . . . Finding a Public Voice

AT AN INFORMAL LUNCHEON at the White House early in 1975, the late Walter Cronkite had been asked how we might, as a whole people, best celebrate the bicentennial, in the following year, of this nation's independence. The nation was still under the shadows of Watergate, and President Ford had already instructed that each federal agency develop for the occasion its own bicentennial project that might encourage citizens throughout the nation to appreciate and take pride in its work on their behalf.

For the military, as an example, this might have meant merely another, and larger, parade; and Americans who are now pushing middle age may recall the fire hydrants that suddenly turned red, white, and blue throughout the country in 1976. But as host of the nation's most popular nightly television news program (in the decades before electronics enabled us all to become each other's correspondents), Cronkite was already a virtual "immortal"; his quick response was that we should find a way to encourage the whole nation to reflect thoughtfully upon the now clichéd phrases about America that we tend to utter and take for granted on such patriotic occasions: "life, liberty, and the pursuit of happiness," for example; or "the business of America is business"; or "In God we trust."

For the young and tiny federal agency known as the National Endowment for the Humanities, which had no bands to march to and no uniform to wear, nor hydrants to paint—and of which the present writer was Deputy Chairman at the time—Cronkite's idea (not to mention his presence) was manna from heaven. The National Endowment had been established, after all, to help people—not just in schools and universities but in their communities, as citizens—come to grips with and understand the implications of the history and values that shape our life and culture as Americans. So with Cronkite himself as chair of an hastily put together advisory committee, we began to develop a little national bicentennial program whereby, in town and village, big or small, and in church, library, and college throughout the land, citizens each month might meet to discuss the implications of a different, thoroughly American topic or "motto" throughout the bicentennial year.

It was not argued that we should expect citizens to be "better" for the experience; nor did we anticipate that such community conversations would continue subsequently (even though "humanities councils" were already being developed in every state to facilitate public deliberation about local community problems). We nonetheless took some pride in our institutional contribution to the nation's bicentennial consciousness, and we were quietly gratified when for a few years thereafter, what was then known as the American Association for Community and Junior

Colleges subsequently adopted the monthly discussion as an ancillary public program in community colleges nationwide.

Called "The American Issues Forums," this oddly "occasional" program, however, was not insistently associated with politics, and it was relatively short-lived, in fact. Yet, the value of public deliberation about what is important to us as a people, and of its practice in democratic societies, has become increasingly recognized—and to a degree, formalized—over the past quarter-century. We were still in the 1970s when Daniel Yankelovich—the "dean," as it were, of public opinion analysts and president of the small research organization in New York called Public Agenda—began to suggest deliberation (although he may not often have used the term) as a means by which people might "work through" the troubling contradictions that their responses to public opinion polls appeared inevitably to suggest. Toward the end of the 1980s, James Fishkin (at that time at the University of Texas, later at Stanford, as director of its Center for Deliberative Democracy) began to orchestrate what he dubbed "National Issues Conventions" in nations around the world: weekend-long gatherings of large, representative, random samples of a given nation's citizens, to offer—following deliberative discussions among themselves and intermittent interrogation of political and professional authorities—their settled sense of what national policy might best be fashioned with respect to an immediately critical national issue. In the 1990s here in the United States, with unflagging energy and commitment, Carolyn Lukensmeyer created America*Speaks*, which has enabled us routinely to hear the deliberative outcomes of what a large mass of interested and articulate citizens have thought about a good many issues that have affected us all.

This present study, however, is not intended as a comprehensive report on American public opinion or even public deliberation over the past 30 years; nor on the public's responses to the policies of its political leaders or to the grand or awkward moments of its history. It is, rather, an exploration of some of the patterns of public thinking about a dozen or so of the most critical, and sometimes controversial, challenges that we have faced, as a people, in our journey from the midst of the Cold War, early in the 1980s, to the still-bewildering 21st-century era of new crises in the Middle East; inadequate and unaffordable health care; and the fears of energy shortages and global warming. The subject of our study is not the substance of such problems, per se, but rather of the way in which small, deliberative groups of American citizens, gathered informally in institutions like colleges, libraries, churches, service clubs, community centers—and even hospitals and jails—have together talked their way through such problems until they have found a kind of agreement on what they think should be done about them.

In the 1980s, when Daniel Yankelovich was first drafting, for presentation at Syracuse University, the series of lectures that would ultimately comprise his book called *Coming to Public Judgment,* some of us at Public Agenda were lucky enough to be, bit by bit, as it were, a trial audience for the thoughts he was shaping. His brilliant analytical mind and cool passion for politics and policy were always inspiriting, perhaps particularly because all of us in our different ways, shared very similar political persuasions. What most struck some of us who were privileged to work with him, however, was that despite his astute perceptions of the failings of parties, governments, *and* the public, he clearly did not doubt that a particular kind of progressive logic marked the way we humans think about and respond to our collective plight. His approach revealed the patterns of human responses to particular predicaments, as well as an extraordinary sophistication and skill in both citizens' and their government's not-infrequent evasions of their responsibilities. Still, the outcome of his analysis invariably pointed to the possibility of improvement in our practice of democracy.

A sense of the possibility of a "public will," even of its inevitability, is always what the work of Yankelovich has ultimately offered. His analyses persistently seem to be part of a search for truth and a means for hope and an invitation to work at the process of self-government. It seems that however sharply he could show the failings of particular parties and particular interests, he never for a moment doubted that the wisdom of a public judgment could ultimately rule.

As this kind of understanding became more widely shared among us at Public Agenda, Kettering Foundation, and with an increasing number of other practitioners, enthusiasm grew and evidence mounted for the prospects of what came to be referred to as "public deliberation." We knew the work was eminently worthwhile, if difficult, and purposeful, although often disappointing, because it was based upon both an understanding of the extraordinary human capacity for "working through" difficulties and disappointments *and* an awareness of the outcomes of all-too-often neglectful and self-indulgent passions. In our very earliest days of this kind of work, the research analyst John Doble (at Public Agenda), was engaged with a distinguished Harvard physicist, Gerald Holten, in a study of the ways in which a public comes to share and sustain what had seemed to be some of the professional values that nuclear scientists, at their best, retain in their work. It was a small study, done at a time when concern about nuclear arms in the Cold War was at its height. It was not a study that necessarily breached or reclaimed one's confidence in the current practices of governments, or experts, or the people; it was, however, genuinely encouraging in its revelation of the ways in which, through careful and informed *collective* thinking, "ordinary people" could arrive at and stand firmly on particular principles as a basis for action, even in a context as remote from popular understanding as the implications of nuclear weaponry. It was this kind of revelation—by now reinforced year after year, issue after issue, through outcomes of the National Issues Forums—that, some of us are convinced, helped the kind of deliberative work we had begun to undertake on the public side of politics, 30 years ago, to grow into what is sometimes now referred to as a "movement."

Setting aside the unusually robust civic demonstrations of the Vietnam period—the marches on Washington, the hundreds of citizens temporarily incarcerated in the DC stadium, Kent State, even—it seems, nevertheless, that the American public has for a long time been somewhat skeptical about government, even its own government. Even in the relatively mild, brief years of the Ford administration in the 1970s, David Mathews reports that, as head of the federal government's largest agency, the then Department of Health, Education, and Welfare, he had become more and more concerned about the obvious differences between what government set out to do and what citizens seemed to think important or useful. When he resumed his presidency at the University of Alabama in 1977, that preoccupation led him to invite other educators to join him in considering ways in which this apparent weakness in the functioning of our democracy might be addressed. A few years later, having recently become president of the Kettering Foundation, he sought and encouraged other foundation executives to turn their interest, too, toward this concern. Their response was initially not helpful: then, as perhaps even now, many foundations tended to think of their constituencies as institutions rather than as individual citizens; only Deborah Wadsworth, then at the Markle Foundation, had words of encouragement for him. "You should talk with Dan Yankelovich," she said.

It was then 1981. At the Kettering Foundation, Mathews had already gathered a small group of individuals from academic institutions and not-for-profit organizations, intent upon forming what (for want of a better term) they dubbed a "domestic policy association" that would organize public discussions on contemporary issues, within communities around the country. For his part, Yankelovich, along with former Secretary of State Cyrus Vance, had established the Public Agenda Foundation (now quite simply, Public Agenda), where a small group of young professionals had signed on to explore and analyze the ways in which the public approaches—or resists approaching—critical current issues on the political agenda. So, when Yankelovich, Mathews, and a few colleagues gathered one morning in the fall of 1981 in the Markle Foundation's conference room in New York City, both a concept and an institution were engendered. The meeting of these two institutions at the Markle Foundation ended with the understanding that, while Public Agenda would seek to frame and present a few critical issues each year in terms that a broad public could readily understand and respond to, Kettering would encourage nongovernmental, academic, and community groups to engage citizens in such discussion throughout the country, and would find ways of communicating their outcomes—essentially to media and the political leadership, who are professionals thought to be charged with pursuing the public good.

Yankelovich was, of course, profoundly respected among survey analysts, and much of his conversation at that time revealed his concern about apparent contradictions in individual responses to serious problems in the polity, as recorded in public opinion polls. Simple questions invite simple answers, but to complex *topics*, people react in complex ways. Particular questions in a survey instrument reflect different aspects of a topic; the response that each secures may be honest, yet nevertheless seem incompatible with responses given earlier and later to other questions on the same topic.

To address what he called this "mushiness" in public opinion with respect to policy matters (which are "official" framings of problems very much at issue among the public generally), Yankelovich argued that people need to be presented with just a few—perhaps three or four—recognizable alternative approaches, explained in straightforward and accessible fashion, shunning the technical or prejudicial coloring that often appears when such matters are presented either by expert professionals, political leaders, or members of the press. A modicum of significant information, in similarly accessible fashion, with an acknowledgement of the drawbacks that arguably might attend each different approach for citizens under different circumstances, would also be necessary, in effect providing a simple public equivalent of the "decision memo" characteristically prepared for presidents and senior government officials faced with actually determining policy. Borrowing terminology from his professional training in psychology, Yankelovich anticipated that people, talking together when such choices had been presented, are better able than they would be individually to work through their attitudes toward a given public dilemma—just as, differences notwithstanding, people, over time, work through their natural bouts of despair, loss, blame, guilt, denial, and so on, in what is called the "grief reaction" that all of us must occasionally cope with in situations of extreme personal distress.

So each of the first three issue guides that Public Agenda prepared in 1982—for use (as it turned out) in about 150 communities across the country, in what would eventually become known as National Issues Forums (or, soon, NIF)—presented 3 or 4 different, if not mutually exclusive, proposals for handling an issue that was high on the nation's agenda. The implied presumption was that after the assembled participants in a local forum had talked together about the competing approaches presented to the issue, along with the drawbacks or "trade-offs" that each respectively would entail, they would make an informed decision about which approach, or aspects of approaches, they were ready to follow. Anonymity among the participants—as typically observed by pollsters—was certainly not anticipated; nor was it assumed that the participants would in any scientific sense qualify as technically a random sample. But all of us who were engaged in the experiment at that time anticipated that what would emerge from the forums as a whole would be an acceptable indicator of a potential public judgment about what *should* be done; and that it would be sufficiently well thought out—and sufficiently in command of a general public understanding—to be presented as a viable indication of a course of action that the nation might confidently follow.

This process in the forums, at that time, was dubbed "choicework," a typically straightforward and communicable Yankelovich term. The term *deliberation* was not at first used to describe the nature of the anticipated dialogue, nor was the concept of "judgment" articulated (although it may have been implicit). An underlying sense, however, at least at the Kettering Foundation and Public Agenda, was that this forum process would provide, for a research organization, a better handle on where the public was in relation to a given issue than did the over-worked and too often abused public opinion poll; and that "leadership," advised by the "policy option" that a deliberative public had made its own choice, would presumably chart a politically and popularly viable course of action. Clearly, what we had in mind was the production of a documented insight into public concerns that would be helpful, even perhaps persuasive, when it was narrated to those in authority, leaders who had the power of decision and the authority to command action.

A constant tension—if not an historic dilemma—was inherent in this work. For although Yankelovich was clearly as valued an advisor on public matters in the political sphere as he was to executives in the commercial world, in contemporary *political* life, what a public believes *should* be done must further be weighed against what particular specialized but influential interests demand, at least for the short term. Thus, Kettering's classical ideal of a *sovereign* public may not be reflected in the majority vote of a given electoral district at any one time, granted the specialized interests there that may prevail. While groups of citizen participants profit from each other's different experiences, their collective range of understanding may still be limited; the driving force of other powerful interests, institutions, and organizations—who are not voting citizens, yet remain critical to the nation's good—may not come through clearly, even in the pages of careful and impartial issue guides prepared for the NIF discussants. The concept of a sovereign public judgment would thus need careful elaboration and qualification—and a good many tests of experience—if it were ultimately to become a powerful factor in the contemporary democratic state. Developing the concept of a public coming to judgment was a challenge Yankelovich took on himself over the ensuing decade, and the practice of annual, nationwide, deliberative National Issues Forums, engineered by the Kettering Foundation, has, for more than a quarter of a century now, been a means for illustrating and testing the value of that concept.

Meanwhile, in the spring and fall of 1981, about two dozen community leaders had gathered at two conferences that the Kettering Foundation had sponsored at the Wingspread Conference Center in Racine, Wisconsin. In all, at the close of the second meeting that fall, just 17 of them agreed that they would hold community forums, if Kettering would provide appropriate promotion, discussion guides, and the promise of some feedback both to themselves and to the nation's policy leadership.

Eventually, in fact, in the late summer and fall of 1982, an estimated few thousand people, tackling the first three issue books, participated in forums sponsored by groups around the country. Then, in February 1983, the leading participants assembled at the Gerald R. Ford Presidential Library in Ann Arbor, Michigan, to consider collectively what had been accomplished. Former presidents Gerald Ford and Jimmy Carter presided over the event; David Mathews and Daniel Yankelovich acted as masters of ceremony; and a distinguished group of experts, government officials, and political leaders (including 6 former cabinet officers and 6 White House advisors from 5 administrations) joined some 60 citizens, representing 145 community forums, scattered across the country. As an event, if not also the launching of "a movement," the enterprise had obviously started successfully.

In the ensuing four years, 1984 to 1987, comparable annual "end of season" events were hosted by the Johnson Presidential Library, the Kennedy Presidential Library, and the Carter Presidential Library, and then again, by the Ford Library. As if that were not enough evidence of "national" activity, during each of the years 1983 through 1987, a week-long, early summer assemblage of National Issues Forums participants from around the country gathered in Washington, DC, where the week's events included visits to Congress and the White House for citizens' presentation of the outcomes of the season's public deliberation. Informally, throughout these three-day events, individual participants as well as professionals from Kettering and Public Agenda exchanged their individual experiences and expectations of this (to most of them novel) practice of "politics in public." Each time, too, as the conclusion of this "Washington Week," Public Agenda was able to present a preview of the issues and issue guides that were being prepared for the anticipated next set of forums, in the coming fall. To the degree that one of the original concerns of this forum enterprise had been to give the public the sense that, if it worked seriously on an issue and had something to say that mattered, it would be heard by "the powers that be" in Washington, DC—that goal seemed to have been shown accessible. But of course, there's a lot of talk in Washington. And not all of it is heard.

The Public and Public Policy

The first three issues that Kettering and Public Agenda had chosen for their groups to consider—jobs, the federal budget, and Social Security—were, all of them, what the press and Congress had adopted at the time as "hot button" issues. Yet with the advantage of a quarter-century of hindsight, now it may seem that in those early years of nation-wide community deliberations, the National Issues Forums were much more successful as a *movement* than they were as a means of conveying, to elected officials and the media, an understanding of public judgment on the topics at issue. Or, to put it another way, what *was* of value for the *polis* in these public deliberations was not necessarily influential among, or valued by, the *political leadership*, formally charged with coming to grips with the issues being discussed. This very lack of connection was precisely what had begun to trouble David Mathews back in the 1970s, as the concept of public deliberation was beginning to take shape.

In part, this lack of leadership interest may be because outcomes of the forums were invariably reported as though they represented the considered judgment of an influential interest—namely the public itself. Although undoubtedly the forums, from the start, presented a "public" just slightly better educated and probably slightly more "middle class" than the norm, their intent was actually to suggest the ways of thinking that are current among that least considered part of the *polis* in the American democracy, the "ordinary folk" who have, or consider themselves typically to have, little influence in the corridors of power. The premise of public deliberation is indeed that people, talking to each other in tolerably patient, varied, and coherently led groups, can begin to work through in their conversation the trade-offs that virtually any response to a shared problem may demand of them; their accepted response as a group could therefore be a profoundly useful guide to policy in a democracy. Yet ill-thought-through responses to questionnaires or polls may in fact be a safer guide to public whim and its relationship to imminent votes or political decisions; and powerful interests with seemingly unlimited funds for sympathetic candidates may be more influential than the uncertain wisdom of individual citizens unaware of such interests or the importance of such stakes. Ironically, the challenge that forums sought to address—and that Yankelovich was to take on very seriously in his exploration of how a public comes to judgment—was to capture a carefully articulated "voice of the voiceless" on problems that affect them variously as individuals but are seldom presented to them in a terminology or with a rationale that the inexpert and unprofessional can readily understand. That the expert and professional may not expect to hear this voice, or may not understand it when they do hear it, or may think it to have a relatively low claim on their attention—such outcomes have become, ironically, more and more challenging in the ensuing years.

They are the substance of this book because they continue so—for the Kettering Foundation and Public Agenda, and among a steadily increasing number of organizations and individuals who do find the analysis of this *public* political process professionally rewarding and democratically worthwhile. The publicly accepted purpose of this public movement was to engage citizens in considering what should be done in the context of given nationwide problems, to which government, with the support of its panels of experts, and attended by representatives of particularly relevant interests, had already turned its attention. The citizen dialogues would inevitably be about policy in that broad sense, although all of the organizers and participants were intent that the conversation not be about ideological or party differences, nor be presented in terms of given or proposed legislative programs. The intent was, from the outset, to discover the degree to which people's values—recognizable, common, human values—come into play as citizens make their own judgments about the threats and promises of situations of concern as different citizens differently experience them in their communities. The issue under discussion, in this sense, had to be generally recognized and accepted, even though different individuals would almost certainly have different interests in various proposed ways of dealing with it. Thus, for example, in international matters—and these were the days of the Cold War—the issue would never be whether "communists," or "the Russians," were right or wrong, but about the relative wisdom of different ways of preserving some things we valued, albeit sometimes at the expense of others: peace, perhaps; or security from nuclear mishap, despite another power's adherence to oppressive rule and threats of force. Or concerning Social Security, or the problem of caring for elderly people no longer able to command solid wages and without adequate accumulation of personal funds, the issue would not be about whether to ignore their quandary, but about different ways of ameliorating the impact of this predicament within the nation's communities in coming decades.

In the long run, it seemed that the deliberative approach might produce an outcome as "readable" as the public opinion poll, yet more closely reflecting broadly shared public understandings than the particular ideologies or interests that are otherwise typically circulated and elaborated both by political leadership and the press, sometimes giving voice to what may be valid but somewhat "special" interests. Most important, having shared their concerns with fellow citizens who find themselves in different circumstances, participants from these public forums would have inevitably worked through (at least to a degree) the trade-offs, disadvantages, and accommodations that any chosen outcome would have to acknowledge. The deliberative public forum, in effect, may yield not so much a *decision* on public policy but a *judgment*—or even merely a way of approaching judgment—about actions that may appropriately serve the needs of their communities. Despite some shared traditions and a conviction about the virtually sacred value of individual opportunity, US citizens seem to acknowledge that, for a democracy, the *public interest* must ultimately rule, not a majority vote: the vote is a mechanism, valid as a means to verify the public interest, rather than to secure the interest that is private. Public deliberation, then, is a burden accepted by citizens who share values that provide a means of coming to judgment about interests that are *not* shared.

When the outcomes of the first year's discussions were reviewed at the Ford library in February 1983, both Presidents Ford and Carter were warm in their applause of what the citizens had done. President Ford welcomed the guests, both the unnamed and the distinguished, with this observation:

> The proliferation of government and our well-intentioned, but often misguided, attempts to make it more responsive have led to a widespread feeling of helplessness. Many citizens do not know who is really in charge. . . . They have given up on the electoral system.
>
> The responsibility we all face is how to restore that feeling that each one of us can and does make a difference. That is why the

> Domestic Policy Association, whose first report to policymakers we are inaugurating today, is so important. The Domestic Policy Association can provide the mechanism to broaden public knowledge of issues affecting our national well-being. It can bring the public's badly needed common wisdom to bear on pressing national issues. It can help those who must make policy see—with far greater insight than that provided by standard public opinion polls—how people really feel about issues, and where they are willing to modify their own parochial positions for the greater good.
>
> In discussing issues we often forget that policy, which is so often discussed in abstract terms, is really about what happens to people.

Yet in fact the outcomes of these wonderful public discussions yielded no new suggestions about policy; nor did they reveal freshly particular deficiencies in the various approaches to policy that were being currently voiced in official Washington. Nor were they meant to. What they did, however, was provide a dense portrait of the world for which those policies, under legislators' discussion, were intended.

Writing at the time of the Ford Library meeting, Keith Melville—who was in fact the creator of most of the discussion guides used in the first decade of the NIF—noted that

> Most of the associations that are formed to influence the political process are devoted to a specific ideology, a special constituency, a single goal. Yet a working democracy assumes that public decisions are made in a system where a majority of concerned but disinterested citizens will oppose policies which favor special interests. . . .
>
> What is conspicuously lacking today is some way of accomplishing what used to happen in the New England town meetings. Those meetings offered something different from the contending views of special interests that one hears in today's public policy debates. They were an occasion for seeking the

> common ground—and a reminder that each citizen's future is inseparable from that of the community and the nation.

But of course, common ground for the feeding of a few families' sheep in a tiny, colonial 18th-century, New England village is a long way from the agreement needed when the problem is to find a common ground for action, nationally, on preparing a workforce for the 21st century, during a recession in the 1980s; or managing inflation; or continuing some modest allowance to older citizens, no longer employable, while worrying about the national debt and the high-tech workforce needed for a newly technological world. Yet these were the issues taken up in 1982 by this first season of forums, one by one. A wise citizen, working with Spanish speakers in the Archdiocese of Los Angeles, perhaps came closest to the real import of this first season's forums:

> We welcome the National Issues Forums because it provides an opportunity for people to have an input into the issues that affect their lives. Most of the time—and this is true not just of Hispanics—the issues are defined *for* us. Decisions come from the top down. We have no input, and often little comprehension of what is being said. This forum gives us an opportunity to express our deep interest in national issues, to sit down together and have a communal sharing of ideas and interests.

In his assessment of the Ford Library meeting, Keith Melville made much the same point—that the NIF gave citizens an opportunity to sit down with their leaders.

> Today, at a time when most pressing issues are national issues, it is not often possible for citizens to sit down with their leaders. The National Issues Forums provides a way of doing that.

And so, at the Ford Library, momentarily, for some 60 of them, it did, quite literally.

Hasty Judgments and an Emerging Voice

Yet no one would claim that participants had "come to a judgment" on the three issues they had discussed. The issues in that first year have since proven to be among the more consistently difficult for the public to handle deliberatively over the subsequent quarter-century, and those looking to these early deliberations for policy insight on jobs, the federal budget, and Social Security found little to record.

At a forum on inflation, for example, a local reporter in Cincinnati is quoted:

> We're always demanding increased benefits, or cost-of-living adjustments that make it even harder to keep prices from spiraling upward. Or we support a candidate who proposes to reduce taxes without reducing spending. If we're homeowners, we rise up in arms when Congress talks about changing the tax deductions for mortgage interest payments. We're all to blame—and we're all victims.

As another woman observes, "there seem to be more problems than solutions here"—echoing, as Melville points out in his assessment, "a sentiment that policymakers have so often felt when confronted with the question of what to do about inflation." Much of the time, what emerges from the community discussions about inflation, he says, is

> deep resentment about excessive salaries paid to corporate managers, and anger about the tight money and high interest rate policies which have elsewhere been defended as the most effective anti-inflationary tools.

But rather than concluding, as Alexis de Tocqueville did in the 19th century, that people are bound to make hasty judgments, Melville insists that "we are obliged to ask whether—through efforts such as the National Issues Forums—people can make more thoughtful, reasoned choices." This pilot year was by no means an instant unmitigated success, he acknowledges, but "however well-conceived and thoughtful these community discussions might be, the forum process shouldn't begin and end in these local meetings."

Certainly, it would have been unrealistic to expect that these community discussions would resolve into a clear consensus about what course of action is in the nation's best interest. They were intended neither as referendums nor as meetings that would reveal sentiments that are typical or representative. Indeed, no clear consensus emerged from most of these meetings. But the forums *did* provide an occasion for thoughtful discussion about what would be best not only for us as individuals but—in a larger sense—for us as a nation.

In truth, what they give us—even now, reading the pages at this almost 30-year removed—is the beginning sense of a public voice. There is the man from Oklahoma, for example, who says:

> We've come through a period—the post-war period—when many people prospered, when they expected that things would get better year after year. But I think that a lot of people here in Oklahoma know that that's changed, and we're willing to make some adjustments. The question is what we need to do now. That's why I wanted to be here, to be part of the forums, to be part of the solution. Why we need leadership so badly today.

And a man from Cincinnati:

> What's critical in these forums, is that they have to be something more than a cry of pain. A lot of people I see are frightened about the prospect of being unemployed. There seems to be, as there is in families that have just lost a loved one, a spiral of hopelessness. And *that's* what's so destructive, the sense of hopelessness. We've got to do something more than just weep about the loss. In grief work, the essential thing is to help the person move back toward reality. That's what we have to do, as a nation.

When that kind of voice is heard, an individual speaking as a member of the larger community and calling for a common effort to help each other, there is surely a possibility of judgment—given evidence, deliberation, and a collective voice. But coming to judgment, in Yankelovich's terms, takes time. Writing of this first post-seasonal meeting of the National Issues Forums, Yankelovich himself had this to say:

> People need time to work through their decisions—particularly if all of the apparent solutions are likely to be painful. Psychologists recognize that people go through a cycle of human reactions between the time they are confronted with a problem and when they eventually make a choice. In the decision period, anyone faced with an unpleasant set of choices regarding their personal life is likely to experience disbelief, anger, frustration, or even despair. This syndrome is sometimes called a "grief reaction." Similarly, when people are faced with difficult choices in public matters, they can be expected to resist and struggle against having to reach a conclusion—until they realize that a choice must be made and carefully worked through. Coming to this realization and achieving consensus based on thorough information and responsible thought requires time. A single speech from a leader, a single piece of literature, a single town meeting—no matter how thoughtful or carefully planned—will not do.
>
> We're talking here about difficult matters, processes that are far from easy. But these are difficult times, beset with problems that offer no easy answers.

A few years later, in his lecture series that would be the basis of his book, *Coming to Public Judgment*, it is not surprising to find Yankelovich focusing on an exposition of a "working through" process that he sees as very much a product of time. The kinds of questions that demand citizens' most careful deliberation before "coming to judgment" will not have arisen suddenly; nor will they quickly disappear; for they are not likely to be susceptible of simple solutions. Deliberation about them is an exploration of our collective life and requires adjustments in that life to be made collectively—a task that is accomplished only in time, "time that takes account of all the world."

In *Coming to Public Judgment,* the major illustrations of the process through which a public comes to judgment are associated with extraordinarily complicated and long-standing troubles in our collective life as an American people. Yankelovich makes reference to the long and painful progress of America's race problem, which has continued to change slowly, even after the civil rights legislation of half a century ago; and he refers to the restrained pace and consistent controversies that have inhibited the United States in attending adequately to the health of all of its citizens.

Thus, while Public Agenda and the Kettering Foundation and the thousands of citizens who have participated year by year in National Issues Forums have insisted on the importance of political leadership getting to hear something of the outcomes of their occasional deliberations, there has been nonetheless a recognition that these deliberative public forums are not necessarily in themselves decision-making occasions; nor are they attitudinal revelations to be simply recorded for the purposes of persuasion and propaganda, as often are public opinion polls. Rather, public deliberations are themselves the actual *means* of working through difficult issues. Their value is not that they can tell the political leadership *what* to do but rather that they indicate our will, our best thinking about the problem that besets us, *as a people.* This does not mean that they are politically useless; it does mean—and this is their value—that they can be read, consistently, over time, for the significance that they hold as we continue to wrestle with what are sometimes referred to as "wicked" problems. That is to say, deliberative forums are instruments as critical to democratic decision making—if not as immediately decisive—as the ultimate decisions of legislators and executives. For the problem we face as a *polis* is always multi-faceted; it challenges different values that we, as people, variously hold; and it is dependent, too, on circumstances and values and judgments that are not always within our control, *as a people.*

"Working through" toward satisfying responses may sometimes last as long as the problems themselves. In the case of wicked problems that may be almost inevitable, by definition; for they are problems to be lived with, seeking adjustment. As the poet A. E. Houseman observed:

> The problems of our proud and angry dust
> Are from eternity, and will not fail!

II.

Searching for Balance . . . America's Role in the World

ALL OF US, I SUSPECT, while we were still young children, encountered some history-making event that we knew was to change the comfort of our little world. We did not surely understand it, nor even really "know" what it was; but we knew that it "happened," that it "meant" something, and that someday, therefore, we should have to cope with it. To the now elders among American citizens, such an "event" may have been Pearl Harbor or the atomic bomb on Hiroshima; to a very few, even Poland, or Neville Chamberlain getting off a plane from Munich, a piece of paper (signed by Adolf Hitler) fluttering in his hand declaring, more wrongly than he could imagine, "Peace in our time!" Or for a somewhat younger generation, it will have been 9/11—and new enemies, new friends.

The long and continuing sequence of National Issues Forums—which (as this is being written) have addressed something near 100 issues, nationwide, over the past 30 years—provides now a valuable indication of the progress of public thinking, and the continuities in it, over time, otherwise unavailable, the likelihood of which was perhaps not fully apprehended during the earliest years of the NIF experiment. America's sense of its place in the world is one such continuing theme.

In the 1980s, the country passed through the depths of the Cold War, which, in effect, culminated with the dissolution of the Soviet Union. Well, this was perhaps not the precise "depth" of the Cold War, granted Sputnik, the space race, and the Cuban Missile Crisis; but the period was certainly filled with deeply troubled and passionate concern about the relative nuclear strengths of the two superpower rivals. Three times in that decade the NIF forums took on a consideration of the US-Soviet relationship. Then again, immediately following the end of the Soviet era in 1989, they turned to consideration of America's role in the world. And in the fall and winter of 2002-2003, within weeks of the US attack on Iraq, citizens were again discussing "Americans' Role in the World" in their National Issues Forums.

History does play out on a large stage, where we all can see it and respond. So when listening for a public voice, it is convenient (and it may be helpful, since we have a quarter of a century's records on hand) to begin here, with the way in which Americans have looked at their place in the world. The way we see *others* tells us more about ourselves than about *them*, often as not; so it may be useful to start with Americans' sense of the world, before moving to the delights and dilemmas of our day-by-day domestic life as a people. That way, at least, if historic foreign affairs grow too tedious, the reader may skip at leisure to the continuing satisfactions and distresses of our domestic scene, which will occupy our later chapters.

Questions of international relations and foreign policy present a particular challenge to citizens of democracies, especially if they see themselves as a nation of immigrants. For most of the past century, fortunate Americans thought of themselves as somewhat better off than the rest of the world, and perhaps envied by it! When wars have had to be fought, they have been fought in places other than the United States itself and caused less of its citizenry to be directly involved in fighting. And the outcomes of the Second World War and the Cold War seemed to place the United States in a position where it could provide extraordinary assistance to the rest of the world, while fearing virtually nothing from it. At least, so some leaders and many citizens liked to presume, while others seemed sometimes to prefer to pursue a policy of strength through fear.

Among politicians and pundits, the wise and the not so wise, and quite a few scholars, the common wisdom seems to be that since 9/11, "everything has changed." At least, our relationships (or lack of relationships) with other peoples have changed! After 20th-century wars with Germany, Japan, Korea, Vietnam, Iraq—not to mention the quick or drawn out but relatively minor events in Grenada, Panama, Nicaragua, Haiti, Bosnia, Lebanon, the Sudan, and so on—we have moved to 21st-century wars of a different style and in different neighborhoods. After almost half a century of "cold" war, and "wars" on poverty and crime-and drugs, we have moved to a "war on terror." If we take these all to be genuine states of war, then we have been at war for more of the past hundred years than we have been at peace. But Americans have always been addicted to the metaphor of warfare; ideological divergences that Europeans take as the very stuff of democratic politics are, in America, argued as moral commitments with divisive implications for both social ethics and patriotism. So change attributed to 9/11 may turn out to be less than meets the eye.

Yet the record of deliberations among the American public, over the past 20-some years, about their nation's place in relation to other peoples of the world is, if sometimes sketchy, nonetheless surprisingly persistent. Some patterns of thinking have emerged from those deliberations about the ways other peoples govern themselves, ply their trades, develop (or fail to develop) their societies, and deploy what might be forces of destruction against what they think to be hostile or threatening powers. Indeed, as we shall see, some public judgments have been made.

An absolute or world-without-end judgment about America's role in the world is of course unlikely. Political leaders tend to articulate policies to which they are already (often for very good reason and sometimes for bad) committed; media tend to reflect the rhetoric and personality of those same leaders, their critics, and their advisors; and pollsters analyze only aggregated responses to carefully worded questions designed, more often than not, to reveal respondents' reactions to those same policies, as articulated and reported. The concerns expressed by citizens, however, as they have talked together and shared experiences together of the impact or anticipated possible impacts of international events upon their own lives, and on the interests and aspects of life that they value most dearly, are revealing.

Now, the records of a deliberative public available to us begin in the 1980s. For the 1950s, 1960s, and 1970s, we do not have such deliberative records. We cannot therefore formally compare attitudes of deliberative Americans toward Iraq or Iran today with those of citizens during the oil crisis of the 1970s; nor compare divisions about this nation's presence in Iraq with divisions in the 1960s and 1970s about our presence in Vietnam. We cannot compare people's feelings about the hostages in Iran, 25 years ago, with comments about hostages taken by insurgent groups in Afghanistan today. Americans over 50 may recall the OPEC (Arab) oil embargo of the 1970s as a trade threat, different of its nature from one associated with religious fundamentalism and military force. We may genuinely remember students killed on an American campus by American military, or tear gas in the streets of our nation's capital, and thousands "imprisoned" at a stadium in that same city—yet think that the nation was less clearly divided then than it has been, in this 21st century, between the "red" and the "blue." And we may or may not think it reasonable that no heads rolled, nor was impeachment called for, over the "Irangate" conspiracy. These are merely remembered crises, about which "public opinion" is on record, but there are no reports of public thinking. Perhaps it is only nostalgia that talks to us about such remembered events. Or perhaps it is just, as Yankelovich has argued, that judgments, by the public, take shape only over time. To trace possible continuity in events of the past and traits of today's public thinking is a challenging task.

Fortunately, however, since the fall of 1982, the National Issues Forums, convened in American communities by local institutions, have deliberated on issues both of national policy and community practice. Although these groups operate nationwide, they don't constitute an association or even a formal network; and they are not the kinds of random samples from which social and political analyses—let alone national policies—are generally persuasively to be made. Yet they do tend to be representative of American popular life. And the records of these deliberative discussions we have, from various forums. Through more than 20 years, now, the convenors of such forums, with the help of the Kettering Foundation, have invited reputable analysts to visit and formally report the outcomes from such forums; further, some of these forums have been recorded on videotape each year and presented at the National Press Club, where members of Congress and the Washington Press Corp have "responded," as it were, to what the citizens are saying. (The videotapes *and* the responses have then been broadcast as an annual public television program called *A Public Voice.*) From resources such as these, we can venture some retrospective observations about patterns and changes, *over the past 20-some years,* in what seem to have been compelling concerns (or aspects of interest) in the reactions of American citizens to the impacts of international accidents and policies upon their sense of America's place in the world. We may report, at least, about reports.

The Illusory Flight of Hawk and Dove

The Cuban Missile Crisis in 1962 was perhaps among those events that, from time to time, change the way Americans look at the world. It was by no means the *start* of the Cold War. That had begun when the victorious allies drew a line across Europe at the end of the Second World War. And cold "battle" had been first joined, so to speak, with the actual Soviet blockade of Berlin in the late 1940s. In the intervening years, the Soviets had developed nuclear arms, brought down the U-2 spy plane, and got into space before us; and Mr. Khrushchev had rapped the heel of his shoe on the table while delivering his "we will bury you" thoughts at the United Nations. Such images linger still in the popular mind of older Americans. But it was the confrontation, the crisis of nuclear fear of 1962, that occasioned the calculated stalemate of arms control agreements whereby the two superpowers rode out the remainder of the life of the Soviet Union.

From the time of the understanding between Mr. Kennedy and Mr. Khrushchev that limited the testing and production of nuclear weapons, until another understanding a quarter of a century later, between Mr. Reagan and Mr. Gorbachev, Americans' alternating postures of threat and ingratiation in relation to the Soviet Union determined their responses to the rest of the world. Strictly speaking, America's interest in the world was not confined to its concerns about the Soviet Union; nor were those concerns only about the comparative nuclear strength and nuclear arms strategies of those two nations. But, by and large, each saw the world as prize or prey coveted by the other; and since both possessed nuclear arms, the apparently endless stalemate that evolved seemed to enfold all of the other possibilities of domestic and international life within the shadow of a mutually assured destruction (referred to often as MAD) that could follow the exercise of nuclear force, by either nation. MAD was, in effect, the basis of US Cold War policy, although a number of studies make it clear that neither experts nor the American people were confidently of one mind about that policy.

Without the threat of nuclear holocaust, the years of the Cold War might have filled themselves with North Koreas, Vietnams, Grenadas, and Iraqs, anyway. But both the early NIF issue books in the 1980s and the reports of public deliberation that they engendered suggest a people whose future may have been uncertain but whose frame of reference was—especially when contrasted with the first decade of this 21st century—remarkably sure in itself. Foreign policy for most Americans had become essentially a *defense policy*, designed to maintain the credibility of the threat itself of nuclear destruction as a means of keeping alien ideas and practices from infecting traditionally American principles. In this context, conservatives and liberals became either hawks or doves; the differences between them became degrees of anti-Soviet rhetoric;

and their differing approaches to international relationships were measured by their relative willingness or reluctance to engage in talk and treaty. Three issue books produced for NIF during the 1980s reveal the currency of this preoccupation with defense; the few formal *reports* we have from the forums are dictated by its singular pervasiveness. As we shall see, commitment to the goals of containing communism and avoiding nuclear war framed public thinking, while reaction against the war in Vietnam had eventually come to color its expression.

Given the few formal reports from public forums and the fact that there are no *Public Voice* videotapes from this period, remarks from the forums are not plentiful. But enough can be found to elaborate upon this now historical mind-set, characterized by images of hawks and doves, and to reveal the reservations that appeared to be growing within it.

In the fall of 1983, when Public Agenda, in collaboration with The Center for Foreign Policy Development at Brown University, launched what was to become a four-year study of Americans' attitudes toward the Soviet Union, it began with the observation that "the chasm in understanding and perspective between the public and its leaders could hardly be more stark or more potentially troublesome." Public Agenda based that preliminary judgment on a long series of polls, some of which were to prove misleading, with conclusions that differed significantly from what Public Agenda would learn in its ensuing study of the *deliberative* public.

In one such poll that Public Agenda had examined, for example, almost two thirds of those questioned had given, Public Agenda observed, "answers more consistent with the world of the 1930s than the world of the 1980s." In the event of a US/Soviet war, that poll had suggested, people thought "that a son or husband might be drafted; Americans might have to go abroad to fight; there might be shortages of certain goods and some economic hardships." But "only 36 percent had mentioned the possibility of massive death and destruction." The public, it was assumed therefore, held views that were "disparate, unfocused, and disconnected," and its "thinking was marked by anxiety, confusion, unreality, a sense of powerlessness, and a rising tide of alarm." This presumption proved accurate. The sense of powerlessness and the rising tide of alarm, the Public Agenda study learned, were certainly characteristic—as they might also be said to have been characteristic of the American public as a result of 9/11, twenty years later. But public deliberation in the three sets of NIF forums on the Soviet-US relationship in the later 1980s revealed divergent but considerably more sharply focused views that, as it turns out, did in fact offer increasingly clear indicators of what would eventually become a more appropriate policy—a more balanced public judgment—for greater national security by the end of the decade: attitudes both more realistic and increasingly less divisive than both political leadership and the media of the preceding 30 postwar years had presumed. By the middle of the 1980s, it had become abundantly clear, both from polls and from public dialogue, that an overwhelming sense among the American people was that the United States did *not* enjoy nuclear superiority over the Soviet Union; that they (like the rest of the world) would have little chance of surviving nuclear war; and that therefore nuclear arms should not be used except in immediate response to another's nuclear attack.

A deeply rooted antipathy toward foreign ventures had been planted by the war in Vietnam, the last quarter of the 20th century had gradually become used to a kind of peace—albeit peace punctuated by occasional adventures, in, for example, Grenada, Panama, and, more consistently, in the Middle East. An ameliorating relationship with China had begun to enlarge the international marketplace; and that may have had more to do with the decline in people's sense of a "communist threat" than had the posturing of the fictional Rambo character of Sylvester Stallone and the illusion of a Strategic Defense Initiative (or "Star Wars"), both of which had a following, at the time. Increasingly, Americans in the 1980s were coming to think of foreign policy in terms of defense against the *potential* of the Soviet Union; so, energized still by the fear of communism and the love of profit, they went about their Cold War business—with growing reservations.

Thus, to suggest a people divided between "hawks" and "doves" does not accurately represent the American public that revealed itself in deliberation through the 1980s. Certainly, these labels represent attitudes commonly recognized and often talked about. The two images were consistently used—and public concern moved back and forth between them: between a commitment to "peace through strength," through arms control strategies, to the goal of a bilateral freeze on nuclear weapons, and even, now and again, of unilateral nuclear disarmament. And vice-versa! Keith Melville, who had written the first discussion guide used nationwide in the National Issues Forums confronting this international problem in 1983 (and who has an unusually sensitive ear for the complexity of public thought), reported:

> Most of the people in these forums concluded that it would be foolish for us to renounce the use of nuclear weapons. It is one thing to conclude, as many people in these groups seem to have done, that the Soviets aren't as implacable an enemy as they are often made out to be; it is another thing entirely to hand them military advantage by taking the radical step of unilateral nuclear disarmament.

This had the appearance of a public judgment: the Soviet Union apparently wasn't all-powerful, but that didn't mean we should renounce the use of nuclear weapons. So much, then, in these early forums, for both the hawk and the dove—who, Melville noted, tended, insofar as they *were* extremes, to become *more* extreme in their assertions as deliberation proceeded, while others moved together by a process, largely, of exploring contradictions.

> Participants in these forums had little interest in the subtleties of deterrence theory, but its underlying premise came up again and again as a topic of discussion. What seemed so striking to people who confronted its meaning for the first time was the contradiction it contains. Its goal is to ensure the peace, to protect our sovereignty, to promote international stability. What it requires of us is to build and threaten to use an arsenal capable of massive destruction. In brief, we are keeping the peace by threatening annihilation.

This is clearly what Yankelovich had anticipated as the kind of tension that a public must face, working its way to judgment. As evidenced by the forums that Melville was describing, the US public apparently was facing it, albeit without conclusions that could promise comfort over the long haul.

It was apparent, then, in the analyses of public deliberations at that time, that the popular movie images of Rambo excited the imaginations of large numbers of Americans in a way more appropriate to World War II than to the occasional unhappy and indecisive military confrontations of the Cold War period. Still, the threat of the Soviet's SS-18 (dutifully articulated in the discussion guides for these public forums) certainly occasioned in many minds an enthusiasm for response by way of the MX intercontinental missile (first test fired in 1983) and a "Star Wars" defense. The flexing of muscle and ostentatious military power, it seems, has long been a standard US response to fear or the threat of military force from others. Yet no less pervasive (and also fully described in the discussion materials) was a view that presented the chief danger to the

United States as being *not* in the number or the nature of the weapons we had to defend ourselves with, or in the intentions of our adversaries who had similar nuclear weapons, but in *the very existence of those weapons.* This view encouraged some to consider immediate steps to eliminate weapons of mass destruction from our arsenals as the only effective means toward our safety. To that degree, perhaps, hawk and dove were still circling.

Between these two poles of "Star Wars" and nuclear disarmament, official policies moved back and forth among strategies of arms *control* and debate about the occasions that might justify the unilateral *use* of such weapons. But what is most valuable in the relatively meager reports of public deliberation during the 1980s is what they reveal about the profoundly influential tension that existed between these two ideal (and sometimes ideological) postures of the American public mind. It is because this consistent tension is captured in public deliberation that we can recognize slow modifications represented in what was continuing national policy—earning somewhat tentative public support—with respect to the Soviet Union and nuclear arms. The reports of public deliberation in the 1980s reveal a continuing (and growing) public reaction—only belatedly accepted by political leadership—to the dangers of that policy in the then-contemporary world.

Since the Cuban missile crisis some 20 years earlier, arms control agreements had been reached between the 2 superpowers at a rate of about 1 per year. While the policy of "mutually assured destruction" ensured both a continuing arms race and a continuing fear, it also provided a tenuous stability in the minds of a fearful public. Over time, however, there developed an overwhelming fear among some Americans (estimated as many as 75 percent by Public Agenda in 1984) that, as forum participants put it, "if we and the Soviets keep building missiles instead of negotiating to get rid of them, it's only a matter of time before they get used." "I'd like to think that it won't happen," said a student from Indianapolis in 1984, referring to the *use* of nuclear weapons.

> I'd like to think that the people running both countries are smart enough to know that if it did, everything would be destroyed. But then I think, why are they making them? If they really don't intend to use them, why are they making them in the first place?

To the retrospective view of a series of deliberative public forums in the 1980s, it might seem that the two widely held and popular formulations of "policy" within the parameters labeled "hawk" and "dove" made an apparent *domestic* struggle highly likely if not inevitable. Such different approaches would inevitably suggest a divided nation; and certainly a great deal of time and energy and rhetoric was expended on the aggressive articulation of the various conflicting views as a basis for US foreign and defense policy during the 1980s. Polls in the period focused persistently on that struggle. Yet closely examined retrospectively, the record of public deliberation during this same period reveals not a divided country and divided communities but divided *individuals*: it shows differing views presented in individual voices, but, in all these groups, among the discussants *each appears to understand the import of the other's concern*. They present us with people—apparently honest and often principled—still less than satisfied with where they stand, and eager to identify the trade-offs that might bring them closer to a shared *purpose*, despite competing strategies.

This inching toward a shared purpose was important. In the fall of 1985, public deliberative forums already revealed quite clearly that collaboration with the Soviet Union on a wide front of activities was a viable choice for the discussants. Then, as if in accord with this view, in

1986, President Reagan—who just a few years earlier had characterized the Soviet Union as the "focus of evil" in the modern world—met in Reykjavik with Soviet leader Mikhail Gorbachev, and startled the world by discussing the abolition of nuclear missiles. That event gave rise to an extraordinarily energetic increase in trade, scientific research, and cultural exchanges between the two countries.

In the spring of 1988, at Newport Beach in California, a group of National Issues Forums participants—citizens from around the nation, in fact—met with a visiting contingent of senior Soviet advisors who were formally in this country to consult with their US counterparts (within the structure of the bi-annual "Dartmouth Conference" that had been in place to facilitate off-the-record US-Soviet exchange dialogues for more than 20 years), to discuss the relationship between the superpowers. One young man, describing himself as a heavy equipment operator from Colorado, concluded that it was time to

> find a way to work with each other. You just can't judge the Soviet system or the people from a standpoint of ignorance. It's time for American public opinion to prepare to receive the best rather than just the worst about the USSR.

And in a discussion between the Americans and the Soviets produced for broadcast on the same occasion, another NIF participant, president of a branch of Goodwill Industries in Orange County, California, said he had "arrived with an expectable Orange County conservatism, combined with a Missouri show-me skepticism." But he left discussions with these distinguished Soviet officials, he said, "impressed with the seriousness of their intentions."

This was, of course, the time of *Perestroika*, and one of the Soviet advisors, Nikolai Shishlin, a member of the Central Committee of the Communist Party of the Soviet Union, had told the NIF citizen group:

> We asked ourselves who we are, what our history has been, what is the state of our economy, what our morals are like. We discovered very quickly that aircraft crash not only in the United States or other countries, but also in the Soviet Union. We discovered that failures and disasters occur not only in other countries, but also in the Soviet Union.

Analyzing these Newport Beach public conversations at the time, Yankelovich gave President Reagan high marks for insisting on military strength while opening the way for collaboration in other areas. "I don't think his attitude changed public opinion," he said. "I think public opinion changed, and he changed along with it." Later in 1988, reporting on "A Public Summit"—an unusually far-reaching study of public thinking about Soviet-US relations in five cities—Yankelovich observed, "There is a profound hope and conviction that collaboration is the preferred model." A poll taken *following* the public deliberation in this project had also shown that an astonishing 76 percent of respondents favored a future built upon collaborative problem-solving by the United States and the Soviet Union. A retrospective look at records of public deliberation, however, suggests that public thinking may not in fact have "changed" dramatically: it had throughout the decade been tending in that direction, President Reagan's earlier rhetoric notwithstanding. The combination of Reagan's insistent "hawkishness" (which reflected one sector of public opinion) with the increasing recognition of the dangers implicit in such a course (which reflected another) opened the way, eventually but inevitably, to a kind of cooperative, internationalized endeavor that was the only way to respond acceptably to the powerfully felt demands of both hawk and dove. The ambivalence—for it appears to have been a genuine ambivalence, rather than a modeled attempt at compromise—between hawkish and dovish inclinations in the public mind reflected not hostile but complementary values that a combination of fear and vanity (plus a degree of ideological pretension) had served to confuse.

Yankelovich had this to say:

> When the focus is on the short term, Americans tend to be somewhat "hawkish." They tend to want to stand up aggressively from a tactical point of view. When the focus is on the long term, American tend to be "dovish" and want a much more peaceful relationship than is present at the moment. But you can't get from A to B; you can't get through hawkish tactics to a dovish, peaceful future. So it is necessary to confront that kind of contradiction and conflict that people have—and that is "choicework."

"Choicework" of course, is precisely what is revealed, actually taking place, in these public forums of the 1980s. Yankelovich continues:

> It is illuminating to contrast this process with public opinion polling. It is very different. . . . The purpose of a poll is to learn people's views, and to inform leadership of people's views. The purpose of choicework is to help people *form* their views. The end product of a poll is a statistic—numbers. The end product of choicework is changes in people's outlooks. The method of a poll is the method of taking a snapshot with a camera: you look at a viewpoint in a moment of time. The method of the choicework is dialogue, engagement with an issue. The effect of a poll is to leave people unchanged: when you take a poll you don't change people's views. The end product of choicework is usually change. The role of a democracy in a poll is to inform leaders of the opinions of the people. The role of choicework is to advance intelligent participation in public policy issues. In a poll there is no conversation with conflict and contradiction. The very essence of choicework, when it is successful, is confronting the trade-offs and the contradictions. The public's view may start with the media input, but it ends as something very different.

When we are patient, and committed, it may end in a public judgment.

Seeing Ourselves . . . and Our Responsibilities

Granted what we have already noted about the crepuscular but perhaps ultimately shallow roots of antipathy between the Soviets and the United States—and the constraining of the two powers' belligerence within the bounds of rhetoric, arms control, and regional conflicts—it may not be surprising that the American public so quickly should have dropped the specter of the Soviet Union from its mind. The concerns that had for some time popularly justified Cold War policy no longer played an important role, once the Soviet state itself had imploded—perhaps most dramatically in the fall of the Berlin Wall in 1989—and the communist ideal been shown to be empty. Yet what remained apparent, through the final decade of the century, was that the citizens of the one remaining superpower did still prefer to be just that: the remaining *superpower*. And this outlines another genuine tension or ambivalence in American public thinking, a little short of what we might term a public judgment.

The ending of World War II had been marked by fireworks and bonfires and dancing in the streets, around the world. The ending of the Cold War—except for the still-awaited collapse of the Berlin Wall—was neither as dramatic nor as satisfying. Its accomplishment was that, by the simple act of talking with the enemy, a way had been found to achieve the impossible dream: to have power, and not to use it.

But that remarkable paradox sheds light on three other not-always-compatible preoccupations of the American people, which emerge when they have deliberated about their nation's role in the world over the past quarter-century. These preoccupations are revealed in expressions of certain recurring American ideas: their inclination to like being left to themselves (isolationism, in effect); their pleasure in acting as "sheriff" of all the world, keeping order; and their interest in the dispensing of human rights—through American-style democracy! And since these impulses have been reflected in conversations in public forums about US relations with the Soviet Union, with China, with Vietnam, and with Iraq, they are worth some attention. Deliberation, after all, is a spoken path toward the American public's judgment.

It is not altogether surprising to find that in 1987, when the National Issues Forums chose to deliberate on relations between the superpowers for the third time in a decade, one of the options they considered was that of isolationism, harking back to an historical American attitude that had been not much in evidence over the preceding 40 years.

George Washington, in his final address of September 19, 1796, had advised his countrymen that they should avoid "the evils of foreign intrigues." And with seldom more than an occasional clenching of fists or rubbing of elbows, the United States had followed that advice. America's intervention in the first world war had been decisive, but brief; and although the second world war was fought over principles central to America's way of life (and the United States had offered significant support to Britain in the form of supplies through its war's first two years), the United States did not join forces with the allies until the Japanese attack on Pearl Harbor inevitably brought this nation's full military response. Following the war, however, Washington's advice had little weight. US troops had remained stationed in Japan and Europe as armies of occupation for some years; in 1949, the NATO agreement had committed American forces, in a continuing way, to the defense of Europe; and there were bilateral treaties with the Philippines, with Australia and New Zealand, with Latin American nations, and with various Asian nations (including South Korea and Japan). By the time of the Vietnam War in the 1960s, the United States' military presence extended to 25 foreign countries. Still, Americans do not underestimate US expenditure on defense commitments abroad; and as the country's involvement abroad grew, there were plausible reasons among the public, as the 20th century wore down, to consider reining in our interests.

When the Cold War genuinely ended with the demise of the Soviet Union itself, while the United States (significantly) did not turn a blind eye toward the world after the first Gulf War in the early 1990s, a new kind of "isolationism" had begun to suggest a slightly different tone, a quality of thinking that was to prove of increasing importance through the turn of the century. Despite oddly aberrant acts in relation to both allies and the United Nations as the next century's war against Iraq approached, if there was one clearly shared judgment in all of the early, post-Cold War, public deliberations on US foreign policies, it was that the United States could no longer, as one young woman in Madison, Wisconsin, put it in 1992, "think or act as though the world were our empire." There was widespread sentiment that the United States needed now to look after itself in the context of a differently perceived world.

> We have to get back to basics and build this country from the bottom up again. The people are really hurting down here and they really need it. So we have to help our own people. If we keep helping everybody else, eventually there's going to be nothing left here to give. There comes a time when charity begins at home, when help begins right here and now.

In all the relevant public forums that were monitored at the time, there were strong expressions of concern about what seemed to be a fragmenting of American society and there was reflected a proliferation of need that had grown up at home during the Cold War. The metaphor "coming apart at the seams" was heard in several forums in the 1990s:

> Our first priority has to be our own country, and I think it's very hypocritical of us to go prancing around the world, trying to protect the world order when, within our own country, we're falling apart. I think that we have so many children below poverty level that to me it is a human rights issue. How can we be champions of human rights around the world if we're not even concerned about our own children? To me that is the greatest hypocrisy of all: to say that we have to protect peace around the world, and we're not concerned about what is going on at home. And I think we are in danger of doing the same thing that happened to the Soviet Union, when they were considered a military power—a superpower—and they channeled all of their money into that military strength, while their country fell apart because the people got nothing. And I think that this is probably the greatest danger that we face: that we're going to fall apart at the seams, trying to control the business of the world; that we're not looking within at what needs to be done here.

Consistently, 9 out of 10 participants in deliberations of the early 1990s viewed "domestic problems like unemployment, homelessness, and crime" as serious threats to our country's national security interests. At times, in many of these discussions, it seemed that the subject moved from foreign policy to the consideration of what would seem to be national domestic crises, and from the discussion of international affairs to the discussion of the competitiveness of the American economy.

That juxtaposition—from an international to a domestic perspective—should not be misinterpreted, but it could not be more important. For although received wisdom, as the century wore out, had it that Americans were no longer much interested in foreign affairs but were preoccupied by the domestic scene, forum participants were clearly not Americans who had given up on the rest of the world, turning inward in a kind of *fin de siècle* isolationism. Far from it! Rather, they were citizens attempting, with seriousness and with a genuine sense of the complexity of the task, to re-envision the role of the United States in the world. For them, America's role in the world had to do inevitably with how we see ourselves. Hence, they moved repeatedly into considerations of US competitiveness, of the lifestyle to which we are accustomed—even, indeed, to questions about the environment, recycling, and the way we address disposable waste. Discussions directly about these questions often were interrupted, too, by serious exploration of what was seen by some to be growing inequity within this country.

In the fall and winter months of 1995-1996, midway between the collapse of the Soviet Union and the catastrophe of 9/11—between the Cold War and the no-less-euphemistic "war on terror"—the National Issues Forums had again chosen to focus their seasonal deliberations upon the international picture, billing it this time as a "Mission Uncertain: Reassessing America's Role." Early in the spring of 1996, John Doble Research Associates, Inc., had published the first of what were to become its annual reports on the outcomes from the deliberations of the National Issues Forums in communities around the country. Looked at now, from our vantage point on this far side of the military and political expeditions in Afghanistan and Iraq, what Doble reported seems prescient. The public attitudes he describes are remarkable in themselves, but perhaps even more remarkable for their divergences from what have subsequently emerged as the foreign policies of the United States.

In his executive summary, Doble presents seven major findings about public concerns at that time:

1. Domestic needs have been neglected at the expense of foreign affairs.

2. A return to isolationism is unrealistic and unwise.
3. It is in America's self-interest to remain a superpower, yet our allies should shoulder more of the load in dealing with international conflicts.
4. The "vital interests" of the United States offer a sense of national definition that includes economic factors, stability, preservation of international law, and the alleviation of human suffering.
5. Mixed feelings are voiced about promoting democracy around the globe and defending human rights.
6. Military intervention is appropriate only under certain conditions.
7. A vein of suspicion of the government, its motives, and its competence runs through forums all across the country.

Not all of our boats had been lifted (as President Reagan had promised) during the preceding 15 years. We had spent—and in some peoples' mind we were still spending—far too much on securing our military strength; needs at home now pressed again for help from the public purse. Guns and butter are both persuasive priorities in the United States, and now was the time, apparently, for a leaner defense and a heavier table. Implicit was an understanding that everybody else will pitch in if serious trouble, anywhere, needs to be addressed. Our side of the bargain is that we will never intervene militarily unless asked to do so by virtually everybody else, including those who are to be the objects of our intervention. During that final decade of the 20th century, then, between the nation's two expeditions to Iraq, the *traditional* concept of "isolationism" thus seems to have dropped out of public dialogue. In none of the public conversations recorded over this 20-plus year period, in fact, had there been any *clear* sign of the principle as George Washington first articulated it in the earliest years of the Republic, although it had been encountered as one vein of thought in the Cold War deliberations, influenced by a desire among some Americans to be free to go their own way and pursue their own ends, with neither interference by—nor responsibility toward—other nations with different practices and principles.

The tension of this historic strain in American thinking is strikingly absent from more recent public deliberation about the United States and the rest of the world. Public deliberations about our relationship with the Chinese and Russians at the turn of the century, for example, took as their *a priori* assumption that what the rest of the world does *is* a matter of importance to Americans, and the dialogues that are responsive to actions in the Middle East and that derive from concerns in the Middle East have not suggested that *there* Americans should "leave well enough alone." Distinctions are being made. For example, forums on the subject of Americans' role in the world *since* the terrorist attacks of 2001 reveal a continuing uncertainty about the justification for America's actions in Iraq, on the one hand, and the nature of American actions in Afghanistan, on the other. In short, the concern about whether we are "doing things right" is not related to an *a priori* reluctance about our being engaged in foreign enterprises, *per se*.

Indeed, attentiveness to others is now linked to taking care of ourselves. Expressed concern about our inability to be what others suppose us to be characterized many of the 1990s deliberations of the National Issues Forums. In a nation described as "coming apart" internally there is an evident attempt to explore the degree to which Americans could help solve their *own* problems by a more effective understanding of their relationship to the problems *that others face*. One participant developed the theme in this way:

> We need to rebuild our own country. I agree with that—except that I think we need to take a broader view. What happens in our country affects other countries; what happens in other countries will affect us, in one way or another. And I don't think we can stand back—as we did 100 years ago—behind the big sea, because there isn't one anymore. We can no longer have the luxury of *only* looking at *this* country in terms of problems that are affecting the majority of the world.

Images that participants present often seem to have a remarkable influence on public deliberation about purpose and action—about policy, in effect. In part this has to do with people's dependence on narrative when they deliberate: principally they tell stories from their own experience as they frame problems and take positions on broader concerns. So when the resolution of the Cold War left the United States as unmistakably the most powerful nation in the world—in a way that historically had no precedent—the immediate and fundamental question that American people thought about was their responsibility for maintaining order (which might or might not mean maintaining the peace) in the world. But in forums of the 1990s, what at first was largely rhetoric about the needs of the poor and oppressed at home became more and more closely intertwined with expressed concerns about America's ability—or its qualifications—to be judge, jury, and executor in matters that have to do with "law and order" *internationally*. Whence came the notion that we needed to consider the situation of other countries in order to "rebuild our own country": it is another revision of how we ought to relate to other countries.

To be the world's police officer had a kind of appeal, as in the Rambo character of the 1980s, but an episodic and apparently diminishing appeal thereafter. Tension between the need to "flex muscles" on the one hand, and the skepticism of "war against whom?"—as two forum participants put it in 2005—was most dramatically revealed in responses following the terrorism of 9/11; yet similar concern had also been captured in the early *Public Voice* tapes on foreign policy, 10 years earlier. A kind of skepticism about the supposedly "quiet American" —as sheriff, supposedly—was moving clearly through American public thinking, and ironically, was to be brought almost to a head in conversations about Americans' role when the United States took overt actions in Iraq without UN endorsement, in 2003. Occasional echoes of Cold War arguments could be heard, arguments that had been used to characterize the conflict between "hawks" and "doves": "Americans have the feeling that we're number one, and we're not at all ready to give that up now," a man in El Paso said, suggesting that clear military supremacy is still comforting in an uncertain world. But to view such exchanges as a continuation of the old US conflict between "hardliner" and "peacenik" would be radically to misunderstand them. And it would certainly misrepresent the tenor of the more recent, 21st-century forums. For overwhelmingly, and virtually everywhere, participants appear to have come to view the role of lone superpower as an occasion for worry rather than triumph.

In the deliberations of the early 1990s, a Texas woman had remarked, "Now all of a sudden the Soviet Union is no longer a superpower. We've bankrupted them, and now we're the big guys. The power of that is very terrible." That the United States itself might, as the surviving superpower, employ its strength in the role of world police officer was clearly unpalatable. "If the United States tries to continue to be the policeman of the whole world, it's not going to be a superpower much longer," concluded a woman in Albany, Georgia, at that time. And another woman had responded:

> Going around, pretending that we are in charge of everything, that we take care of everything, and that we have the answers—we have a lot of hostility out there toward this country because of that role. There's a distaste and disdain for anybody who's out there, pretending they have all the answers.

A man in Madison, in fact, had defined the term *superpower* itself as "an arrogant use of power, without any regard for other nations, other interests." That sense left participants unhappy, and the general sentiment, in all of these forums well before the century's end, was that the United States should not be, as a man in El Paso put it, "the Lone Ranger of the world." By the close of the 1998 forums, indeed, fully 70 percent of the participants had agreed, in an "exit" questionnaire, that, "it is no longer necessary for the United States to act as world policeman."

An overwhelming preoccupation in forums of the 1990s, in fact, was not differences in strategies or values or personalities, but a set of unmistakable concerns, expressed in forum after forum and generally shared by the participants: first, that the role of superpower could not ultimately be sustained economically; second, that defense (in the Cold War, or military, sense) was no longer the principal interest of the United States or of the world; and third, that any attempt to force our values—our concept of "rights," in effect—on other nations, without strong support from the international community, would be perhaps unwarranted and certainly unwise. The attitude of defender of the right is an appealing one, but recognition that "rights" are not all equal suggests a more persistent evaluation than many of us would be able to sustain. Should one dispense human rights, then, or democracy? That is a question that would create public tension and demand delicacy in judgment.

Values, Interests . . . and the "Rights" of Others

The language of "liberty" and "freedom" seems always to have described Americans' intentions; but in the latter half of the 20th century, US assistance, civil and military, had been provided to and through other nations primarily so that they might remain anticommunist, rather than to the end of their becoming necessarily democratic—or even committed in principle to the exercise of human rights. "Liberté, Égalité, Fraternité"—this was distinctively *not* the rhetoric of American democracy. It may have therefore been inevitable that "the ugly American" was to become well known, even in Southeast Asia *before* the Vietnam War, and that "Yankee, go home" was to become a sustained and familiar injunction internationally throughout the decades that had followed World War II. Nonetheless, in the 1980s and 1990s, a foreign policy that made—or at least claimed to make—the provision of American assistance dependent upon an improvement in matters of human rights (democratization, bit-by-bit) had become increasingly used. The linking of US assistance to a declared commitment to democracy and human rights—even of concessions to communist nations, insofar as they agreed to observe American-style human rights—had thus become "respectable" topics of public conversation.

But such assistance was not always viewed favorably in regard to all countries. In 1992, two-thirds of National Issues Forums participants, responding to an "exit" questionnaire, had expressed agreement with the sentiment that "working for short-term gains with dictators like General Noriega or the late President Marcos is immoral." In Madison, a man similarly pointed to the hypocrisy of a stand on behalf of democracy when we have clearly supported leaders who do not pursue our ideals, whenever that suited our purpose. A woman in El Paso thought we generally should mind our own business: "Especially in Latin America, the United States is not perceived as benign and is interfering constantly in the affairs of certain countries. I don't think we should involve ourselves in the internal affairs of other countries." "Do we ourselves really know our democracy?" one young man asked, admittedly somewhat more extreme in his rhetoric than most. Another insisted that although we claim to support human rights and democracy elsewhere, we have tolerated human rights violations among allies. And a man in Albany, Georgia, said, "Let's face it, the United States has been guilty of economic exploitation of the Third World.... This is something that will have to be addressed." These discussants professed themselves to be variously liberal and conservative, and they clearly shared a determination to reassess the moral imperatives behind American policy. Yet when asked, "What role should the United States play in the world?" only 1 in 20 of forum participants responding to exit questionnaires placed the highest priority on "promoting democracy and human rights, whenever they are threatened."

It now becomes clear that these Americans, in a post-Cold War world, at a time when the nation did not feel itself directly threatened, were reassessing their judgments about themselves and their own nation. "It worries me to speak as if we're the good guys," said a Texas woman, in the late 1990s. "It seems like we have the idea that we do it so right and so perfect that it should be what everyone else does." "I don't always feel that what we have in this country is necessarily the best for everybody else in the world," echoed a woman in Georgia.

In context, the purpose of such statements was evidently not to declare *mea culpa*. The deliberations here have a more meditative, less accusatory quality. With apparent sincerity, these forum participants, trying to redefine America's role in the world, were coming to grips with a hard and very American question: how to reconcile some of the clear moral imperatives that Americans have always honored in theory, with the proper and necessary *self*-interest that they perceived might always tend to shape the limits of foreign policy.

In one forum, a woman with her own command of recent history pointed out:

> Every time we decided to continue to support the bad guys in the world, not only have we not won, but we've gotten something that was worse. We decided to support Chiang Kai-shek, hoping that we would rescue China from communism—and we got Mao; the day before Castro marched into Cuba, we supported Batista; when we got rid of the democratically reelected person in Iran, we got the Shah. And so every time we have tried to do that, we have gotten something worse. It's a strategy that simply hasn't worked out historically. Aside from the moral value that what we did I think is terrible, politically it never works out; we always end up getting something that could be worse than what we had before. I don't think that is a very good strategy.

From this followed a corollary, which quite apparently settled as a bedrock principle for foreign policy among these groups in the 1990s, following the collapse of the Soviet Union: we have no obligation to make others in our own image, nor any right to do so; each nation must offer and pursue its own definition of human rights. Perhaps paradoxically, in group after group, after the 1989 demonstration of Tiananmen Square was cited, discussions of our relationship with China underscored the point. Disgust with what Americans had seen broadcast from Tiananmen Square still registered strongly, years after the event, but the determination to affirm that judgment was consistently coupled with a widespread reluctance to have it influence our *policy* toward China. Sixty-three percent of forum participants at the conclusion of the NIF discussions in 1993 had agreed that, "We should develop working relationships with countries like China, even if they are guilty of human rights violations." In dialogues at the start of the new century—one in 2000 focusing specifically on Americans' concerns with respect to the Chinese, another in the spring of 2003 relating to Iraq—the "right" of the United States to adjudicate the "rights" of citizens of other nations was broadly called into question.

Whether or not to spread democracy through the use of American power was to become a matter of increasing public concern in 21st-century deliberation. In the summer of the year 2000, for example, in forums held in 20 communities across the United States as part of a larger, ongoing US-China dialogue, participants had considered the degree to which the United States might "promote and foster human u hvbjnrights" in China. Initially, participants characterized human rights by reference to various contexts: some were concerned about acts of civil disobedience, still recalling the image of the young man facing the tank in Tiananmen Square, years before; some were concerned about the ideal of justice, asking, "Why did this have to happen?" and, "Why is there no monument or sign indicating what happened?"

Yet the published report of these dialogues on US/China relations goes on to say that participants then

> became more reflective about US incidents that have created the need for harsh measures. The Los Angeles riots fueled by conflicts between Koreans and African Americans were mentioned. Some brought up the Watts riots. As the discussion turned to the need for internal order in our countries, in a forum held in the southwestern United States, one person asked, "Comparing Kent State versus Tiananmen Square, are

> we really different?" Another responded, "It's like calling the kettle black."

The report on these forums also cites one participant's observation that "Americans cannot expect traditional human values to be the same in every country." The report continues:

> At an Ohio forum one participant offered this analysis: "As Americans, we tend to think of human rights as civil rights, such as the right to vote and a fair judicial system. The Chinese think of human rights differently, such as the right to work and to share in their economy. Everyone is taken care of materially in some way." One person said, "The United States should be willing to give and take, but not dictate," when it comes to human rights. "We stress human rights too much," she went on. "This is important but should be staged in policy over time."

The report concludes, "the more they deliberated choice, the more all the participants emphasized a summary that one person offered up: 'Whatever solutions to Chinese problems there are, they must be Chinese solutions, not American solutions.'" So, as in the much earlier deliberations about US-Soviet relations, there is an important tension evident in these public deliberations about the US-China relationship, and it is by no means a subtle one. The Americans in these forums are prompted both by an interest in *spreading* their idea of democracy and by a reluctance to *enforce* its adoption. For they have a far from unblemished record themselves, they think, as they move between the ideal and the convenient.

A slender and careful study by John Doble, reporting on a "National Issues Convention," a large-scale public deliberation in 2003 on Iraq, bears on this point. When Americans talk of democracy, Doble's study suggests, they think primarily in terms of the procedures and the institutions of the US model, and very little about people engaging in essential civic activities outside the formal processes of government. And while people believe that the spread of democracy will enhance our national security and increase global stability, they are persistently opposed to what they see as "imposing" democracy by the use of military force. Their inclination either to "require" or "overlook" effective democratic practice in other nations is largely contextual. Thus, again, one may find a nation divided—not between citizens of different convictions, but in individual citizens themselves.

Of American attitudes about the adventure of 2003 in Iraq, Doble wrote:

> Some saw the war and democratizing Iraq as absolutely necessary, saying Saddam posed a direct threat to the US and the war was a heroic sacrifice and a highly ethical response to a tyrant. . . . Others held the opposite view, saying the US should not try to democratize Iraq; the idea is unrealistic. And that the war was unnecessary, of questionable legitimacy, being carried out without international approval or assistance, or worst of all, diverting attention from the real threat of Al Qaeda.

Doble was reporting on the National Issues Convention in Philadelphia, a large-scale public deliberative event organized by Jim Fishkin, of Stanford University, with the collaboration of Kettering and *The Newshour* of PBS. But his comment recalls the experience of people deliberating together in forums a decade earlier, following the ending of the Cold War and the first military confrontation with Iraq, in the first Gulf War, code-named Desert Storm. The individuals in each of these sets of deliberative public groups, separated by about a decade, are very different one from another, and their ideas of tactics, on both occasions, vary enormously. In 1992, there had been those reluctant to trust other nations, and still sold on the idea of remaining a superpower. There were those obsessed with the inadequacies of our own democracy, and inclined to emphasize needs at home, rather than the troubles of others. There were those, with the Cold War behind them, eager to reduce military spending and turn their backs on war. And there were those not at all ready to give up our military position in the world, no matter what the fate of other powers might be. There were those, then, for whom the experience of the Gulf War had been a step toward multinational peacekeeping efforts. And similarly, in 2003, there were those who still found it hard to accept a United Nations role. And everywhere, there were differences of opinion.

Yet these differences did not entirely mask the commonalities of concern through these different times. Paradoxically, different voices, coming from contrary directions in each Iraq crisis, fixed the common interest all the more sharply in focus. The two sets of continuing public deliberations, over time and focusing on different moments in recent history, reveal for us a public generally opposed to the use of force for the purpose of developing democracy (for "a host of reasons," which Doble catalogues), that remains nonetheless, as all the polls indicate, overwhelmingly committed to the idea that the United States should promote democracy globally.

This prospect of promoting something *globally* may again require some attention as a question of moral imperatives. Through the preceding 20 years of public deliberation about international affairs, the most remarkable and consistent change in attitudes had been a slowly increasing interest in the fates and destinies of other nations. This is neither a theoretical interest, nor an abstract one, but a slowly growing, almost offhand or back-of-the-mind awareness of this nation's existence in the minds of others, and of the impact of the nation's occasional adventures on other peoples' lives. The first Gulf War, "Desert Storm," may have been important in that it was a war fought with American troops, outside America, but not against communist or international factions. It was preceded by open debate among this nation's leaders, conducted in almost a "popular" manner, and unlike some other military interventions over the past several years, it involved territorial rights and an apparent US interest (that is to say, an economic interest). It appeared to involve, in other words, the kinds of questions that foreign intervention and foreign policy are popularly supposed to be fraught with, and in a context where the international community was also clearly involved in the councils of war, although America, as the one "superpower," was commanding the field.

It may be useful, here, perhaps, to step back to 1986, when Public Agenda had sought the considered opinions of local community leaders in a series of extended workshops in mid-size cities—the likes of Cleveland, Des Moines, Minneapolis, San Diego, and so on—around the country. The premise at that time was that

> in every community there is a handful of citizens who are acknowledged leaders, leaders by every useful definition of the term, who yet remain very close in interest, temper and understanding to the communities in which they live and which they serve. They reflect their communities' thinking and share their interests; and as leaders they are prepared to respond readily, thoughtfully, and perceptively to complex issues.

The groups had included, in fact, archbishops and justices; educators; a police chief and a hospital administrator; bankers, corporate executives, and labor negotiators; even, in two communities, retired military officers of staff rank. The subject of their conversation on this occasion had been, broadly, America and the world.

Summarizing conversations among such "community leaders," Public Agenda reported that in every discussion at that time there were expressions of frustration at our seeming inability to "sell" democracy in the third world. "We are preparing for a war that will probably never happen and we are ignoring the reality of what is happening in the third world," one group participant had observed, pointing to levels of human need to whose urgency this country's preeminently anti-communist agenda appeared a less than satisfactory response. By the time we had moved from the period of *Perestroika* and the end of the Soviet Union to the turn of the century, these skeptical voices had become stronger.

At every one of those earlier, "leading citizens" meetings, Public Agenda reported, participants had discussed, at length, US behavior in the world. And it had found, to Public Agenda's surprise—this is 1986—that these community leaders had argued that the main focus of our attention should be on the third world! Most of them apparently felt that "the United States did not understand the third world and often thwarted its own best interest by its actions in the third world and by those whom it chooses to support there." These discussions all took place, to be sure, during a year of well-publicized terrorist actions in Europe, and there were indications in the groups that concerns like these were not merely "alarmist." Rather, participants showed themselves to be genuinely troubled by what they took to be inadequate attention to the third world and a lack of "purchase" by the United States upon third world inclinations.

One woman in Wilmington, Delaware, remarked, "we can get along with the Soviet Union in the coming generations and [still] find ourselves in a world of people who don't share our values and interests, and who are antagonistic to our interests, from Central America to South America, to Africa, the Middle East." In many communities, people saw US policy toward other nations as poorly informed and often ignorant of local history, rivalries, and culture. "I never heard of Sunnis or Shiites until we got into trouble in Iran and Lebanon," one leader said. Another remarked:

> There appear to be fundamentalist movements shaping the Middle East. Now they didn't start five or six years ago. And I think that there are other kinds like this in our world that we know very little about. We don't know what motivates people, what their hopes or aspirations are, what they want to do. I think the first thing we ought to do is to try to understand the world around us.

A woman in Seattle concluded that, "We are way beyond the point in history where one can build a buffer for oneself in terms of territory. The whole world is our territory at this point."

The time, again remember, was the late 1980s, and the policy of containing the spread of communism still determined US practices in the world-at-large. So when participants complained that "the leaders of this country for the past 20 years . . . have not faced up that we need a total change of our foreign policy in how we are dealing with other nations," they were referring to an official attitude that may or may not be any longer precisely relevant. Yet, the conviction that drove these remarks would turn out to be no less pertinent 20 years later. As one professedly conservative gentleman said, "I've never found that there would be that much harm in talking to somebody and trying to establish some kind of relationship, assuming that you can maintain sanity while it's happening."

Such remarks may have seemed—indeed, did seem—dramatic to Public Agenda at the time because they were at odds with the accustomed commentaries of political leadership and the media in the 1980s. But hindsight, more than 20 years later, places them in a continuum. The record of public deliberation during the period reveals this concern about the world beyond Europe as an increasingly *popular* sentiment, a sentiment that has become articulated more clearly as a different cast of mind has shifted the focus of American interest, pushing it toward different kinds of problems in the third world—and toward the Muslim world in particular. Americans have been coming to judgment about the country's relation with the rest of the world under pressure, especially in the past decade of difficult circumstances.

In gauging the value of public deliberation, it is useful to consider the occasional tendency (an occupational hazard) of political leaders to see their options in black and white, the "other side" as the enemy. The political class has other priorities than public interest, sometimes, and for them it is difficult, professionally, to confess to having been wrong. In talking, then, of what we may learn from public deliberations during the past quarter-century, we can observe that public judgment sometimes embraces (rather than settles between) apparent polarities, and that successful public policy may sometimes be best founded not on one or the other of opposites that appear to be mutually exclusive, but on embracing a tension that may tie the two irrevocably together.

In the case of the Cold War, this may not have been as remarkable as it seemed at the time; it represents, after all, no more than the classical myth of Mars and Venus. But it is worth noting that in the immediate sense, Venus inevitably has the best of that marriage, for hers is the victory of conciliation; and if Mars does not *lose* his weapons (as Samson did his hair), at least he renounces their use. In a sense, in modern America, this always puts the exponents of realpolitik and the political leader who acts with the presumption of absolute power somewhat out-of-kilter, over the long haul, with the American public. So the Vietnam episode ended in ignominy, with pain that still has a personal sting today, 30-some years later. And thus the dilemma in the Middle East has long been couched in terms of the right or wrong of having got into it, or the speed with which we should get out; whereas the intense and lasting public deliberation—in forums of public deliberation since 2003, in fact—seems rather to posit the problem as "having got in *wrong*, how shall we get out *right?*" The "public voice" in effect recognizes tension and assumes sacrifice, in the interest, perhaps, of possibility. (Interestingly, the public mention of Vietnam in the Iraq, let alone Afghanistan, contexts remains relatively infrequent, and not so much grim warning as cautionary tale.)

Homegrown myths, too, sometimes have equally awkward implications for foreign policy. The first European Americans were consciously emigrants: they had *left* something behind in order to build their own "city on the hill." And if latter-day immigrants are no longer driven by so specific a metaphor, they are nonetheless here to realize a kind of life that had been denied them elsewhere. Despite George Washington's wishes that we let the rest of the world be, however, as we have noted above, that city seemed not possible to be built, let alone preserved, unless we were sometimes willing to play sheriff to the rest of the world. Hence, one tension that we have noted is that tension between the American instinct toward isolationism ("to be left alone") and a sense of the *duty*—that goes with the *power* to act—as sheriff of the rest of the world. After all, one needs a system of laws and enforcement to preserve one's own way of life; and that enforcement ends up entailing interrelationships with others powerful enough to bring trouble. A sheriff—even a global sheriff—has to act *on behalf of* the community in which he maintains order. (Every aficionado of the Wild Wild West knows what fate awaits the gunman and his posse who ride without that public "star.") Yet the gulf between Americans' general understanding and the at least comparably intense interests of other parts of the world (noted in the Public Agenda's extensive interviews with "community leaders" in 1986) seems to have persisted, rather than narrowed, in the intervening years. And now, if there is more widespread awareness of this problem of independence and leadership, the American public seems still not yet secure in its judgment of what should be done about it.

COMMONALITIES OF CONCERN . . . IN A NEW CENTURY

Maybe the United States ultimately is not an *imperial* power; Americans lack the will and the discipline for that kind of obligation. Perhaps like the Spanish, more than the French and British, we are too self-indulgent. Missionaries, yes! And commercial explorers, always! But unlike antique Roman or imperial Brit, we don't have the will to make over all that we see. "My country, right or wrong!" is the imperial patriot's cry. In America, we prefer to think, "My country, always right!" So we tend to invest our leader, once elected, with the divine right of kings; and presidents, unlike the rest of humankind, do not admit often to having been wrong. Indeed as merely *elected* leaders, they try very hard to *appear* right!

We have observed a tension between proponents of a policy of mutually assured destruction and the advocates of a nuclear freeze—a tension that appears to have been (in retrospect, again) not an unyielding opposition between two ideologies, but a reflection of a complex public response to two compelling concerns that could only in fact be laid to rest by precisely the kind of cooperative attention to problems between ourselves and other peoples that Mr. Reagan and Mr. Gorbachev promoted in their culminating series of summits. It was the call for cooperation between the United States and the Soviet Union that won the day in the Cold War, even though, at the time, to call for it seemed, to some, revolutionary almost to the point of sedition. It is a nice irony that the most hawkish of our recent presidents should have turned out thus to be the one who gave life to the more dove-like side of the nation's aspirations. The public dialogue opened up a *course* of action toward which Mr. Reagan was not intellectually sympathetic, but he had an uncanny, extraordinary, and perhaps instinctive sensitivity to the complexities of the public mind at critical times—like elections and international appearances. As the journalist Roger Rosenblatt once said, in a Fourth of July essay referring to *The Star Spangled Banner*, "Mr. Reagan may not have known the words too well, but, boy, could he carry that tune!"

It's perhaps a problem for us, trying to follow a public judgment formulating itself over time, that the 1980s discussions of international matters were always put in the context of the Soviet Union and a nuclear arms race, so that the outcomes are in a sense predetermined. Yet this in itself may be an interesting phenomenon in longitudinal research. Americans may be thought to have difficulty accepting a world that is not bipolar, "multinationalism" being a concept of experts and policy wonks. Yet the possibility of a relationship between "their" interest and "our" interest, and the influence of "the one" upon "the others"—or of "the others" upon "the one"—has clearly been growing in the American public mind, as the National Issues Forums over this past quarter-century evidence.

There have been historical assumptions about American immunity *from* the rest of the world; there has been extraordinary evidence of America's cultural influence *upon* the rest of the world; and there is little doubt that, in a conventional sense, America has more power overseas than any other nation or any other likely combination of nations militarily. Yet the price of goods, the loss of jobs, the loss of a war, the loss of lives, the loss of two towers, the loss of allied confidence, and the apparent difficulty of asserting influence and control in places like Somalia, Afghanistan, Iraq—not to mention North Korea, Iran, Palestine, Israel, Pakistan, and so on—are all reflected in the seemingly incidental but endlessly repeated detail of public talk about the larger world of nations of which Americans are quite evidently increasingly aware. The awareness of a world of different peoples that is revealed in the deliberative public forums on terrorism and the forums on China and Russia in the new century is utterly different from that which emerged from conversations (primarily about the Soviets and "other communist nations" like China and Cuba) in the forums of the 1980s. Early references to the United Nations tended to posit it as almost another nation (if not another world!) in itself: although "liberals" may have cared about that sort of thing, Americans didn't necessarily have to! Public talk in the past few years, however, has been consciously about our nation among other nations.

It was in January 2003, just three months before the US attack on Iraq—and when that outcome seemed increasingly likely but not yet quite inevitable—that a random sample of 344 US citizens from throughout the country gathered at the National Issues Convention in Philadelphia—which we have already referred to earlier in this chapter—for a weekend, to consider together "Americans' role in the world." Called a National Issues Convention, the event was created by MacNeil/Lehrer Productions, in association with the Center for Deliberative Democracy at Stanford, whose director, James Fishkin, had first conceived the idea of such events and, over the past 20 years, has successfully staged many such experiments on critical national issues in Europe and Asia, in Australia, Britain, Japan, and North America. Such occasions remain—necessarily—exotic; for deep pockets are called for to gather such a sample of participants and experts from great distances to devote (and be compensated for) a weekend together in one place, then to broadcast a suitable summary presentation and to analyze the implications of not only the recorded dialogues themselves but also of the survey questionnaires administered to participants, both before their arrival and immediately before their departure.

From a technical point of view, the sampling and the survey analysis—undertaken by the Survey Research Center at the University of California, Berkeley—were impeccable. The resources and experience of MacNeil/Lehrer Productions provided participants the opportunity to punctuate their own conversations (in small deliberative groups of about 15 people each) with "Q & A" sessions with 2 well-balanced panels of experts and political leaders—and also provided subsequent public television broadcasts that gave to the event a serious credibility. The Kettering Foundation (which, as a research institution, deals precisely in the exploration of such democratic and deliberative practices among both the public and professional leaders) provided an issue guide in the style of that for the National Issues Forums, as a framework from which to develop the deliberation; and it helped recruit two-dozen skilled and scrupulously impartial small-group moderators from the National Issues Forums network. Around, behind, and under it all, the generous stewardship of The William and Flora Hewlett Foundation made the event possible.

On this occasion, Kettering also provided a team of observers experienced in the analysis of public deliberation to monitor and record their experience of the event at firsthand—and these essays have been collected in the volume, *Public Thought and Foreign Policy* (edited, as he is happy to acknowledge, by the present writer), which provides perhaps the most complete record we have of public deliberation about concerns that have surrounded a specific and current issue of foreign policy. But what is of particular importance here is the quite remarkable degree to which, at a time of extraordinary crisis in our still young 21st century, the reports in this book throw back clear and recognizable echoes of what we had heard from a deliberative American public 10 and 20 years before, in times of relative stability during the Cold War and, after that, following the first Gulf War.

Looking through the records of public deliberation in the 1980s and 1990s with 21st-century eyes, we are struck by the recurring concerns expressed then about terrorism. While the apparent driving concern in the 1980s was with the twin threats of communism and the Soviet Union, in all of the reports in those decades there are indications that the need to guard against international terrorism is one of the powerful "felt" reasons for questioning Cold War policy and looking for greater collaborative, international arrangements. "Terrorism," notes Public Agenda, describing its "community leaders" project in 1986, "was a continuing preoccupation through all of these workshops over the 10-month period; it was identified as a common problem that might invite cooperation or even require collaboration for its solution." Public Agenda quotes a Seattle participant who said, "You think ahead 15 years, and that terrorism is going to become more common . . . possibly other countries are going to have some interest in restraining terrorism and cooperating when it occurs." A decade and a half before 9/11, terrorism may not have figured prominently in US political considerations, but it was clearly present in the public mind.

In this context, the National Issues Forums on terrorism in the year 2002 and on "Americans' Role in the World" in 2003 are peculiarly revealing of a people struggling toward a judgment on terrorism and the apparent need for joining with others to avert or contain it. Throughout the year after 9/11, and during the six months or so before and again immediately following the invasion of Iraq, public dialogues are particularly interesting, therefore. They not only gave people an opportunity to engage their more-than top-of-the-head reactions to the events of 9/11 itself, but also to react to policies, or plans for actions, or expressed needs in relation to them. The deliberations on terrorism, for example, that continued during the weeks immediately before and following the actual US invasion of Iraq, gave relatively little time and virtually no credit at all to the policy of the "preemptive strike" featured in the Bush doctrine. Our history books would no doubt be shorter had this nation never used a preemptive strike; and people's resistance in the 2003 forums—it was genuine *resistance* in these forums—seemed therefore to have less to do with its employment as a tactic than with its articulation as a principle. Winning may be everything, in war as in sport, but for these Americans there seemed nonetheless something a little disquieting about hitting the other guy before he hits you—or saying you plan to do so!

More important, however, and more pragmatic, seemed to be the fear that the preemptive strike—whether by Japan at Pearl Harbor, or by the United States in Vietnam or, in this instance, in Iraq—may turn out not to be preemptive at all: not an end, but a beginning of trouble. Claire Snyder, one of the Kettering observers at the January 2003 National Issues Convention, wrote of these dialogues (held, it is perhaps worth noting again, just before the actual US invasion of Iraq):

> Self-defense clearly went hand-in-hand with multilateral cooperation in the minds of participants. Remarkably, there appeared virtually no support during the discussion for the current administration's doctrine of "preemptive strike." One man bluntly said, "What, are we going to start a Hatfield-McCoy thing with the whole world?" No one said we should "go it alone"—despite the ubiquity of that phrase in the mass

> media at the time. As one person put it: "I disagree with acting unilaterally. Just because we have power does not mean we shouldn't work with others. We need discussion with allies. Our role should not be policeman of the world. But we should be ready to go if people ask us for help."

John Doble (some of whose comments on this convention we have examined earlier, and also a Kettering observer on this occasion) picked up on this concern about acting without persuasive reason.

> A woman in one of the observed groups said, "Proof [about weapons of mass destruction] has not yet been shared with the American people," while a man in that group said, "I have a problem going in and beating a government before the facts are known . . . before we send our sons and daughters." Another man said he "wouldn't know what we would be fighting for if we did go to war now." A moderator noted that people in his group "felt that there is an absence of proof that Iraq was involved with 9/11." The questionnaires administered to the departing delegates on Sunday, January 13, 2003 also picked up this sentiment, with researchers reporting that "only 22 percent of the deliberators . . . thought that the US should invade Iraq 'if there is no new evidence found by the [UN] inspectors that the US still has reason to believe that Iraq has weapons of mass destruction.'"

Doble adds the familiar American recognition among the participants that war elsewhere affects life at home:

> When the citizens considered the costs and consequences of military action, they voiced concern that waging war without broad international support would mean the US would pay the lion's share of the costs. "The dollar costs of war, especially if we act unilaterally, were a significant deterrent to my group," said [another] moderator. A number of people said the need for jobs and health care for all Americans should top the national agenda, adding that war would mean putting off action on them. [A] group talked about "their personal finan-

> cial struggles and having enough money to feed their families." [Another] was concerned about policing other countries "while we are still having problems here at home."
>
> Others voiced concern about how promoting the spread of democracy would be perceived internationally. For example, [one] group felt that what seems like patriotism in this country "might feel like ethnocentrism" to foreigners. Saying her group was concerned that democratic values not conflict with indigenous norms, [another moderator] added, "People in my group were trying really to be considerate of other people's values and culture."

Another Kettering monitor, Scott London, described in this way what he heard from the small group he audited at the National Issues Convention: "While Americans tend to judge themselves based on their intentions, the rest of the world judges the United States on the basis of its actions. Our values are basically fine but our behaviors don't reflect them." This juxtaposition of intention and action captures a now familiar dilemma that Americans face whenever they think about the rest of the world.

It was at a deliberative forum two years later, in 2005 in South Carolina, that one participant said, "You have to know when to flex your muscles," only for another, sitting across the room, to expostulate, "But war on terror! War against *whom?*" In other words, the public question becomes, not whether or not to fight but, in effect, "who are you fighting, and for what?" The two men appeared to be presenting two views at odds: one of strong-armed intervention and the other of a more subtle purposefulness. Further discussion showed otherwise. Both men were middle-aged African Americans, one apparently a teacher, the other a retired foreign service officer; and each clearly understood and shared the other's seemingly different impulse, as it turned out. Of the war on terror, one of the men said,

> We're not going to declare victory. There's not going to be a signing of something on the Battleship Missouri. This thing is going to go on for a decade or so—and if it gets over, we won't know when it's over.

In other words, we are, in effect, not fighting a war in the traditional sense.

So, in these public deliberations the "cause" for which we were supposedly to be fighting became something more than "military," its impulse other than "democracy." The concerns expressed by the participants embraced AIDS, the environment, international justice, economic development . . . a host of global problems, in relation to any one of which, it seemed, America's reputation might be at stake. "Choicework" becomes difficult, apparently, when so many different "causes" are at stake, incidentally but unavoidably. As another Kettering observer, Dorothy Battle, reported from this 2003 National Issues Convention:

> Delegates shared individual views about how the US could help people throughout the world with problems such as hunger and AIDS. "Environment and disease are common amongst all people of the world," one delegate remarked; and these common concerns seemed generally to be thought of as, in the long run, more of a threat than terrorism.

Battle went on to identify a growing pattern of concern during the deliberation (although not a new one, for we had heard it recurring since the 1980s): that what other peoples think of Americans matters.

One delegate explained that he had traveled to many countries, as a civilian, throughout the world and noticed how people in foreign countries felt about Americans. In his opinion, Americans were seen in a negative light, as being arrogant and self-centered. Another delegate, who also claimed that she had traveled abroad quite a bit and, therefore, had direct interactions with people in other countries, corroborated what he had said about foreigners' perceptions of American arrogance.

The Trace of a Collective Will

That public deliberation always comes to bear so powerfully upon dilemmas that entail reluctant trade-offs is what makes it an invaluable tool of democratic self-government. A public forum does not tell us what a majority of Americans believe; nor does it move people toward some middle-of-the-road consensus that satisfies few of them on either side of an issue. On some aspects of any given issue it might succeed in doing either or both of those; but its real purpose—and, at best, its real achievement—is to lead us to discover what we have in common, with such assurance as will enable various of us (individually, or within our political parties, or in special-interest groups, or in ad-hoc attempts) to effect what we have collectively willed. Deliberative forums are not a substitute for political parties, or for government, or for particular lobbies; they are, however, instruments by means of which broad-based political parties, while representing their own historic and philosophic priorities, can nonetheless effectively govern *for the public good*, because the deliberators capture the preoccupations, the patterns, and the purposes of public thinking. Where public deliberation is neglected (as it is much of the time in modern democracies), partisan governments are left to—and are often elected to—sustain merely the interests of particular factions and to seek goals that, not having been adequately examined, are pursued at a risk to the common welfare.

"Poetry," W. H. Auden once wrote, "makes nothing happen. It is a way of speaking, a mouth!" And being a wry old poet, what he was really saying is that *without* poetry, *nothing is known*. That's the way it is, too, with public deliberation. So it may be salutary—although probably not comforting—to recognize that, sometimes, *official* policies and practices (that through the past 25 years have been accompanied by considerable domestic stress) may turn out, after looking back at public responses over time, to have been merely too eagerly and too narrowly conceived to define *carefully* (for example) America's role in the world; they may at a given time have aborted the kind of collaborative international experience that might ultimately prove necessary to fulfill our imagined American destiny. In contrast, the deliberative public has been ahead of political leadership in important instances; at least it seems to have hovered about a judgment—or leaned in the direction of it, from time to time—that retrospectively appears to have been not unwise. Hawks and doves turned out not to be ideal birds to fly in the Cold War, for example; and preemptive strike and hurried abandonment may, neither of them, turn out to have been appropriate to the situation of Iraq. In retrospect, there might be a more persistent coherence in American public thinking than is represented in the annals of the nation's capital, if it were consistently pursued, over time.

The problem, of course, is in the pursuit. For the kind of "judgment" we have been tracing is more ambience than edict; policy is to be found within it, rather than shaped as response to it. The concept of public judgment implies no less; analysis of the patterns of public thinking in the National Issues Forums on foreign policy over the past quarter-century suggests that the public—albeit changing, sometimes overstating, and always highly charged—given opportunity, and time, and necessary information, may in fact be capable of assuming a sovereign role to which the ballot box is, quite properly, *merely instrumental* in democratic government. What we see in this cursory exploration is the actual process of public thinking: working through, in a sustained process of dialogue, something close to those stages through which a people reconciles itself, from among contraries, to a place where a judgment that can be implemented in action is possible.

Of course, not all steps in the "process" that Yankelovich has elaborated are completed in sequence; for we are victims of argument; and instruments, from time to time, of circumstance or the influence of others' whims. Put broadly, however, the movement is from a state of anxiety, puzzlement, blame, defensiveness, or anger, toward the place where contraries meet, where unavoidable tensions remind us that no life is lived without risk . . . or collaboration. That is the point at which a deliberative judgment becomes possible. And there begins collective decision making. A deliberative public begins with opinions but *shares* experiences; it recognizes shared concerns or "values" in unexpected, sometimes unfamiliar circumstances; it responds to the divisive with restraint. And *sometimes* it begins to imagine itself as a public, acting.

The movement in forums across the country did not start from a concern for America's defense, then nudge toward domestic issues, because the Soviet threat had suddenly diminished. Rather, it is as though foreign policy had become a domestic issue itself, a popular interest. It did not begin with anti-communism, then become a crusade for human rights; participants were not making a choice of one strategy rather than another, a hard-line Americanism rather than liberal internationalism, or a balance-of-power *realpolitik* rather than a new commitment to international machinery. Absent the "blinders" of the communist and nuclear threats—and perhaps despite the mirage in the desert and the mistakes attending 9/11—participants have been groping toward a new policy: one infused by a kind of internationalism that has not been typically American, historically. And one impelled by a sense that America has problems that need to be addressed as a priority but that are not unrelated to the experiences of other nations and the ways in which we deal with them.

It is perhaps worth noting that in those first "peace-time" public forum discussions of 1991-1993, after the Cold War and the first Gulf War, the name of the president came up scarcely at all and the name of the Secretary of State—even the title—never! This may not be what one typically expects when Americans settle down to serious discussions of foreign affairs. Quite apparently, the concern of the Americans who joined in discussion at the forums at that time was not with what had passed, but with what was to come—a future about which they thought there was no policy and for which they feared there would be none unless they, as a people, could articulate their interests afresh.

A dozen years later, and in every one of the forums on international relationships that we have documented and analyzed since 9/11, there has remained, at the close, an uneasy sense of foreboding, much like that reported 10 years earlier in 1993. It is as though one world had gone, not entirely happily, and no new one had been described to replace it. There was an abiding sense that a chance may be—may have been—missed! A woman in Albany, Georgia, remembered:

> To me when we saw years ago, the wall coming down . . . I remember also that New Year's . . . Tiananmen Square was devastating, but everything else that happened . . . we were united as a world. And it was the most wonderful feeling. I don't remember feeling like that, except maybe back in 1969 when there was the first landing on the moon and we all

> looked, as people from the Earth, up to the moon and thought: "We're in this all together; there, representing all of us, is a world." And they seemed to be an ideal; but we have to strive for the ideal. And if we don't, we're really going to have problems. If we could just get together and talk about this! There are so many other things, so many gifts that we have to offer one another that we're wasting because we're so concerned about our military strength. How are we going to appear to the rest of the world? We want to be the superpower. But I think we're losing sight of what life is all about and how to really protect our world.

In 2003, just one week before the invasion of Iraq, a man in a Portland, Oregon, forum said this:

> Many years ago, I served in . . . the Peace Corps. In 1963, John F. Kennedy was assassinated . . . and all these Tunisian mechanics stood there with tears running down their eyes. . . . These were people who liked us in 1962 . . . and I don't think things have changed all that much. I think just after 9/11 we had tremendous good will from around the world. Everybody was on our doorstep . . . and it seems to me that we have squandered a lot of that good will.

III.

Shared Experience and Collective Understanding . . . the Outcomes of Public Deliberation

THE BLESSING, AND PERHAPS THE CURSE, of history is the easy wisdom of hindsight that it offers. We know that times change; and when we examine that change it may be comforting to see it as rooted in the genes of national history. If we have a sense, too, of how public judgment on a given issue or problem in our collective life might (or should) relate to the institutional judgment of our leaders, we will find it illuminating to track the ways that public dialogue has reflected, or was confused by, or failed to anticipate what in fact subsequently happened. But when Yankelovich describes, in his book about public judgment, the exercises of intellectual discipline by which a public may come to an actionable judgment, it is only for convenience that he cites them as stages through which the public awareness will pass in sequence (from becoming aware of an issue to making a responsible judgment), as though in a relay race where only the handing off of the baton gives license to proceed along the next lap, toward a finish line already known and accepted. The real truth of public deliberation—and it is implicit in the psychology that informs Yankelovich's work—is that people move back and forth between the stages he identifies: one stage may virtually "embrace" another, so that to have passed through one may accomplish the work of two. Further, as these pages may suggest, a given dilemma as understood by any one person may itself change over time: its features may "morph" into another's dilemma, and any "judgment" we may think we have come to may turn out to be merely a temporary reprieve, or a turn in the road. Perhaps more significantly, the "finish line" is not known but emerges from the deliberative work of the participants.

To understand this particular phenomenon of *public* deliberation, approaching a judgment, is to contrast it with that of a jury that has to decide firmly between innocence and guilt, and even sometimes to measure the sum of penalties that its judgment should determine as appropriate. Public deliberation, for those who see and hear and analyze it—and for all of us who depend upon it—in effect reveals not a verdict but *the making* of a "public," the formulation of a *public will* that can be described and put to use, even though it may not be measured in the sense that a public survey or poll may measure public opinion.

The survey analyst asks a series of questions (all of them based upon extensive research) of participants to be surveyed, then analyzes the responses as they relate to the predetermined purpose of the questions asked, reporting the outcome as agreement or disagreement, metrically. In analyzing public *deliberation*, however, having already identified a handful of different kinds of citizen that we think will be, overall, not *un*representative of the nation or the community whose judgment we are seeking, we search out, in the course of a group deliberation, the various aspects of the substantive problem that participants have seemed to be interested in addressing, discovering both the range of their interest in those aspects or subtopics and the motives or values or risks that appear to have driven particular dissensions or agreements as the subtopics have become, by turns, the focus of discussion. An ultimate distinction between the two ways of capturing public attitudes—polling and deliberative conversation—is that while the first approach (the survey) pursues established points of difference, or conflict, in knowledge and opinion and intent, then reports on them metrically, the second (the deliberative forum) is a means of revealing—for commentators, politicians, or other citizens to pursue and capture narratively—*substantive points of interest and concern* that people think they might usefully address collectively as citizens. In public deliberation such concerns are modified, expanded, even merge into each other, recurring, or fading, as groups of people talk judiciously together for sustained periods of time.

Both the likenesses and the differences between findings from the two approaches are of course ultimately of interest to us in the pursuit of democracy, or self-government. But in pursuing an inquiry, we always have to remind ourselves that the questions asked in a survey are dictated by something other than "the public"; the survey, although it is informed by focus group research, ultimately is designed to illuminate and understand the likely public outcome of expert, official, or special-interest attitudes toward a substantive and already defined problem at issue. The public deliberative approach, by contrast, is intent upon finding out *what* it is that interests people, broadly, and *why* it is that they are interested in—or quickly cease to pursue—particular aspects of the problem or its consequences. What we have to report, ultimately, from public deliberation, to policymakers or various leadership elites, is not "what *they* (the policymakers) ought to do" (although that may be implied), but what aspects of the problem at issue *people* are interested in; and why—this is most important—*why* they are interested in those aspects of the problem, and in what has been suggested might satisfactorily be done about them. What we have to report from the public's deliberations is not what action or policy the people appear to favor, as pollsters might, but how (or to what degree) the people have come, collectively, to understand the demands that a recognized dilemma may make upon themselves, collectively.

This is an enormous step forward, for this kind of public *judgment* is an essential aspect of a democracy's political practice that is simply not included in the formalities of our Constitution, nor much noted in the present institutional realities of our American democracy. Yet, as a collective dialogue among citizens—like the *demos* of the ancient Greeks— it is fundamentally what democracy *presumes* to characterize the community that is called "democratic." Democracy demands a deliberative citizenry; an elective government is merely thereafter instrumental in effecting (or sometimes, alas, frustrating) what that citizenry wills.

Different as it is from conversation or argument among family or strangers at a table or along a bar, public, political, face-to-face, group deliberation is inevitably and of its nature significantly different also from both deliberation through the newspaper, or by mail, or online. Fundamentally, it seems that mail, print, or online kinds of communication tend to take shape as question or statement invoking or implying an answer, the varying responses being direct, oppositional, or sometimes ingeniously diverting reactions to a stated question or "position." In deliberative groups, however, each successive respondent seems inevitably to add to or modify the nature of the original question or observation itself, frequently with reference to personal concern, so that others, eager to respond, slowly change the nature of the understood question—which has (perhaps in some sense, not even consciously recognized) already been changed between speaker and listener so that a deliberative "narrative" is itself being formed without reference to an agenda or issue book, or position, or any recognized rule of process in the consciousness of the deliberative participants. (That on-paper, on-wire, or online respondents are not physically recognized as participating nonverbally—by gesture, notion, murmur, or intriguing changes in physical reaction—may further exacerbate the difference.)

Such deliberatively offered considerations are important in varying degrees on different occasions, of course; yet we do well to remember that the core of a group deliberation, as we have traditionally valued it, is the *unfolding of a shared story* among a modest-sized group of individuals, with some shared values but differing experiences, as they consider a common (or shared) "public problem." This is not to say that our experience of the problem is shared: the health-care problem strikes me differently if I am a stockholder in an insurance company than it does an uninsured teen-aged mother. But in public political deliberation, as citizens, we recognize similarly the problematic nature of our mutually affective individual interests. Public communication among strangers who do not assemble as a community, however, even if it can be realized online with a visible component, tends to reflect a focus on immediate responses, or answers. And even if a range of individual narratives of discomfort in search of answers comes readily in some instances, the one-at-a-time accumulation of individual responses—rather than a continuing sequence of experience and interaction—remains a significant difference between the deliberative *group* and the casual or one-at-a-time read news-sheet, online communications, or in audited argument. This is perhaps why there are so few examples of written literary deliberation; even great collections of correspondence, like that between Paul Claudel and George Bernard Shaw, turn out to be, in effect, debates among researchers—carefully thought and highly opinionated ones, at that!—rather than deliberative searches for shared understanding. In a deliberative conversation a shared story unfolds, taking the place of argument, while in the debates of legislators or partisans, predetermined *interests* are argued and attacked.

Public deliberation does not need a teacher or an umpire, and certainly not the kind of moderator we are familiar with in news programs, where typically hosts and reporters tend to adopt consciously (and sometimes condescendingly) the pattern of professional commentators. Popular domestic news media, deliberation online, and formal political campaign activities all tend to be valued among individuals who consciously represent a given *interest*. They are favored instruments of government and elective politics. Public politics, however, takes place within groups whose members must come to share an *understanding* strong enough to generate action by means of an extended exchange of experience. The value of public democratic deliberation, then, is that it opens the way toward shared understanding and thence collaborative action. Experience tells us that this is a difficult process, however, that requires extensive exchange among citizens. And *public politics*, in this sense, is never a conflict of interests, always a shared endeavor. The recognizable deliberative process of democracy is one whereby we citizens, in groups or as group, together exchange (and to varying degrees change) our understandings of problems that confront us all, as a people. We appear to value the options that such conversations offer us, and so recognize the trade-offs that the various options will inevitably require.

To assume that the outcome of public deliberation is, ultimately, the making of a decisive quasi-legislative decision—as, to a point, James Fishkin's National Issues Conventions (an example of which was described in the preceding chapter) and Daniel Yankelovich's research group, Viewpoint Learning (which designs and conducts dialogues for both business and public policy) both have sometimes seemed to suggest—may actually undervalue the public's distinctive role in the political life of a contemporary democracy. To government, always, belongs the task of framing and enforcing law; and in a fully functioning democracy, it will do so in response to a manifest public understanding—if you will, to an expression of public will. The image of the classical *agora*, as a place of relatively well-centered concern, comes to mind; but, in a vast and diverse country like the United States, where the business of one interest often seems necessarily to depend upon the exclusion of another, the notion that this kind of harmonious will can be satisfactorily achieved by the skills of representatives, elected *by* those interests, is open to question. The formulation of a coherent public will—indeed the taking shape of a *public*, itself—depends on *the process of its citizens, collectively, coming to judgment*.

Except that the outcome of public deliberation is not ever quite a "judgment" of the kind we associate with courts of law, or professional examiners, or ideologically driven legislators!

In the very early years of the National Issues Forums, we learned quickly that individual participants in a deliberative forum very often did not change their minds (or their opinions) on the question at issue, but that they did change their judgments of the opinions of others. The voices that they heard in the public forum were voices recognized as responsive to a shared dilemma, even though they might tend toward different courses of action, reflecting the somewhat different circumstances or prior concerns of individual participants. The more we have heard these public voices, confronting more (and sometimes more complex) issues, the more clear it has become that, in deliberative *public* politics, the movement is always toward a closer, collective understanding, both of shared dilemmas and of the kinds of trade-offs that must be considered in deciding how those dilemmas might best be handled. And more clear becomes the effort that needs be made to that end if we are genuinely to share our life as a people!

When our goal, then, is an actionable, collective response to a societal problem, our interest is not merely in what individuals in groups want to do, but in why they want to do it. What citizens' deliberations have always revealed—if we hear them fully enough and consider them carefully enough—is the *relationship* between the "whys" rather than merely a *tension* between the "whats." The "what" and the "why" are each related in their proponents' eyes, those of the deliberators, but acknowledgement of the tension that attends any action is valued variously by different individuals—and recognizing that is the means, the indispensable means, toward the making of citizens' relationship as a community. The achievement of that relationship—of a community that consciously shares its destiny—embodies the concept of government to which democracy aspires.

In this sense, whenever we listen to, or participate among, a deliberative public—no matter that the issue be complex, the deliberation together all too brief—we become a part of that public, coming to (or at least moving toward) judgment about what should be done, in the context of our shared problem *and a shared sense of others' experience of it.* It may often be that in deliberative politics—as in psychiatric medicine—relative to the time available and the complexity of the rooted problem, the ultimate "cure" remains elusive. Nevertheless, what is achieved, what is learned or "worked through," session by session, may be critical in determining what follows. And the patient (we, the people, in this case) may progress therefrom! Politically, the psychological metaphor of "working through" is particularly illuminating to those whose interest is in the question David Mathews is wont to ask, "What will make democracy work as it should?"

Such deliberative dialogue is itself what makes democracy work: deliberative citizens are doing the work of democracy. In a culture like ours—that tends to think of "government of the people" as essentially associated with a representatively elected *institutional* government which, once chosen, governs pretty much as do other kinds of hierarchic governments—it is not conventional to accept that a people talking to itself is ultimately setting the terms within which effective policy is designed and legislation shaped. Yet although these deliberative citizens—some of whose recent deliberations on various topics we are in this volume just sketching—may still not know quite what to do or who should do it with respect to any given issue, it is nonetheless their dialogue that leads us to an awareness of what *should* be done, and why. In the last resort, public deliberation is not well fashioned to make policy or frame legislation, but it reveals to all of us the concerns that policy and law must embrace. It sets the stage, turns up the lights, and sometimes itself becomes the overture of the show that we look forward to. As Daniel Yankelovich says, it sets "the boundaries of public permission." As a deliberative public, we may not actually decide upon what actions might be taken by ourselves, individually or collectively, and which by our governing institutions. And contrary to sentimental expectations, the deliberative public forum seldom leads directly to individual citizens' actions. It is, however, the *people's politics*—as distinct from the politics of elections and legislation—in the functioning democracy.

The Modes of Public Politics

In 1991, the Kettering Foundation inaugurated the annual television program called, appropriately, *A Public Voice*, that was to be broadcast by PBS for 16 years, presenting each year—sometimes twice a year—a synopsis of public deliberative discussions on one (or occasionally more) current issues, videotaped and carefully analyzed, then edited into formal, coherent video sequences that both political leaders and the press might evaluate and respond to, live, on camera, in the broadcast public television program itself. The videotaped public deliberations were drawn each year from half a dozen public forums held in different parts of the country, each of them having initially been videotaped in its entirety. The panel at the National Press Club in Washington, DC, included US representatives or senators, or representatives of the administration, members of the press, and often professionals knowledgeable about the particular subject under discussion. The group would listen and, in a moderated discussion, respond to the judgments, tensions, or evasions that they observed on the edited videotapes of public forums. The eventual broadcast program, then, one full hour in length, would include three 10-minute sequences of *public* dialogue on a chosen issue for the year, each followed by a 10-minute dialogue among the dozen or so panelists—members of Congress, the press, and professional experts—commenting on the just-viewed segments of public deliberation.

In one sense, the program was to provide, to an outsider, the opportunity objectively to note how the relationship of politician and expert, on the one hand, and the public, on the other, might unfold. More significantly, it showed us how public thinking, when people deliberate together in an organized way, comes to sharpen itself as citizens face up to differences in their individual experience, acknowledge the values they share, and focus eventually on what they, collectively, think needs to be done in response to the "wicked" problems that are the subject, in each instance, of their deliberations. From these videotapes and further written analyses, we have learned a great deal about democratic politics—and about public deliberation as a unique and essential part of our political life as a democratic whole. In the carefully edited video presentations of *A Public Voice*, we watch the progress of a public, struggling toward judgment, and we get some sense of the relationship—or the absence of a productive relationship—between the "public voice" and that of the Washington professionals.

To those of us who analyze public dialogue, then try to represent it within the constraints of the television hour, the challenge is always to look at the main contours of a half dozen or so deliberative forums on the same subject, to see just how much depth and movement, common to all of them, can be captured in order to give viewers (including viewers at the Press Club in Washington, DC) some sense of an emergent public thinking. Those of us on the production end of these programs had always been conscious that participants in National Issues Forums are in no sense being invited to choose literally between three or four choices of possible courses of action, examined in turn; we know, of course, that when colleagues prepare an issue book, they have not been submitting their own framing as an alternative for people to consider in competition with the current or partisan political framing, or the press framing, or the experts' solutions, or special interests, already well publicized. The NIF pattern is simply to use three or four formal points of entry into an issue—different ways of approaching it—as a means of introducing the known public concerns into a somewhat formalized public discussion, without the need for people to see them, specifically, as representations of any already chartered course to which they need immediately to say "yea" or "nay" as though it were a world-without-end, absolute answer. Each "choice" presents a legitimate sense of what is "problematic" about a given issue, and reveals the pros and cons that might be entailed by each different way of responding, as a people, to its challenge. The public forums do not merely refuse to take a vote or headcount on any eventual disposition toward given "choices"; they actually anticipate that, as people work their way through those choices, they will begin to formulate and wrestle with options that have not yet been fully fleshed out on anybody's agenda at the time. The issue itself may take on a slightly different shape.

Habit and custom—television viewers' habit and custom—had pretty much determined that the *Public Voice* videos, when shown as a finished broadcast program, would follow the approximately 10 or 20 minute "attention" periods that viewers of commercial television are attuned to; but the *Public Voice* videos have always used these periods to track and represent the movement of people's *thinking about* the subject—the recorded thinking of participants in deliberative forums, that is, rather than what might seem to be people's too quickly judgmental responses to the "approaches" outlined in an issue book, or the easy reaction in casual "coffee-shop" conversation, or the "party-line" response that recognizes no "shades of gray." An issue book is meant to stimulate deliberation, not to prescribe an agenda for it. Summary statements of individuals' *opinions*, whether informed or not, are not the business of public deliberations. The analyst's task is to discover and more clearly reveal the *patterns* of people's thinking.

This is fundamental—and fundamentally important. Anyone who chooses to look back at the *Public Voice* video programs and at the originally published discussion guides may notice that the first video sequence of the deliberative public does tend to align itself fairly closely with the first choice in the published issue guide—generally a policy option or strategy addressing a fairly broadly recognized aspect of popular concern about the issue—while the second filmed sequence tends to reveal a more expansive view than the option presented as number two in the issue book. Often, however, the third sequence moves in a somewhat different direction from that specified as the third alternative approach in the original printed discussion guide. In fact, when participants in the dialogue move to the second approach, they are already bringing with them the experience of talking through the first approach; and that experience frequently challenges them to explore in some directions other than those that were anticipated and presented in the second approach of the issue book itself. In deliberative public forums, as a practical matter, the moderator has to cope with this, to a degree, and that usually means that participants do, to some measure, start their discussion, as it were, over again with each successive approach, although not quite as they might have done had each indeed been the first choice presented to them. Quite naturally, that's a hard row to hoe; and if anything, *deliberation* over the second approach to the given problem in the issue guide tends to be engendered by rubbing the first two together. So the second choice may be an Aladdin's lamp in a world darkened by the first; and if there is a growing sense of a shared focus, it will become more visible as the forum (or the video made from film of multiple forums) moves into its final option for discussion.

The upshot of this natural progression in deliberation is most often that a sense of direction begins to emerge in the middle of a public forum. None of these forum occasions, of course, leads necessarily to what Daniel Yankelovich would call a "public judgment." But it frequently does lead to a restatement of the problem as "actionable" in the final stage of the forum, or to the exploration or syntheses of perspectives on it that were not noted before, even in the issue books that served as a discussion guide. This seems always to have happened, for example in deliberation about freedom of speech issues; it tends to be the case in forthright political (or "governance") issues; it has certainly been true in Social Security deliberations and in those on health care where, by the close, people have generally been seen as putting the lie to suggestions of intergenerational warfare or ideological insistence in *any* particular direction. Some of the most dramatic examples, recently, were in the forums on terrorism and on America's role in the world, in the latter of which (as we have already noted in the preceding chapter) participants gave a surprising prominence, toward the end of the forums, to a concern for this country and its reputation in the eyes of the world. Our deliberative people may not often have decided upon a policy that wins all their allegiance or fits them all like a glove, but they have moved slowly toward an understanding of something that matters in their lives—because it is, collectively, important enough to provide the "litmus test" for a policy.

Public deliberation does not proceed in a directly linear narrative; nor does it "see-saw" as does "principled" or self-serving debate. More tango than foxtrot, it tends to reveal hesitations, cross steps, bends, and reversals in its course. Nonetheless, it is in fact progressive; recognizable strains of thought have beginnings, middles, and ends; one leads to another, or at least gives rise to it. Thus the end understanding of a deliberative group is more widely shared than—and to a degree different from—the *individual* opinions and understandings that have been first voiced in the process. It is a dialogic process in which people weigh alternatives on their way toward collective judgment about what they should do collectively, as a public. Over the years—and particularly while analyzing discs and videotapes of deliberative forums—we have been able with some confidence to identify distinctively recognizable kinds (or "modes") of conversation through which the deliberative undertaking proceeds for short periods at a time. And we can see their functions in the process of coming to a public judgment.

An *argument,* for example—in a public forum, as anywhere else—suggests the simple, always useful, momentary clash of opinion that most of us in America seem to anticipate (and all too often employ) in political discussions. But deliberation typically avoids the open and unyielding clash of opinion; people speak their opinions, certainly, but the character of the deliberative gathering is such that opinions tend to be weighed and accumulated in a context of comparable but variously differing experiences from other participants. Emerging as they do in the context of described individual and personal hopes, fears, and experiences, they are not usually in themselves the focus of interest or the subject of *argument,* but merely illustrative of different people's handling of a generally recognized predicament. Inevitably, too, when facing controversial issues, there are occasions when somebody is particularly eager to advance a pet concern, a favored remedy, a distinctive or cultivated mistrust, or the like. Generally this sort of thing doesn't get very far in a deliberative gathering: other participants don't pick it up; they have another experience (of their own) to narrate; and the good moderator won't allow the event, anyway, to degenerate into a "he said, she said" contest. Yet there are occasions when one participant's spoken, deeply felt concern is so thoroughly at odds with the trend of the continuing deliberations that a number of others will loudly exclaim about its irrelevance, or possibly wrong-headedness—and the force and weight of their collective rejoinder is enough to move the ongoing deliberation forward to related but distinctly different concerns.

An example of such an *outlier* concern occurred in a public forum taped for use at the National Press Club in 2005, when one of the participants attempted to make 9/11 and terrorism relevant factors in a deliberation about the nation's illegal immigration problem (which we shall look at more fully, later in this chapter). In the full tape from which the broadcast excerpts were made, the comment serves as a demonstration of the way in which people sometimes try to insert their own agenda into a discussion—and how a public deliberation handles it, to move itself forward. The fact that 9/11-style terrorism may involve immigrants, either legal or illegal, was quite apparently unrelated to the "immigration problem" that preoccupied these forum participants; in a number of forums on the topic, it simply was passed over whenever it had been introduced as though a significant factor in the issue of immigration. To some citizens, certainly, "immigration" implies increasing threat from foreigners, but clearly to most discussants the immigrant was not to be *confused with* the terrorist.

On the other hand, a common feature of any deliberative public meeting are individuals whose own distinctive experience and powers of articulation equip them to sum up and in a sense put to rest an uncertainty about which fellow participants have been deliberating for the past several minutes. This kind of *weighing in* is featured, more often than not, during segments in which participants appear to want to separate their different individual accounts of experience too personally, but it often ends up characterizing the different steps by which a deliberation seems to progress. We encountered such a *weighing in*, notably, in the comments and voices of a retired hospital executive and an anonymous but knowledgeable African American VA patient, both featured on film from an Ohio forum, presented in the 2004 televised healthcare deliberations that we shall refer to again later. At this forum, both men contributed to a highly articulate and clearly "felt" panegyric on the accomplishments of the Veterans' Administration's provision of health care to the injured that simply overrode—quite simply, brought to a stop—suggestions of unease or doubt about government's capacity in such matters.

Another example of *weighing in* occurred in the 2007 forums on immigration, where the former supervisor at a chicken factory in Georgetown, Maryland, offered a modest example of this kind of intervention from his experience. He knowingly tells his story at an opportune moment in the dialogue, which crystallizes our sense and other participants' sense of what it means for a very different and seemingly ill-mannered alien—which he had appeared to be—to take on a hard and relatively thankless job which might before have been—just *might* have been—another US citizen's legitimate means of support. In such moments, the temperament of the speaker is necessarily important: such episodes serve their purpose in the movement of deliberation because the speaker seems to be in tune both with people's fears *and* their generous expectations; the speaker at such critical moments is always a generous spirit, though not necessarily to be agreed with, routinely.

Conscious *trade-offs* are another deliberative mode in which a small group of people, coming with different experiences and differing points of view, face up to the fact that to secure a desirable end, they will all have to make one *trade-off* or another—in fact, a sacrifice—that will have such serious ramifications that the end, desirable from various points of view, will be readily recognized although perhaps not so eagerly undertaken. *Trade-offs* are much more common in public deliberation than we may realize, although such trade-offs are very seldom carried on with the sustained intensity of thought that characterized the remarkable conversation taped during the course of a forum on health care, in Pittsburgh in 2004. The *trade-off* in this classic Pittsburgh forum (to which we shall return in the next chapter) entailed consideration of the question, "to what extent should we, as taxpayers, provide expensive and demanding medical assistance to the patient—hyper-typically, someone's beloved family member—who seems unlikely to benefit from it in the long run?" The deliberation was clear and compelling because participants were able to introduce and focus on a persuasive real-life example that one of them presented, so that others clearly shared the recognition that a decision was inescapable, even as the outcome, *either way*, would be painful. The speaker was a young widower whose wife had died after a long dependency on publicly provided dialysis. "Somebody paid for that," he murmured; then in wide-eyed shock: "It wasn't me!" In its ultimate form, then, this experience presents an insoluble mystery that can be accepted only by an act of will. It does not appear often in such persuasive and dramatic form as we hear it in this example, but the *trade-off* mode is central in the course of public deliberation, for it presents, in a sense at least, a metaphor for the process of public deliberation itself. As we embrace another's experience, we recognize that we share similar values, if somewhat distinctive experience, and therefore must be prepared sometimes to bend to accommodate what we might prefer not to know about.

Such *narratives of accumulated understanding*, occurring within deliberative forums and sometimes embracing a forum in its entirety, are generated among people who are trying to come to grips with the full complexity of a problem that they recognize has already become a part of their shared lives. In the televised 2005 *Public Voice* video presentation on immigration, the entire first segment (composed by editing down several forums together) is an example of this. Somebody wonders to what degree immigrants did and may still today become assimilated into the host culture—and whether willingness to master the host country's language would be an indicator of this assimilation. But immigrant patterns of behavior, participants revealed, may influence their judgment in this regard. Perhaps, beyond language, the *appearance* of difference (and the fact of it) may make some host country citizens nervous, perhaps even revealing traces of invidious prejudice. The difference—the awareness of "the other"—is in itself unsettling. Even though, once immigrants are assimilated, the newly diverse outcome within a community may be seen as enriching, nevertheless some citizens will continue to regret the resultant change—despite the fact that this is a narrative theme in the story, toward the telling of which narrative some 30 individual comments, recorded on film from 6 forums, have contributed. It is not that contributors to the deliberation knew the end of the story before they started; rather, each sentence in the discussions to which they contributed compelled their interest anew, and (eventually) their personal contribution.

Essentially, in the first half hour of every one of these recorded half dozen deliberations on illegal immigration, participants themselves laid out the complex features of the issue that they had to reconcile, from their family histories and direct personal experience, before any satisfying or acceptable action might be taken. The outcome is neither consensus, compromise, nor a general sharing of one opinion; but it is a slowly developed, shared awareness of experience. Such *aggregated story creation* is perhaps the norm of public deliberation on critical political issues. Its outcome is a shared understanding of the nature of a problem, though it may stop short of a shared public judgment about what should or can be done, collectively, about it.

The narrative of such accumulated, contributory understandings comes close to delineating a sense that all of the participants, whatever their opinions, recognize at the end as a *collective* awareness of the issue's challenge—the comprehensive narrative of a shared experience that demands action. Another sequence of the deliberations on immigration, shown at the 2005 taping of *A Public Voice*, offers an example of how this somewhat rarer kind of public comprehension from the deliberative process unfolds. The *Public Voice* film presentation first uses a few clips from Cedar Rapids, Iowa; El Paso, Texas; and Mesa, Arizona; but the essential story of a civic experience is then presented, *from beginning to end,* by participants in Georgetown, Delaware. These are not participants thinking together, as is the case in the mode described above, modifying opinions, and changing their individual senses of the problem as they go. Rather, here participants add unique perceptions of experiences that *aggregate* to a shared and more sophisticated whole. The story is about a body of strangers (undocumented aliens) who, it is perceived, perform a very necessary job, cheaply. In the course of doing that, being strangers, they sometimes seem troublesome; yet that may be nothing compared to the trouble they endure themselves, being unable to speak the language and subject sometimes to victimization. Yet clearly, it is recognized, there *is* work for them to do: *they* come because "we" want them—even though we don't "want" them. Here the deliberation is not the weighing of a "choice" in the sense that "choices" demand a judgment; nor is it the weighing of a trade-off against the value of what is received at its expense. Rather, it is a case of weighing each perception one hears in relation to the next perception that it occasions. This process of responding to perception continues until everybody seems to think the "story" is complete and has (so to speak) its appropriate "moral" injunction at the close—even though that "moral" may still prove to be ambiguous in its application to individual concerns.

All such variants of deliberative exchanges that we note as "modes" in public deliberations are very much there for the recognition as we analyze the movement toward judgment in a deliberative public forum. We would not want to suggest that any public deliberation is essentially made up merely of these, strung together, however. While we have isolated them and present them as illustrations of kinds of exchanges that make clear the points of contact where differences meet and modify understandings (or misunderstandings) between individuals, we recognize that in the course of a deliberative forum these modes may themselves be spread out over time, overlapping and intertwining, one with another, to make the conversation more natural (and the analysis a little more difficult), but the eventual judgment more secure. What matters is that these modes reflect natural, human means of communication. The expression of opinion, even of half a dozen differing opinions, communicates merely that: the existence of half a dozen differing opinions. From a deliberative public, however, we can capture a far more important kind of communication: the slow, often circuitous sharing of *understandings* that reflect—or at least hint at the possibility of—a shared and actionable *judgment*.

Framing a Public Purpose . . . the Immigration "Problem"

This said, it may be appropriate here to begin the narrative examples, promised in our preface, of three distinctly different public deliberations that exemplify what we mean to imply in the phrase *circuitous sharing of understandings* which, as we have noted, often describes and assists in the deliberative journey toward a public's judgment. Further, to see how deliberation can fairly be described as "the people's politics," it may be useful for us to look now, not at Americans' perhaps slow and uncertain progress toward judgment about one broad and "wicked" problem, entangled and difficult to resolve over the decades—as we did in the preceding chapter, exploring our foreign policy—but rather to examine the ways in which deliberative citizens in a democracy can formulate a shared attitude from a shared understanding of difficulty, talking through a given problem that seems immediate in their present domestic life as a people—a problem now desperate for response, if not exactly a solution, in a limited period of time. That was the concept with which the National Issues Forums first started their work, and it has remained their most consistent concern. Theirs is a conscious *political* act, a planned interference in history, through the attempt to explore, and if found, assert, a *public* will on the basis of a shared understanding of what should be done in the people's collective interest—something in which the people themselves might play a conscious part, if not quite literally "do," individually!

To this end, it may be of further practical value to illustrate the public deliberative process by considering the concept of public judgment as we see it unfold, not in one forum nor in multiple forums over a slow space of history, but in a number of forums on the same topic, carefully analyzed, but taking place in different communities, over a limited period of months, so that a determinedly relevant and recognizable change may be begun in people's lives. Attempts to do just this, and to make what was discovered available to politicians and the press, with the sense that it might also be useful to them, have developed significantly in this past quarter-century. What we shall now explore, then, are patterns of "public thinking"—of a public coming to judgment—as evidenced in a small number of public forums, over just the past few years, on each of three troubling and nationally critical issues—immigration and energy in this chapter, and health care in the next. The forums on each of the given topics, each comprising about 2 hours of deliberative talk among 20 or so people—a manageable group—were recorded on videotape within a few weeks of one another during the past few years, each in 5 or 6 different communities across the United States.

The movement toward change—and the impediments to it—is classically demonstrated in the immigration videos used in the program broadcast from the Press Club in 2005. It is not that the individual immigration forums provide the ideal illustration of this kind of movement, but it is abundantly clear that in these forums, overall, people's thinking did in fact change, enlarge, and (I think we dare say) mature between the beginning and the end. So they may be worth further retrospective exploration.

The panel of experts who reviewed the tape of citizens' deliberation on the immigration problem at the National Press Club in 2005 had been invited as a sample potentially responsive to the increasingly collective public awareness of this issue's importance—and of its controversial nature! The panel included two members of Congress, Representative Silvestre "Silver" Reyes, from Texas, and then-Representative Jim Leach, from Iowa; Richard Harwood, president of The Harwood Institute; Mirta Ojito, a Pulitzer Prize winner who herself had been, as a teenager, one of the Cuban "boat people"; Doris Meissner, a former INS commissioner who was described by everyone we consulted as a thoroughly remarkable woman with a profound knowledge and broad human understanding of our subject; Tamar Jacoby, a former writer and editor at *Newsweek*, who had recently published a widely esteemed collection of essays on the new complexities of the immigration topic, *Reinventing the Melting Pot*; and two articulate conservative intellectuals, John Fund, from the *Wall Street Journal*, and Dan Griswold, from the Cato Institute. We were confident that, for them, our tapes would project, in sum, a "public voice" about immigration at that time, whose tenor might be somewhat different from the news stories commonly found under the heading "immigration problems," and that this difference would make their own engagement at the Press Club directly responsive to the concerns and interests of citizens who had been approaching (if not unanimously reaching) a judgment in the forums around the country during the preceding year.

The deliberations that we had analyzed as raw video footage were perhaps more than usually circuitous and sometimes seemingly repetitious. At least, let us say, at first sight no one of the half dozen forums we had filmed seemed initially to suggest a particularly coherent set of tapes that would make the Press Club conversation generally useful both to members of Congress on the panel and to the viewing public. What was really going on in these public conversations clearly had something to do with the extraordinary challenge that widely spreading and multinational 21st-century immigration presents to what is, ironically, a professed "nation of immigrants." It seemed that a lot of ground had to be circled, then covered again, at each forum, before participants finally could begin to see themselves as responsibly *doing* something. Careful scrutiny showed that in fact, participants had to explore three layers of interest, as it were, to reveal a pattern of understanding.

The task of the analyst—in this case, the video producers—was to discover and chart the underlying choreography (so to speak) of the public dialogue, and thus to reveal the nature and the extent of what may be happily conceptualized as *movement* toward a judgment. We found that people did, in every forum, start with and keep coming back to their sense of what being "a nation of immigrants" really meant. Once they had satisfied themselves there—and acknowledged the tension between what they knew and what they might wish for (the first layer of interest)—they could then look more squarely at the problem of a flood of immigrants who arrive to do work that we want to be done, but for whom we find it rather difficult to assume responsibility or to recognize mutual obligations—in effect, a second level of discovery. And it was only toward the end of the forums, in every instance, that people then began to face the thought that, in a nation of laws, the laws have to be enforced, but that they also have to make coherent, practical sense in the context of our contemporary life—the third layer of interest. So, we presented the outcomes of deliberation to the *Public Voice* panel of political and media representatives in that three-tiered pattern: the *public's* pattern that was more self-consciously expository, as a narrative, than the actual individual community deliberations may have seemed to be at an initial viewing—to citizen participants or to those who filmed them.

The contrast between the progression that the deliberative public revealed itself to be making and the persistent stalemate of government on this issue, however, turned out to be dramatic, as (then Congressman) Jim Leach bluntly acknowledged at the Press Club, on camera. We, the producers of the video, hadn't invented the progression of the deliberation; we hadn't made it up; nor had we distorted anything that had been said in the forums to make it apparent. And certainly neither the Kettering Foundation nor the NIF had done so. A process of analysis and synthesis, illustrating the formula first elaborated in Yankelovich's *Coming to Public Judgment*, however, makes it clear as a process of "working through." Or, to change the metaphor, that formula, exposited in Yankelovich's Syracuse lectures 20 years ago, enables us to read—much as an MRI or CT scan "reads" the body—to "read" what is working, and how well, in a democratic public mind.

Now the "expert" panelists from both left and right, in their own conversations that followed each segment of the video, were referring very clearly to the same human understanding that emerged in the forums; and that, too, is captured in these videos. But it is particularly evident that the politicians, reluctant to talk too clearly or too openly on this subject (perhaps because they know where their campaign support and their votes have to come from), are somehow caught in the middle. Immigration is, as people on the Press Club panel said more than once, an extraordinarily powerful human issue. So even the politicians call for more political leadership, and, as one representative from Congress phrased it, ask for "a pass out of Washington" so that they can come to grips with the issue more firmly in their home districts. That's an odd awareness to emerge from a videotaped session at the National Press Club, and it may suggest the possibility that a slightly different relationship between members of Congress and the public—or as David Mathews would put it, between "institutional" politics and "organic" politics—could be desirable and may yet be possible in the future.

There certainly were manifest differences between those citizens in the forums, on the one hand, who mistrusted the unfamiliar, and those, on the other, who imagined America as refuge for the poor, the rejected, and the hungry. Initially offered by participants as two virtually antipathetic views, this tension grew more troubling, harder to take any firm grip on, as participants began to acknowledge more clearly this nation's characteristic and time-honored dependence on cheap labor from "other worlds." And finally, that tension itself was transmuted to a sober but disquieting recognition of a more fundamental tension—between the impulse to change the law to match realities and the impulse to change reality to match the laws. Such progressively deepening understanding of *dilemma* is often the real challenge and a politically significant accomplishment of deliberation by a *public* on its journey toward a judgment. The clear relevance of this process to various proposals from our political leaders underscores the importance of the development of a *public* judgment within a democratic system. So we may take the immigration "problem" as an example—since here we have conveniently sequential videos, first of citizens engaged in the deliberative process, then a finished broadcast program of political and expert people doing likewise, over the shoulders, as it were, of the first group.

People begin by talking to each other about what they think the problem is—the first tier of interest—and at first we all seem to have just different opinions. But opinions uttered in a deliberative community meeting are related to personal experiences; so instead of fighting with attitudes as if they were convictions (which opinions are too often pretended to be), participants respond to them as *experiences*. We learn—and the citizens on the tape are obviously themselves discovering—that while immigrants typically have assimilated, learned the language, found jobs, made homes, and raised families, there are nowadays so many new immigrants, scattered so widely through the nation, speaking so many different languages, and revealing so many "strange" looks and habits and beliefs, as to give at least some of us citizens pause, even though we do cherish deeply certain American values—including that embodied in the Statue of Liberty's welcome. The pride of now middle-aged participants in their immigrant grandparents visibly came up against—repeatedly stubbed its toes on—their seemingly instinctive mistrust of immigrants (legal or illegal) who "don't speak our language" or "don't celebrate Christmas."

At the Press Club, Richard Harwood summarized what he had heard from such video presentations:

> I'm struck by how different this conversation is from the conversation we see in the news media and on Capitol Hill. Those debates tend to be acrimonious and divisive; in this debate what I heard people doing is joining these issues and saying: "I'm trying to figure out how all this fits together; where I fit with it; where the person coming from some other country, coming into the United States fits with it; I'm not quite sure where I end up on that."

And Doris Meissner, a senior fellow at the Migration Policy Institute and former Immigration and Naturalization Service Commissioner, spells it out:

> Some things have changed, some haven't. This is the oldest story in America, and it's also the newest story. Today's immigrants come from more parts of the world than ever before in our immigration; we have a much wider variety of countries that people are coming from, so they bring more languages, different traditions, etc. They're settling far more widely in the United States. It used to be that people settled in New York, Chicago, that was about it. Now we have the large cities that we've always associated with immigration, but at the same time we have immigrants settling in many, many different parts of the country. And it is also the case that today's immigration is a very robust legal immigration, which goes according to the laws that we've written, but it is accompanied by almost an equal number of illegal immigrants, unauthorized immigrants.

This is a naming of the problem to which each forum participant has contributed: yes, the man who wants (as we learn later) to build a wall around the borders; the woman who accepts that this cannot any longer be simply a "Christian" country; and the woman who complains about that; the woman who is afraid of change and the man who believes that if we don't change, we die; a congressional representative of each party; men and women, both young and older; and people from the border states, the east coast, and middle America. They don't have answers, yet, so what is "at issue" is not yet clearly framed; yet a problem's parameters are clear and a challenge has been engaged. While some are more fearful than others and some more hopeful, a *concern* is shared.

It is this recognition—marking, in a sense, a clear stage in the deliberative public journey—that enables the people in these forums to begin to focus (and it really is a matter of focusing) on a clear and nationwide manifestation of this "problem"—the second tier of interest: the clustering of large groups of *illegal* immigrants—or technically, as someone is always quick to point out, "undocumented" immigrants—in communities where it is hard for them to become quickly assimilated, where their language and behavior may seem strange, where they are in many ways victimized, yet where they are in fact eagerly sought to perform menial and largely unskilled jobs that Americans will not often accept at the minimal wages that are offered. Some complain that they do in fact take jobs from Americans; some say that this, as Representative Silvestre "Silver" Reyes puts it, has "cheapified the work force." But such concerns are quickly lost in the almost universal recognition, during deliberations, that this use of cheap immigrant labor is critical to our local and national economies in the United States today.

Because she is skilled at this kind of summation, let's again quote Doris Meissner's summary appraisal, at the close of this segment of the deliberative public video at the event at the National Press Club:

> What you had here was a textbook example of what our problem is. Our problem is that we have jobs available in this country; we have—they stated it very well—we like our cheap products; we particularly like our cheap food; and what we have, as policy, is a situation where we say, "We will fortify that border as much as we can, but if you get past it, there is a job waiting for you in this country." And we are not upset about the fact that that is a complete contradiction. As long as those jobs are there, people are going to cross that border.

In a real sense, the issue has been "joined" by the mid-point of the forum, and the trade-offs, in fact, have been emerging in different contexts, sometimes scarcely half-understood, from the very beginning of the deliberations. What may have seemed like odd or iconoclastic opinions about immigrants and what to do with them, at the start, have slowly come into focus, now that the cause-and-effect dilemma that the American people face has become clear. The "immigration problem" that seemed so fluid, even alarming to some, because it was hard to grasp, hard to be specific about, is now specific; it is real—not easy, but *addressable*. Soon, indeed, people will start venturing on solutions!

Instead of trying to summarize the thinking of the third segment of the tape, representing the third tier of interest, let us therefore go directly to Tamar Jacoby's articulation of it at the start of the third conversation among the panel at the Press Club, following the very last word of the videotaped "public voice" from the public forums themselves.

> What I thought was remarkable, was how well they understood the problem, and really the solution. They said: we need laws, but now the laws are out of sync with the reality; that's creating burdensome enforcement. We need more realistic laws that we could enforce more effectively. I mean, they got the whole program, right there.

One seldom hears such a clear movement toward a public judgment (in the sense in which Yankelovich first used the phrase) as occurs in these forums—and indeed did occur in most of the other forums collected in summaries of research on the topic, provided to the Kettering Foundation. When some of her colleagues on the panel seemed a little hesitant to bring closure to this experience of public deliberation—or perhaps were reluctant to finish without a final citing of their own favored response—Tamar Jacoby reiterated what she had seen.

> They were saying, "Get control of it. We want control of it." And the answer is, "realistic law" is how you get control of it. Think about prohibition versus what we have now. Unrealistic law is impossible to enforce. But law can make steps.

Doris Meissner, ultimately, perceived that this answer is viable insofar as it is *public*: not one person's or one party's or one interest's plan, but responsive to the multiple needs that the conversation has articulated.

> I would agree that this was a very intelligent conversation. These people do understand, and they understand really more clearly than an awful lot of our political class, it seems to me. The thing that's so difficult about the answer here—and the answer is a multiplicity of answers: there's no one single element that is going to solve the problem—is that the concerns on that tape about the border, and controlling the border, and porousness of the border, can only be addressed if you basically open up the system and bring it above ground. And that's a hard thought to get. . . . It means that you can manage your border only if you're able to really regulate who's coming in and out of the country, and if you recognize that there are people here that we need and want to have here.

Occasionally, one wonders if there may not be some brooding problems that escape the public voice, and fears that our political leadership does not readily share with us; yet such problems and fears may *demand* a public voice, broader and more deliberative. Richard Harwood—called upon by the meeting's moderator, news broadcaster Frank Sesno, as someone whose "business is to bring citizens and elected public officials together" to close the session at the National Press Club—suggested a hope that we may continue more urgently to cherish:

> I think this conversation should offer us hope . . . about the American public. It's a very complicated issue; it's a tough issue; it's riddled with contradictions in people's values; and I think what we saw in these tapes today was the American public's ability and willingness to engage, to wrestle with these challenges, to acknowledge where they're contradicting themselves, and to try to figure out to the best of their ability with the information that they have, how we might be able to move forward.

The public obviously can put politicians on the spot; it also can help them sometimes when they are on the hot seat. To move in that direction—where the public speaks to the politician—may entail a somewhat more frank assessment of where the deliberative public turns out to be on some issues that have not been adequately tracked. This is difficult to do fairly and persuasively—and it is difficult to do unless we are prepared to be exact in our own analyses and precise in the ways in which we describe *what we actually learn from public deliberation* on given topics—in print reports of public deliberations, in televised deliberations like those used in the *Public Voice* program, and in research materials that circulate among scholarly participants. Lying behind this concern—the concern of describing what we actually learn—is something tremendously important that we know, but to which we have given too little real attention and that we have not quite adequately articulated, although it is absolutely central to our life as a *polis*. It is the difference between public opinion and public thinking, perhaps the distinction between opinion and understanding—or, to be positive, the *relationship* between public opinion, thinking, and understanding.

Fixing a Direction . . . the Energy "Problem"

What is often called "the energy crisis" plops us down right at the start of the public journey toward a judgment: with a faraway and uncertain goal; with a few instant-effect options that would likely harm as many of us as they help; with sacrifices we could make, but wouldn't want to make unless everybody else did; and a wonderful array of scapegoats to satisfy almost everybody's anger, including everybody's favorites (the government and the corporate sector) as well as "the man on the street." And the cliché that "we all will have to help fix it!" This is where we the people usually experience—and still too often fight against—our political role as *a public*.

In the preceding chapter of this book, where the context was international, we had the retrospective comfort of history, reporting with a backward glance how we came to where we know we are, among slow mutations in the light of a third of a century in a changing world. For the two domestic problems analyzed now in this present chapter, however, we have only written reports and videos that provide a precious reflection, in one relatively brief and passing season, of how people were readily and together weighing what should be done in the face of seemingly fresh or increasingly urgent *national* issues to which we have not yet, as a nation, responded in a way that satisfactorily—even if only provisionally—puts the matters at rest.

The rapid rise in the price of gasoline—the energy crisis, if you will—and the impact that a shifting global economy seems to be having on the way Americans think of themselves and how they like to live, these capture a second such problem. At issue here is not one of those occasional but recurring inconveniences that thrive and recede periodically on complaints that temporarily quicken the ideological appetite; nor is it a long-term, historical process that imperceptibly moves toward a shared acceptance that is sometimes more satisfying than momentary partisan triumph. Moreover, the problems of the cost of fuel, the sources of our energy supply, and the lifestyles that it determines or requires—these are not at all the kinds of problem to which we can individually make some accommodation that will at least calm our consciences, if not entirely salvage our customary lifestyles. Here, rather, we face a specific nationwide challenge that demands relatively speedy action, yet promises no easy satisfaction; with significant costs that will have to be shared variously, but agreed upon collectively; and for which most of us have very little experience to help us come to judgment.

The judgment to which we move, at a given time, may be far from final, yet it will no less be the outcome of a process of "working through," as we confront a troubling and complex policy question. It is arguable that the citizens who have deliberated, this past few years, over what the nation should or might do about the clearly not-improving problem of our dependence on fossil fuels, are moving closer to a judgment about how we should, as a people, now address the problem; yet this is not necessarily to say that they agree upon a workable policy. (That may come later, perhaps much later.) This public, coming to judgment, is nonetheless engaging in a process ideally appropriate for a democratic people, no matter how far from judgment they may yet be. We, as people, make choices based upon what we understand at a given time, and those choices often merely posit others yet to be made. The pursuit of judgment through a public political process may be outlined in a broad sweep of history (as we have tried to suggest in the preceding chapter), but public politics in a democratic society needs be continuous. Most of the stages in coming to judgment are steps toward a shared understanding that will be repeated again and again before an actionable outcome is determined, certainly before a problem is "settled." But this public, while coming to judgment, is in fact engaging, in its own profoundly important way, significant political responsibilities of a democracy.

In fact, it had slowly become clear, through the decades of the 1980s and 1990s, that the immediate and perhaps the ultimate significance of the deliberative community forums was not in their impact on the agenda or the accomplishments of legislative programs or party platforms, but in what the process revealed to people about the understandings they shared; and about the problems that arise from the tensions between the different emphases they place upon those values that they share, when they live, variously, under different circumstances, one from another. It had begun to seem that in a democracy, where the people's will is ultimately sovereign, it is of more significance that people—the public—themselves recognize those tensions, understand the obligations that any given dilemma places upon them, and move to discover the degree to which, or even the circumstances under which, although differently motivated as individuals, they might nonetheless address the shared problem collectively. And with some hope, therefore, of accomplishment! This clearly would be an invaluable *public political process*. The degree to which it might prove directly useful, or even commanding, to those whom we have elected to lead us is not necessarily apparent; but that the public itself has views that move, change, sometimes join, as people collectively weigh their various implications—this seems worth broader attention.

What, then, may be thought of, *pro tem*, as "conclusions" (using the word somewhat loosely) that can be derived from relatively recent public deliberations on the energy problem—in 2006 and 2007 primarily—that we have analyzed? And what may be the aggregate impetus of those deliberations as a *public* contribution, ultimately, to the nation's political life and solidarity? The "energy crisis" seems to provide a good current example of critical questions for a democratic society to ask itself.

In the context of uncertain gas prices, and the continuance, with uncertain outcome, of hostilities in the Middle East (although virtually nobody in these forums elaborated on this latter concern, specifically), participants in these public deliberations said we ought to be thinking about other ways of assuring the energy supply upon whose availability our culture seems heavily to depend. It is amazing how many participants remember nostalgically the economy, noise, and exhaust emissions of the cars of their youth. There is a general and even tolerably sophisticated awareness that a growing middle class, globally (in India and China notably), is willing to bid up prices and compete for supplies from our traditional oil sources, many of which are in inaccessible and unstable areas; that in other nations, other fuels are increasingly being used to drive automobile engines that were made, but are not broadly available, in the United States; and that availability of the oil supply has some influence upon international policies and practices—although this last, while receiving nods of agreement everywhere when it is mentioned, is not anywhere elaborated in these public forums.

There was a continued, or continual, sense of a near incredulity on the part of participants in all of these forums (many of whom recall the gas crisis of the 1970s) that so many of us Americans were still driving ever bigger cars that burn embarrassingly large quantities of gasoline. And that American companies had continued to manufacture them—at least until the financial collapse of a few years ago! It is easily established—and will be repeated many times—that Americans recognize themselves to be self-indulgent, or "spoiled" by cheap gas, but also as loving their cars and unlikely to cross the street, or down-size, merely to save a few cents on a gallon of gasoline. While the production of smaller automobiles and the development of vegetable-derived or other alternatives to gasoline seemed to be everywhere called for in these forums, it appeared to be broadly recognized that when and where—and whether—we might explore new sources for oil *in US territories* is a difficult question and perhaps politically unaddressable. There was little indication, however, of irreconcilable hostility between would-be Alaska-diggers and wildlife preservationists, and it did seem everywhere most generally accepted that our own flora and fauna, to some degree, are valuable resources in themselves.

The manner or tone of these conversations may thus seem surprisingly mild: one gets consistently the impression of amiable people, aware that things are not going well—even, indeed, that something is genuinely wrong—but also aware, nonetheless, that some remedies are probably within our grasp. The impression that slowly unfolds, overall, in the course of the early minutes of deliberation (where the focus is always the gasoline crisis *per se*, as experienced, on and off, in recent decades), is that people are just a little puzzled about why they are living the way they are. Their life, apparently, is both expansive and uncertain, and one gets their sense that, as a collective, there is something not quite "proper" about their living that way.

The astonishing—yes, I do believe it is astonishing!—recognition and acceptance of the notion that we Americans should not be spending as much time as we do in automobiles that consume as much gasoline as they do, picks up again and again in these public forums—as when, for example, a clearly British participant recalls a boyhood where he bicycled to school 15 miles every day, only to have a young American respond that all the people *he* knows who ride bikes, "do it for sport—or because they've had their automobiles repossessed!" But the sense that we are spoiled and self-indulgent (and that our mistaken assumption of an inexhaustible availability of energy is absurd) here begins to suggest that to change will make extraordinary demands on us as individuals and have extraordinary implications for our style of living. A man from Cleveland notes that, although static in population growth, his city has multiplied its area enormously—but that, with inadequate density to make public transportation viable, and increasingly expensive fuel, some people might have to give up their jobs, walk miles to work, or find new accommodations—and so on—if our automobile supply or easily affordable fuel should fail.

A Texas woman points out that since we are "running out of dead dinosaurs," we have no choice but to look for alternative energy sources; and in every forum this awareness of shortage is underscored by an equally widespread awareness of the threat of global warming. It's worth noting that while some people feel more deeply than others about that topic, it always comes up at this juncture in their thinking together; yet in *none* of these forums was global warming ever discussed substantively, *per se*. The deliberations were about *energy*, not about global warming or the environment; that the energy we use and the way we use it are damaging to life is, simply, generally understood, never argued. Global warming is not at issue, but the question under deliberation does nonetheless become one of who is to establish dependence, by whom, upon what source, *given the fact of debilitating climate change*.

For all of these American citizens who had taken the time to come out and talk together, "alternative" sources included nuclear, wind, and sun, each of which has recognized advantages and disadvantages that participants in these forums readily explored. A woman asked why we hear so little about nuclear energy—is it still the "No! No!" as in the days of Chernobyl and Three Mile Island? In these forums, quite apparently *not*! Certainly in every forum somebody raised a negative word about the disposal of nuclear waste or its danger to our security, but others offered rebuttals to modify such fears. Further, while nuclear energy was not a familiar part of their lives, some of the participants knew, perhaps surprisingly, that a significant 20-some percent of America's energy is already produced from nuclear plants; that those plants are all very much out of date; that unlike carbon fuels, nuclear energy is "clean"; and that replacing any of the other kinds of power plants with a nuclear power plant has gone virtually unnoticed in ordinary life wherever it does happen. (These participants, we should note, were all groups of 20 or so citizens, young and old, and with few exceptions they did not include individuals with professional experience of the topic at issue.) Wind sources seemed to be acceptable and tolerably familiar as an idea (if not a fact of everybody's experience), although there was some recognition of difficulties with respect to location, noise, and birds! Solar energy was brought in as an ultimate ideal, but recognized as regrettably expensive for domestic use and something whose time, technologically, has not yet quite come. Granted this apparent familiarity and ease of reference to alternative energy sources, but as yet the absence of any energetic development of them in ways that affect citizens everywhere, the common outcome of this exploration was—perhaps not surprisingly, but one may suspect, importantly—a climactic assertion that we, as a people, may need a kind of national and official effort, comparable even, some say, to that associated toward the ending of World War II with the Manhattan Project or the Marshall Plan.

Having put together these summary minutes from an analysis of about 10 hours of public talk in 5 distinctively different locations, we should perhaps emphasize that there is nothing casual or arbitrary about what is found in these discs and reels of tape. In every site, the more participants talked about the energy situation—its challenges and the opportunities we have, even if they are opportunities that have not yet been adequately pursued—the more clearly did the deliberators seem to express a kind of awed nostalgia for the world of more than half a century ago—the 1940s, 1950s, and 1960s—when great projects were undertaken at times of great need, by a nation committed and acting collectively under determined leadership. The references, in fact, to these various historic undertakings (in times before many, if not most, of the participants were born) are repeated from beginning to end in the actual forums of which we have the full taped records; but the idea of a "collective calling," so to speak, really seemed to gather coherence in the latter part of the deliberations, after participants have explored alternative options in the manner of relatively casual, but not quite disinterested, observers.

The discussion guide that had been prepared to encourage these conversations concluded with a look at the topic of conservation—what we as a people could do to save, rather than "reinvent" sources of, our energy supply. As it turned out, however, the entire deliberation was about conservation, in a way—from its very early moments when people had begun by talking about their own gluttony in the use of energy, especially in high-consumption automobiles. So by the time participants in these forums got to their final half hour, people—in Nebraska, Ohio, Oregon, Texas, and New York—consciously and with more passion than at any other time during the course of these two-hour deliberations, had begun to talk seriously about why they hadn't addressed, and how they might come to address, what they had, during this discussion, slowly recognized, with increasing clarity, as a critical issue.

Thus, in the culminating segment of each forum we discover people confronting the idea of *crisis*—which they blamed themselves *and* their political leaders for having, seemingly, agreed to ignore. Participants reintroduce the theme of the self-indulgent American, to explain that we seldom take serious and uncomfortably disciplined action, except in times of crisis. A woman says that it's rather difficult to "incentivize" in this area since a whole industry (marketing) is committed to pushing people the other way. A man indicates that people usually do the right thing as long as they have the information. Another man thinks that taxes on gas and Hummers might be helpful, provided these tax "deterrents" were also used specifically to assist the development of alternative fuels. And although there was some recognizable reluctance to accept that Americans need their government to "force" them into doing good, ultimately there seems to be a ground swell toward the concept of *leadership*. (The Manhattan Project is mentioned again!)

"Why doesn't the government undertake steps of incentive and restraint (carrots and sticks)?" asked participants in more than one forum. "Why doesn't the government . . ?" "Does it have something to do with the system of lobbying, the ability of oil companies and automobile companies to control?" one participant asked, to general nods of approval. The question draws the response, seriously presented in various ways in different forums, but without the apparent vindictiveness of "congress-bashing," that Congress may not be "as responsive to 'we, the people' as it is to sources of the money that gets its members back into office." Overall it is important to recognize that, at each of these sites, after close to a couple of hours of talking about the energy crisis, these citizens *did* talk about a failure of leadership, *political* leadership. It was blunt; it was direct; and it recurred everywhere.

If one follows this dialogue carefully, however, it must be equally apparent that underlying it is a relatively sophisticated (and let's hope thoroughly American) recognition that this is, as one man put it, "a political, and a market, and a money issue." While in every forum there were moments of anti-establishment and anti-corporate severity, even condemnation, it was very clear that, as one participant emphasized—he happened to be a priest, although in layman's clothing—

> I think that if we thought that somehow our nation wouldn't hear us, we wouldn't be talking right now. I think if we had . . . a fatalistic idea about the impossibility of government assisting in this situation, I don't think we would even bother to be here.

Nonetheless, an older man, in Texas, countered with one of the more intense utterances that we have heard in the course of such quite informal, public, deliberative forums. It came near the end, and deeply impassioned:

> We understand the crisis. Now it's up to you to lead us. It's up to you to convince us. And it's up to you to force us to do what we must do. And if you don't force us, we're not going to do it—because we're human beings and we're greedy and we don't care.

Similarly, from a different forum, in New York, at a similar juncture in the forum, a man concluded to his own group:

> There is a disconnect, I think. We see our public officials as being very different from us. I believe very much in a body politic. And if we're truly a democracy, that government has to be responsive to the issues we think are important.

A Deliberative Political Culture

We have here used a narrative reporting form to summarize the deliberations on two national problems, so that readers interested in exploring the process by which citizens move toward a shared judgment may discern elements of that process as real public dialogues, unfolding in the face of a troubling issue, in real time. The import of these deliberative forums and their place in our political culture is that it is *the public* that must work its way toward judgment. As we noted earlier, we know, from almost 30 years of comparative analyses of public deliberations—whether series of forums on the same subject, in different communities within short periods of time, or series on a single subject, across a significant period of time—that people come to such occasions with different opinions; further, we know that while those opinions may not ultimately change during the deliberations, a recognition of shared values that lie beyond or beneath ostensibly conflicting opinions and impulses often *does* lead toward a collective understanding of the possibility of tolerable, potential action. In these excerpts from forums on energy, for example, it is apparent that opinions do differ sometimes on the acceptability of exploiting oil reserves in wild-life preserves; there are similarly differing opinions of the danger to individual life and national security that might result from an expanded reliance on nuclear energy. The conflict between these inclinations, however, is surprisingly, even disarmingly, mild in these public forums. There is, on the other hand, no strong sense of "immediacy" in these exchanges about "solutions," and one gets the impression in all of the forums we have examined that participants, at bottom, feel that *a public judgment has already been made*. No one seems really to believe that we will permit the sacrifice of protected flora and fauna (in obviously few remaining preserves) for the sake of an inevitably short-term lift in an inevitably diminishing fuel supply; likewise, accepting the twin threats of diminishing resources and global warming, no one seems really to believe that we'll wait *much* longer before upping our (already significant) nuclear capacity to match that of other leading nations (although the Japanese warning had yet to be experienced when these forums were taking place).

More interestingly, we have also observed that a public, in its deliberations about critical issues, often quickly encounters genuine tensions when it uncovers the familiar truth that a problem may demand, in our treatment of it, that we relinquish, to a degree, things we hold dear; and that we tolerate, to a degree, actions that we do not entirely welcome. Old hands at these events, and at the *Public Voice* television programs that presented recorded excerpts from forums for nearly 20 years, will again recall the remarkable taped sequence from a forum on health care, of an exhausting and profoundly moving tension that became evident as a relatively young widower told of the eventual death, by renal failure, of his wife, who had been kept alive for years under care paid for with "somebody else's money—not mine!" (Such patients are cared for by public money in the nation's budget.) The problem of how much it may be worth—to a nation—to keep its people living and healthy became both emotionally and intellectually real in those public dialogues, and *shared*, at that moment. Years earlier, a young mother in Mississippi, also videotaped for *A Public Voice*, had recorded that she could not, today, imagine how she herself could have had an abortion. "Yet," she had said, with a kind of saddened awe, "I did, once. I did, then." The moment of realization—a profoundly moving acceptance of paradox—is still short of a judgment, perhaps, but awesomely close to wisdom. And at those moments—in a room crammed with contentious principles—for one long moment, every participant was visibly captured by the shared and tangible pain of human paradox.

The years of careful analysis have taught us that climactic tensions, like these just cited, do not routinely occur in public deliberation—not, certainly, moment by moment, every few minutes. Most often they build cumulatively, and only as the end approaches do we—sometimes quite unexpectedly and dramatically—encounter the problem behind the problem, through just one individual's human experience. Each of the two participants cited above was facing a not-readily-explicable conflict in his or her own sense of values; and, for a moment, without anger or antagonism, every participant in the room shared the understanding of values in conflict.

We found no example of exactly such tensions in these deliberations on energy—unless it be at the one point, where something, suddenly—typified in the comments of the older Texas man, quoted above, who said, among other things, "If you don't force us, we're not going to do it" —did emerge, explosive. Yet a cumulative and culminating tension in these deliberations on the energy problem did in fact prove to be important. The dialogues had begun, as we have seen, with the gas shortage and the cost, for that is where we all now start, apparently, when we talk about the energy problem in the United States. Slowly participants moved to a shared recognition—a good-humored, unexciting, but slowly grasped recognition, nonetheless—that other countries may be coping better than we are, often with our help, so we'd best proceed thoughtfully, while doing nothing rash. This pattern of a well-tempered "getting together" of details continues, with participants beginning to figure out just what "change" would entail, because it is inevitable and may (per "global warming") prove urgent. Apart from changes in our culture, apparently, this will entail more concentrated attention to alternative sources, like wind, solar, and nuclear power—all of which have their upsides and downsides, people tell each other. And, granted what is now needed to make them happen, this may require the kind of formal national effort that we remember (or are told by those who do remember) characterized this great nation, more than half a century ago, when it did indeed find itself ready to save the world.

The coherence here is an emotionally driven—and perhaps necessarily value-based—increase of awareness. And of complexity! The people who had begun by griping about the price of gas (which they didn't stop buying) seem in fact to have found a new collective sensibility, two-thirds of the way through their deliberations. This underlying sense—embodied in the references to Manhattan Projects and Marshall Plans—of a desire and a need to accomplish something collectively, as a people, has recurred throughout the deliberations. And it explodes suddenly into what is recognizably public political thinking—about desire for, and need of, leadership, and a government of and for and by the people. These are citizens of a democracy, who (with us watching and listening) slowly have begun to frame up what they think *should* happen. Recognizing that in this area virtually no one *alone* can accomplish much change—and certainly nothing of broad significance—they call upon their government to perform *its* task. It is what the old man in Texas meant when he said, "We understand the crisis. Now it's up to you to lead us."

And that is where another older man, in New York, is coming from, when he says, "That's the role of government." And a somewhat younger businessman from Nebraska, who says:

> I would normally, personally, not really be for the government making me do it. But . . . incentive will drive change in technology and behavior. It [government] can help drive that.

And the youngish intellectual, who has the last word from New York:

> I believe very much in a body politic. And if we are truly a democracy, government has to be responsive to the issues we think are important.

There *are* times when public deliberation reveals a shared understanding—though that is not to be confused with a single opinion—and a collective judgment—though that is not a final strategy—about *what should be done*. There are times, too, when, in a democracy, such collective judgment is the voice of a public, inviting a government to play its part.

IV.

Facing the Odds . . . When Knowing What We Like Is Not Enough

IN THE PRECEDING CHAPTERS, we have made reference to two particularly intriguing incidents, in almost three decades of National Issues Forums, where individual participants have acknowledged a tenuous and clearly unanticipated self-awareness of their having, in the past, undertaken actions about whose implications they now felt uncertainty, or (in one instance, at least) genuine regret. In each instance, we have pointed out, such confusion clearly generated momentarily a sympathy, a moment of shared understanding that in effect altered every other participant's perception of the topic at issue in a similar and significant way.

When the clearly devoted young mother in a Mississippi forum on abortion quietly acknowledged, with equally evident regret and incredulity, that she had once, years before, terminated a pregnancy, everybody in that room—divided though we knew them to have been in principle on the question of abortion that was at issue—evidenced a single response. In the last act of Shakespeare's *Othello,* when the hero stabs himself, to fall across the body of his wife (whom he has slain, with the same instrument, a moment before), with just the words:

> I kissed thee ere I killed thee. No way but this:
> Killing myself, to die upon a kiss.

the entire audience in the theater shares the moment of cathartic pain. And bound in the circle of that meeting room in Mississippi in 1991, some 50 or so people quite visibly experienced similarly a momentarily unspeakable bond of painful understanding.

In the Pittsburgh forum on health care, the still relatively young widower's manifest yet tentative bewilderment over the public care, that he personally could not have afforded, but that his wife had received before her death, was not a momentary revelation of the same theatrical order; yet it caught precisely the same shared awe of a people's willing if hopeless provision for a fellow citizen's care unto death. The speaker had been recalling, with evident distress, the long, saddening months of his late wife's dialysis, his voice falling to an evident and for a moment stammering wonder: "Someone paid for that. . . . It wasn't me! Somebody else's money . . . not mine."

Unfortunately, however, such humanly acceptable expressions of awe and uncertainty, or even the occasionally striking recognitions of human ambivalence—sometimes self-serving and too little dwelt upon—do not quickly fashion a way toward universally agreeable public *policies*. When at issue is what we and our fellow citizens are to be permitted (or required) to do, then what we sometimes assume to be a common culture quickly frays back—through the distinctive and often divisive strands of faith, education, class, interest, ambition, and sometimes mere convenience—to what may appear to be stubborn prejudice or ideological commitment. And sometimes, almost certainly, special interests that are not clearly reflective of a common good. The public forum is not theater, nor are its participants performing for effect; their scripts are not already written. A momentarily sympathetic recognition that others, too, share our human tendency to perform or fail to perform, at some points in our lives, actions that may seem almost incomprehensible at other points does not change our habitual convictions; nor does it shatter in a moment the values that have grown deeply in our minds out of long experience.

The abortion issue, for example, remains with us and is a "public" question again each time the Senate hears from a newly nominated candidate to the Supreme Court. (It is alive for zealots as well. In Wichita, Kansas, George Teller, then the distinguished leader of the nation's most respected abortion hospital in the middle of these United States, was assassinated at the very start of a new presidency, elected on a platform of "hope" and "change.") Clearly people's individual responses to the suggestion universally to determine the right and wrong of a human fetus' abortion are often *pre*-determined by belief; by circumstance or experience; by pain; by accidents of economy; by the serious threat of danger; by our chosen definition of what it may mean to be human, responsible, or loving; by our valuation of scientific possibilities—and oh! by so many other considerations that different individuals among us may value, from time to time. Thus, there is no reason to believe that moments of shared human sympathy and understanding will in fact change for long any participant's judgment about a contentious law on abortion itself. And public deliberation does not *easily* change either law or individual behavior.

Nonetheless, and despite the Wichita killing and the endlessly repeated questions of "right-to-life" senators, and the valiantly persistent affirmations of religious leaders, there is cause to suspect that in regard to abortion this nation has *in effect* reached a settled judgment—a judgment, obviously, to permit each citizen to follow his and her conviction in the matter, provided that particular assurance has been presented that the mother is sufficiently healthy and the fetus not far advanced. The state's role seems now in practice pretty much limited to that of determining whether or not to assist and enable scientific research that can utilize a fetus brought into the world thus early. And individual citizens may continue to preach at, pray for, or go forward without reference or regret expressed to those of different faiths.

Perhaps this is why the National Issues Forums have only once approached the issue of abortion, in more than 25 years. Contentious and even deadly individual opinions on the issue still remain fixed and deeply rooted: to some, abortion is a sin, and not infrequently also seen as an option taken because of a prior sin; to others it is a practical and sometimes wrenching decision in a world that ever makes devastating demands; and to some it is means toward improvement of the human lot by way of extended stem cell research. A couple of hours of deliberatively soothed talk does not change these attitudes. And yet ... perhaps that moment of understanding in Mississippi or in Pennsylvania nonetheless made its contribution to what we think of as democracy, and its unique way of moving toward a *public* judgment.

The circumstances may seem to be superficially similar, for example, in the apparently fixed and principled positions of the combatants when we analyze public deliberations about the nation's still angrily contentious health-care problem—a dilemma all the more remarkable because it is one that has already been resolved (apparently with satisfaction) by most other nations with whom we tend typically to enjoy comparison. Put bluntly (and with acknowledged risk of oversimplification) our problem is that contemporary medical procedures are extraordinarily sophisticated and effective, but also extraordinarily costly in a society where more and more people, with the help of that sophisticated attention, now may live longer and longer into an active old age—or, under some circumstances, die during or after extravagantly costly but also vain medical care. Our tax burden, then, necessarily continues to grow to accommodate the elderly and sometimes the very young, unable to acquire insurance adequate to cover their own health-care needs. To make matters more difficult, it turns out that, despite insurance premiums that their clients have paid against a rainy day, insurance companies have more and more persistently "unloaded" (or denied payments to) clients whose age or ailments or treatment suggest that they might, shortly, be likely to "collect" a more than *modest* health-care payout from the companies. Employers (especially relatively small employers) are less and less able to afford the tax-abated insurance payments that they have for decades comfortingly paid at a discount (not available to individuals) for their employees.

The results have been increasingly apparent, as witnessed by participants in public deliberative forums over the past 20 years. Large and still increasing numbers of insured US citizens find themselves unexpectedly without means of paying for specific health care that has suddenly become available and appropriate; health-care bills have become the single most common cause of personal bankruptcies in our country; high and still increasing numbers of Americans have no insurance at all and many of them no means of paying for care, when push comes to shove; and the overall quality of health care in the United States, by internationally accepted standards, is inferior to that of other "progressive" or post-industrial countries in the Americas, Europe, Africa, and Asia, although we, as a nation, have health-care expenditures higher, *per capita,* than any of them. In effect, health insurance and medical treatment are coming close to being priced out of the market for a growing number of citizens in the United States today.

Those, of course, were the reasons why various nations (including some that, like ourselves, at one time had become home to dissatisfied European emigrants) have adopted what sometimes used to be referred to, contemptuously and misleadingly, as a system of "socialized medicine," now more commonly and accurately referred to as a "single-payer system." Adapted variously to accommodate differing national cultures and habits, the driving factor of such systems is—as various proponents of the idea in deliberative public forums in 2007 and 2008 explained—that the more people we have paying into a single pool, the more funds we have available to cover the relative few of them who become sick or injured at any given time. The insurance company—in these instances, essentially a government authority—doesn't have to make a profit; and "we the people," as the only customers, also get thus to "bid down" the price of drugs and some related services that may remain "market" products.

That, of course, is a nice way of explaining a "single payer"—that is, government-administered, tax-supported—system that may need yet further exploration, since any kind of such change has been deferred and complicated in this country for a number of reasons.

As a nation, we have a profound faith in—almost a religious reliance on—"the market" as a kind of *deus ex machina* that alone, we like to maintain, can be guarantor of our individual freedoms. We are encouraged to think that we should not, as a people, interfere in the operation of the free market (although that advice may now, in 2012, sound almost as bizarre as it was in 1929). We also have a sense, if not quite a conviction, that we, ourselves alone, *should be* responsible for our individual destinies. We believe that an honest day's work deserves an honest day's pay; we have a peculiar reverence (and an open purse) for novelty and expertise; we associate wealth with success; and we tend to mistrust government *per se* (or at least to doubt its competence).

These characteristically American traits don't always help us readily to develop a *collective* enterprise when it may become necessary. (One sometimes wonders indeed how our forebears ever came to complete a single Constitution for these United States!) We are often told, then, that government cannot do anything efficiently, although we seem to depend upon it, happily, at federal and local levels, for our defense, fire protection, policing, schools, highways, and water supply, which are not generally nor ideally left in the hands of incompetents. With respect to health care, however, we are sometimes told that a national administration of health-care services would preclude our selecting the doctor of our choice, or would discourage would-be doctors from entering the market (although relatively few doctors reject Medicare, and even fewer patients reject doctors that accept it). We are sometimes warned that a national or public program of health care would lead to long delays or inadequacies in the delivery of treatments (although that is apparently *not* the case in Canada, Britain, France, Denmark, Australia, etc.). We are sometimes cautioned that the cost of a national health program would necessitate cutting back other public services. (A few candidates may come to mind!) We are sometimes advised that the extension of coverage to include everybody will necessarily have a negative effect on the *quality* of our health care (which "ain't necessarily so," as the song writer put it, for some other nations that boast such programs are in some ways providing more people with demonstrably better care than we provide in the Unites States). And it is sometimes argued that improved accessibility to health care will encourage overindulgence almost to the point of vice among the notoriously undisciplined American citizenry—who, for some unexplained reason, are presumed, apparently, actually to *enjoy* visiting doctors and entering hospitals, in order to be pricked, cut, and forced to consume foul dosages not typically found at the local deli.

All such assertions and denials were to be heard and rejected to some degree in recent years' public forums on the problem of health care in our country. The reasons *behind* any of these assertions are not broadly presented, however. They remain assertions, argumentative assertions and denials. So, unlike the abortion issue, the problem of health care in the nation has not settled into a matter of careful, deliberative choice and personal election. Indeed, it seems to grow more troublesome year by year. The problem, however, here is *not,* as it is in the case of abortion, a question of whether to allow a choice, but rather how to address the *absence* of any choice for many of our people. All of the concerns listed in the foregoing paragraphs, whether they point toward or away from our adopting a national (or nationalized) system of health care, are concerns worth exploration.

Four series of public deliberations on the subject, however, over the past 15 years, have thrown little light—and that only slowly—on this uniquely American problem of being a rich country with relatively poor health care for its citizens. Public deliberations this past two decades do however reveal that the possibilities of suffering prolonged sickness, or even bankruptcy as a result of it, are more commonly *voiced* in discussion now than they were *thought* about a decade ago; the aggregated plight of the very poor who are sick is more broadly and sympathetically understood; the difficulties in this context of the small business operator (and therefore of the employees of small businesses) are more widely recognized and articulated; and it is generally known that the cost of many relatively common prescription drugs is now prohibitively high—and higher than the price of the same medications, even with the same packaging and labels, in other lands. Insurance here may rise in cost or be withdrawn, it sometimes seems almost arbitrarily, from the sick or the aging; there is increasingly widespread awareness in the

United States of the genuine pride that citizens of other nations (as well as some well-travelled Americans) reflect when they describe their experience of national health-care provisions in other countries. Substantively, these factors remained preoccupations of focus groups and the deliberative forums transcribed or filmed and recorded in the years 2007 and 2008. Yet while the outcomes of public opinion polls were then clear, consistent, and overwhelmingly in favor of what had been referred to in Washington as a "public plan" for many months before the conscious "unsettlement" of the summer of 2009, we cannot confidently describe a "public voice" on the problem—as distinct from "public opinions"—because there seems to be less than a clearly shared (or voiced) understanding of what a changed system would imply for, or demand from, aspects of the nation's life.

Choice-*work* has apparently not taken place!

The Citizens' Challenge— and the Government's?

Unlike the topic of abortion, deliberated only once in NIF discussions, health care has, not surprisingly, been the focus of forums six times in the past quarter-century of the forums. The observations made on these pages are reflected in the reports, videotapes, and discs of those deliberations and of the responses of legislators, experts, and press commentators to them. In two such seasons of nationwide deliberation—during the early years of the administration of President Clinton in 1993 and 1994—the public forums clearly included ideological controversy: implications of a shared *public* direction remained uncertain. Cost, obviously—although this was in the early 1990s, when costs, comparatively speaking, were not as widely troubling as they have since become—was a strong motivating factor for everybody. There was an added sense, however, that life was unfairly difficult for the poor and treatment sometimes hard to find in rural areas of the country. This meant that an undercurrent of the politics of class ran through the conversation in those years, along with a general sense that *something* was wrong with "the system." Yet there was no commandingly recognizable swing toward a government solution, *per se*, and, if the phrase "socialized medicine" was used—and it was, quite often—it seemed to be invariably offered and received with the negative connotations commonly associated with fears of "government control," or even "socialism" during the past century. Indeed, even among the elderly, the Medicare program had seemed sometimes to be seen as the practice of an unsympathetic and incompetent bureaucracy—although, paradoxically, complainants turned out always to be asking for *more*, and more sympathetic, treatment, rather than less, at government expense. The forums reflected a public that might know what it wanted, but was not confident that it would like it, as offered.

The records (written and on video) from these discussions in the early 1990s consistently reveal the ambiguities—and the relative naïveté—in thinking about these problems in those times. There was, for example, an inherent and essentially ideological ambivalence about what "the government" should do and what it should keep out of; there is a palpable reluctance toward change, which sometimes coincides with, although it is clearly not the same as, that ambivalence; and there is, at the same time, a clear concern that not everybody gets a fair shake, that in some way, we are "a nation that does not care" appropriately for its citizens in need—including the elderly, on Medicare. There are also other paradoxes: people believe we don't take care of *ourselves* properly, but that we, as a nation, should take care of the young, the elderly, *and* the needy, whoever they might turn out to be; that Medicare is the best thing that ever came around the block, but that *government* running Medicare is a disaster. In other words—whether because the framing of the issue was unclear or the problem itself was in fact compounded of different interests—*public* discussions remained merely occasion for the exchange primarily of complaint.

Not surprisingly, three fundamental concerns remained when the same topic (essentially) was subjected to further deliberation, through a second successive year, after a well-publicized interest in the matter was demonstrated by the new Clinton administration in the early 1990s. Although it would be difficult to measure, there was an unmistakable sense in the forums of 1994-1995 that more people were thinking of what "government" (or "public") responsibility for the nation's health *might be*; and Medicare was noticeably referenced more often and relied upon with more pride. The inference seemed to be—although, again, we are not talking of measurable data here, as much as of the tenor and pattern of conversation—that the more they had thought about Medicare, the more people had come to appreciate what they value in it; or the more they looked forward to the relief it would afford them when their magical 66th year came around. The first noticeable (albeit still subtle) change to emerge following the consistently publicized Clinton administration's explorations of the topic was that the elderly, apparently, had come to like what they had! And those who were younger—the now-grown children of the elderly—appreciated that fact, noticeably. In this second year, too, the new Canadian health program was widely referred to, and it drew broadly positive encomiums—many of which, perhaps unexpectedly if not oddly, appeared to come from medical professionals.

In the following decade, however, when the National Issues Forums tackled the issue again in 2003, the difference was remarkable. The change appeared radical, although nothing had dramatically altered in the intervening years—except that the nation's budget was in much better shape than it had been when President Clinton came into office. The cost of medical care had steadily risen, too, as had the cost of insurance and the stringency of insurers' terms, even as the sophistication of medical treatment had continued to introduce expensive wonders into the lives of more and more citizens, including the elderly, who had experienced both the misfortunes of accident or illness and the solid reliability of Medicare.

The outcome, anyway, in 2003, was distinctly different from that of earlier forums: a clearly outspoken and relentlessly critical skepticism about insurance companies and the price of medications. A passionate contempt and mistrust of insurance companies was widespread, and almost as strong was the appreciation expressed for Medicare. Some attention in these deliberations was given to the uneven accessibility of care and to the costs of hospitals; and some medical practitioners focused attention upon the impact that malpractice insurance has upon the pricing of care. Most notably, however, scarcely a voice was now raised in criticism of Medicare. By and large, in every forum, that program was praised for the help it gave to the elderly who, as a class, it seems, are recognized as "deserving," and the efficiency and ease of dealing with it. Noticeably, young and middle-aged participants in these discussions, too, seemed to recognize *themselves* as beneficiaries of the health care that government provided and paid for in the care of their retired and aging parents. Similarly, the health care offered through the Veterans' Administration was praised wherever it was mentioned, and several participants noted, with approval, that VA care as technically deserving of the connotation of "socialized medicine." A participant in Ohio closed an extended deliberative session with virtually a panegyric on the government's provisions for veterans like himself.

Four years later, when the National Issues Forums again (and most recently) addressed the health-care issue, in a series of filmed focus groups in 2007 (with forums to run through 2008 and into 2009), that same Ohioan's commentary might almost have served as a keynote. Now, the very occasional voice abhorring government involvement in health care, extensively heard in the earlier forums, was at best "crying in the wilderness"; and pharmaceutical companies and health insurance companies were everywhere the targeted villains of the occasion. Limitations on malpractice awards that tend to raise physicians' insurance costs (and hence what they charge their patients) were again noted in passing but drew little extended public attention, and penalties for those whose "unhealthy lifestyles" may make them prone to sickness were suggested, from time to time, but not made a focus of policy discussion. Complaints from small business owners (or, often, *former* small business owners) were common; stories of former patients' personal bankruptcies were genuinely disturbing (in their frequency as well as their tone); and stories of students at institutions outside their states of residence (and so without their families' insurance protection) were narrated more lightly by the young than they were received by the old.

Even in Massachusetts, then embarking upon its own system of required and subsidized health insurance as a prerequisite for state health-care benefits, the pervasive deliberations focused—in every site—on the expectation that only what is dubbed a single-payer system might be expected to yield a pool large enough to provide for universal coverage. And universal coverage was, in every group we examined in these 21st-century years, now deemed, quite specifically, "a right." Strikingly, when it came to what was wanted, the attitude expressed in these groups, more closely than in any other public forums we have monitored, on any topics, seemed unmistakably to echo what the opinion polls also were telling us in 2007-2008: the American public wanted a national health program of the kind variously dubbed a "single-payer system" or (by the US Congress) a "public plan." *Universal health care* and the *right to health care* were essentially the phrases on which forums and groups seemed to focus. Achieving such a "right," however, clearly remained problematic!

So in early 2009, the Kettering Foundation staged, in Washington DC, a kind of mock trial, with prosecuting and defending counsel calling witnesses to evidence whether the public, in deliberative forums, had or had not come to a judgment about how the nation might best address its health-care problem. The so-called "jurors" included both experts on health care and leaders like Richard Harwood and David Mathews, who are professionally committed to the engagement of a deliberative public in coming to such judgments as may ultimately guide our lives as a people. Witnesses called by both "counsel" unanimously confirmed that the various forums they reported from had affirmed that health care should be accepted as a right by US citizens. Yet after listening to the "witnesses" from among the participants at half a dozen forums around the nation, the "jury" unanimously agreed that this public had not yet reached a viable judgment about what we, as a people, *should* do as we confront the health-care crisis.

Now having examined independently some of these forums—some of which had included as participants these same "witnesses" featured in the DC "trial"—this writer can affirm their reported assertion that citizens had generally agreed that appropriate health care should indeed be provided as a right to any American who needed it—voices raised in objection being, in every instance, few, and associated, apparently, with either a principled, ideological objection to or a failure of trust in such a government role. How, then, are we to understand and reconcile both the outcome of public deliberation as reported in this instance, and the negative judgment of the mock jury, honorable men and women all of them, and experienced listeners, who had only these witnesses' reports as "evidence" to guide them?

Readers who have stuck with us thus far in this book will have recognized that we value the deliberative public voice precisely because it suggests a judgment—or at least acknowledges the potential value of a policy or action—with a full recognition of the discomforts it may entail, the expense it may incur, and even sometimes, perhaps, the merely comforting dream that it will translate henceforth into lasting decisions. Decisions are seldom easy to make, and decisions that will embrace the destinies of ourselves *and* all of our fellow citizens are particularly challenging. Regrettably, too, they are sometimes therefore fought over with both bitterness and deceit. That appears so genuinely to be the case with health-care policy in America that we may usefully spend a few paragraphs on circumstances that render a commanding public voice on this topic more than usually elusive. So here is one small and quite personal example of the tone that overtook the public discourse on health care in the summer of 2009.

The cluster of little villages where this writer has lived for some years is quiet, rural, and prosperous, yet only 30-some miles—by road, rail, plane, or boat—from the heart of New York City. So I was surprised when, late one Monday afternoon in the summer of 2009, in the almost-deserted parking lot in front of our village post office, I saw standing a small handcart, carrying two posters of President Obama's head. The head was whitewashed in each instance, and just below the nose was painted a shiny-black, Hitler-style mustache. A man and woman (whom I took to be in late-ish middle-age) were attending the cart. Neither appeared modishly elegant, nor theatrically clownish. But as I approached—very tentatively, you may believe—the woman shouted: "Paint a Hitler mustache on Obama! He plans to steal our health care."

The instinctive response in my mind, I confess, was, "There may be a dozen other countries in which it's better to be sick—where high quality health care is more broadly accessible—than in America; why would anyone want to steal *this* country's health care?" But being of the quiet, untroublesome kind, I gently (and softly) said: "Fortunately I'm on Medicare, so I don't think I have to worry."

Whereupon the woman responded, "He's going to take millions from your Medicare." Again, my mind instinctively said to itself, "From me? Good luck!" But I quietly said: "Oh! I had hoped he'd invite millions more Americans to *join* me in Medicare." And I continued into the post office.

Was I being cantankerous? Well, it was under my breath—and more mockery than deliberation! What troubled me, though, was not the harshly partisan politics, nor even the confused vulgarity of the display. This village is dyed-in-the-wool, hard-rock Republican territory. (If the names of Merrill and Lynch and Goldman and Sachs and Whitney and Rockefeller aren't still on the mail boxes in the post office, it's only because taxes made it smart to sell-off their 1,000-acre country estates in 3-acre lots, a century ago!) No! What genuinely distressed me was that, at a time when decisions of enormous significance—life and death decisions, indeed—have to be made, and when changes that will affect individual lifestyles and the social order itself are at issue, that freedom of speech, and the responsibility of a voice, should have been so thoroughly and deliberately perverted into the corrupting foolishness by which I had just been confronted. We do not have time, I thought, for that sort of chaotic and deliberate misdirection. That is inappropriate for a democratic people.

Granted, it may not be easy to determine what is "a public voice" on the issue of health care. Had it been put to a public vote a year earlier, this nation (the polls tell us) might possibly, by significant margins, have joined other nations (to whom we are allied, and often related, through long-term and complex understandings) in supplying health care to all of our citizens, as and when it is needed. (Yes, I do accept the opinion polls in this sense, although I would not assert that such a decision could be simply effected or would prove easy to translate into national practice, merely because more than half of the public had found the idea appealing.) While a year earlier those polls had been moving close to the 70-percent majorities that Daniel Yankelovich used to characterize as presenting what reflects, in effect, a "stable public judgment," the vote for universal health care still remained above the pollsters' democratic 50-percent base point, even after a year of calculated bludgeoning in the form I describe above, as well as in its only *somewhat* more civilized congressional counterparts.

So, we do know what the public would like: health care provided, "as a right!" And (thanks to forums and focus groups) we actually know why: for fear that they can't afford adequate insurance and won't be able to pay for it when they need it. But we do not yet know, with the kind of confidence revealed through extensive deliberation about other issues described in these pages, what steps our citizens are most eager to take, and what they might defer (or perhaps even evade, if they could) if we were to make our way, as a people, toward the kinds of "national" health care that are enjoyed by other peoples, while it continues here increasingly inaccessible. The problem of health care in this context is easy to understand and the case for dealing with it, at first sight quite straightforward, is already practiced (with a few modest variations) by other nations whom (size, economy, culture, and actual history aside) we accept as being "our kind of people."

Modern medicine—"health care," to put it broadly—has advanced enormously over the past century, making available ways of containing and countering and curing the effects of accident and illness that had hitherto, over centuries past, seemed inevitably prelude to incapacity, long-term suffering, or early death. Such extensive and rapid advances, however, are enormously costly, both in the process of development and in application; so it turns out that they are less and less accessible to those who are not wealthy or not wealthy enough to purchase substantial insurance policies. In fact, the insurance company (which after all is in the investment business, not the health-care business) tends quickly, understandably, to drop individual insurees when age or illness suggests that they may be likely to submit substantial claims in the near term. Thus, to repeat the litany we recited earlier, in the United States we have a large body of inadequately cared for citizens; the number of the uninsured grows annually; and the largest single category of citizens declaring personal bankruptcy each year is that of those bankrupted by medical debt, some of whom were insured, but not adequately to meet what turned out to be the actual cost of treatment. (It is perhaps not surprising that steadily increasing numbers of Americans carry no insurance, from the start.)

Now when necessary goods are priced out of the market in this way, government is generally expected to step in—for the public good. That is why we have armies and navies to protect us, instead of warlords and private bodyguards; it is why we have public schools, and highways, and water supplies, and firefighters and police officers, and so on. By collecting something (called a tax) from each citizen, in line with his or her ability to give, we gather a pool large enough to take care of the relatively modest *individual* needs that *some* of us are being faced with, *some* of the time, and *all* of us risk. In the case of a couple of nations (the Netherlands and Switzerland may be prime examples), a modest citizen-bought health insurance is *required*; but the annual cost per person is significantly less than that in the United States, while the quality of those nations' health care (by the generally accepted international standards) is considerably better—for everybody—than is ours in the United States. (The state of Massachusetts, in 2008, launched a plan of required citizen-bought insurance, something like those nations' systems; but participants in Massachusetts conversations remain understandably reluctant to make judgment upon it prematurely.) The immediate disadvantage, of course, is that some citizens in those countries pay more in taxes through a progressive system that taxes the rich at a very much steeper rate than the poor. (In Norway, someone tells me, the top bracket demands 50 percent of income!) Still, in times of national crisis (and nowadays, it seems, we do tend to refer to our health care as *in crisis* in the United States), taxes can go even higher than that. (Britain, in World War II, may hold the record.) So all these other nations' taxes are progressive in a way that makes the US patterns of taxation seem almost medieval. (That in those nations the ultimate gap between rich and poor is significantly narrower, therefore, than in this country, is also considered by some there a socially useful outcome—but that's another story!)

DISAGREEMENT, COMPROMISE . . . OR UNDERSTANDING

If this, then, is broadly the case for considering a national—which is to say, state managed—health-care program in the United States, what does the public voice from the reported forums yield us to deliberate about? On the face of it, not a great deal beyond the familiar (and sometimes frightening) sense that we do not really trust our government. Or the (perhaps in this context equally frightening) "hard-nosed" American sense that we each ought to be responsible for ourselves. These two instinctive sentiments (which are noted in other contexts, elsewhere in this study) are at the core of most of the relatively few straightforward "I don't want the government in my health care" objections to proposals for a national health-care program. But their implications were in no useful way weighed in the forum conversations. They are "attitudes," merely.

Associated with this, there is an articulated, evasive, but in some instances clearly cultivated assumption that our present pattern of health care is good *because* it is expensive. That if it is virtually too expensive for the likes of most of us, then perhaps it might not be worth our having *as a nation*—this is *not* a subject of discussion in these records. This is not the place to explore US class consciousness, but to make the point that health care in the United States today is "at issue" because it is a *national* problem. Everywhere we have heard health care discussed in groups like the National Issues Forums, there have been deeply moving comments upon the plight of the really poor, and on the inequities of American society that are felt in this context perhaps even more powerfully than they are when we talk of children's education. Increasingly, the comments continue, there are more and more families that do not receive the health care that they should have because they cannot afford the cost of it, or of the insurance that might cover at least some of it. *This* is the substance of the public talk.

And along with it, therefore, go unrestrained public criticisms of the insurance and pharmaceutical companies whose profits are—and this is widely acknowledged—considerable. But that recognizable cause-and-effect relationship, central to the experience of every market-based economy, is not a focus of deliberation in the most recent forums on health care. Why and to what extent the entrepreneur or investor or employee who is both resourceful and successful should be assessed differently, as a taxpayer, from workers with modest income was a puzzle neither explored nor explained in public meetings, even though the "value" of the individual life, *per se* was widely asserted. Nor was there broad public consideration that unduly burdening successful entrepreneurs with meeting the costs of everybody's health care might negatively affect the nation's economic growth in the future. So, only the gripes are consistent. Except for the broad hint that prices of pharmaceuticals might be constrained, at the very least by allowing citizens to buy necessary medicines from other countries where identical products are more reasonably priced by the same producers; and the notion of requiring insurers to continue coverage of insured individuals as long as they may need treatment—except for these two potential legislative targets, forums and focus groups over the past few years do not often or in depth weigh the possibilities or negative implications of alternative approaches that they thought might correct the underlying problems.

No sooner did preparation for congressional legislation to change the nation's practices in health care begin to occupy the news, in 2008-2009, than there emerged again an apparently irreconcilable division between those who were in favor of a national "public" program and those in favor of "the market." Supporters of the market had not been prominent in the previous years' health-care forums, but, in the context of current political news stories, their pronouncements seemed quickly to be everywhere. A concern about government becoming involved in the health-care market is in some quarters as organized and passionate, it would seem, as is concern about abortion, albeit without similar theological roots. And those who oppose the *idea* of a national health plan sometimes appear impervious even to actions that wise health care, in the nation as a whole, might seem to dictate and does already practice.

So for more than a year or two, committees of the US House and Senate have themselves been considering alternative ways of coping with the acknowledged problem of health care, and, as reported daily in the news media, they may have succeeded in obfuscating the public understanding of a problem by a plethora of non-solutions. The accepted mission on Capitol Hill, where supposedly representatives of the public deliberate, had appeared to be consistently that of avoiding direct engagement of the government in settling a problem that was specifically *about* the (possibly inescapable) need for government engagement. It was therefore an uncanny but surely illuminating moment when, as September 2009, drew toward its end, two members of the Senate Banking Committee presented an amendment proposing that legislation include the establishment of what Washington professionals like to call a "public plan" (and still sometimes, with designedly misleading intentions, "socialized medicine").

There is a comforting irony in it having been Senators Rockefeller and Schumer who presented this amendment to the Senate Committee's plan, which had been long and carefully drawn up without it. Both tolerably rich gentlemen, and blessed by the US government's own insurance plan (as are their colleagues), Senator Rockefeller serves a state with altogether unhealthy amounts of coal dust in its water and its air and its memories, while Senator Schumer serves a city where it sometimes seems that everyone who doesn't own a tenement lives in one. They presumably well know that what people who can't afford health insurance need is health care. But it was Senator Baucus, a prime mover in the creation of the senate's intended legislation, who suddenly opened (and closed) the door to what had remained absent from the public voice that we had heard in forums. To have a "public plan," he explained, would be "unfair competition" for the insurance companies.

And that objection carried the day. What appeared to have been the monster in the minds of a few participants in the public forums triumphed on Capitol Hill. Some senators had pointed out, of course, that the objective of the legislation was to serve the needs of the people, not the well-being of the insurance industry—just as had many in the public conversations we had monitored on the topic in earlier months. Yet it suddenly became clear that in neither case had there been carefully weighed what ultimately might be at stake, might be lost, or might therefore demand modification or recasting from the simple pro and con of the public opinion polls—neither by the House and the Senate in Washington, nor by the people in deliberative forums.

What we generally acknowledge as we analyze "a public voice," however, is neither the "yes" and "no" of the pollster's questionnaire, nor the binding vote of the senate; it is, rather, the expression of an understanding that is a step toward judgment. When the Kettering Foundation, some months earlier in 2009, had asked its "jury" of five thoughtful friends to hear, from half-a-dozen participants of the 2008 forums, some evidence of where they thought the public was coming out on this issue, they heard pretty much what we have here reported: people were quite sure they should have universal health care. There was, however, no indication of how this might be attained or what sacrifices it might involve, or by whom.

The record of the forum exchanges show that participants clearly had not weighed the significance of a national program for the investment industry (of which health-care insurers are a part), against its significance to individual health needs. They had not weighed, in a sense, the cost of keeping people healthy against the cost of their falling sick. They did not weigh the impact of increased taxes on some citizens against improved health for others. Nor the *value* of both profit and risk in the context of the US economy in the 21st-century world. Many questions they did not ask themselves—and quite apparently very few conditions encouraging or forbidding various courses of action had been publicly assessed. The public voice in 2008 was essentially a cry for help. And to a stern "jury," apparently, it was a case not proven. The reported mass opinion in favor of a national program had long been as near to unanimity as one is likely to find from polls among heterogeneous public groups, in one season; but from the analysis of a public voice, we typically expect to learn something more—enough to proceed toward particular objectives, at fairly articulated costs—with confidence. We might expect someone to ask, or to explain, why we willingly still buy insurance for our own lives and our properties, but think government might more responsibly insure our individual health.

If the poor and the young and the old were our primary concern, the public deliberation did not determine what is meant by "young" and "old" and "poor," if they are to be given a privileged priority in public concern. If the prices of pharmaceutical supplies are too high, they did not ask how prices might be controlled, or how the market might be rendered more open or fair. Perhaps most remarkable, if fewer and fewer of us can pay for our own necessary medical attention, they still did not say—or, for the most part *ask*—*who* should pay for *me*, and *how much*. (Again, we may remember the surprise of the man in Pittsburg, five years earlier, and the fact that no one there had suggested it inappropriate to have paid for his late wife's dialysis from public funds.) The seemingly instinctive sympathy among human beings for their fellows in need—and perhaps it is the fruit of their own experience and uncertainty—is always touching and sometimes appears inexhaustible. But we know it is not.

We also know that the practical expression of that sympathy can be costly—even sometimes futile. So when we think to act collectively, albeit for commonly recognized good, the balance must be carefully weighed. Why some drugs sell for more here in the United States than in other currencies remains an innocent inquiry unanswered in the forums. Why incomes above a given level are relatively freed from taxation that could save lives is another. And why the careless and indulgent among us deserve care from those who are more careful—or why some among us call for help in dying, or not dying—these, too, were not deliberative topics, apparently. Or at least they did not generate serious deliberative exchange. Nor—perhaps more surprisingly—did questions arise about what we in our communities and families *do* find connected to, and a responsibility of, the commonweal, as are our schools, our military, or other services by which our daily lives are facilitated within our communities.

Of course, ultimately these issues are the challenges that legislators and the staffs that serve them must face, with the help of sundry "experts" who may include some whom we think of as government bureaucrats. Nevertheless, the public had not come to its own useful judgment, insofar as it had not wrestled with such practical concerns. The value of public deliberation is in the opportunity, ultimately, that it gives for people, together, to weigh the pros and cons, the trade-offs or sacrifices demanded by—and the benefits of—alternative courses of action. Yankelovich places the public *deliberative* phase relatively early in the movement toward an *actionable* judgment; in exploring public forums on issues such as public health care—issues that continue troublesome for long years together—we have noticed how a kind of shared or collective decision from deliberative gatherings is often the critical factor in a process of change that may still nonetheless have ground to cover before it can be fully executed. That seems to be the case with health care. The fight goes on, simply because the fundamental issues that are involved in shaping an appropriately shared response to the recognized problem have not been openly joined and therefore cannot be fairly weighed.

As it turns out, we do not have complete videos and transcripts from the most recent couple of years of health-care forums (in 2008 and 2009), as we did from earlier forums used in *A Public Voice*, so the detail of evidence from forums in 2008-2009 adds relatively little to what we had captured from focus groups and casual man-on-the-street conversations, on camera, during the preceding winter—essentially a widespread public expression of concern, fear, and hope. People fear illness and accident because they cannot afford adequate insurance; they are most profoundly concerned about the fate of the poor, therefore; they see the pharmaceutical and insurance industries as virtually predatory—and unreliable, and irresponsible, to boot; and they largely insist that we should consider the provision of appropriate health care our right, as American citizens. This, the "public voice" has said. And health-care professionals and experts, for the most part, are genuinely set about finding ways to effect necessary change.

But Americans, of course, have historically tended to talk in terms of rights, once their minds are made up on the importance of a given course. This nation was, in a sense, built on concepts like those that the renegade Briton, Tom Paine, dubbed "the rights of man" at the time of the Revolution. Its citizens are deeply conscious of their civil rights, of their right to speak freely and to vote, their right to fair trial and to emergency treatment—and, granted what they now hear of other nations, their right, as citizens, to appropriate health care, too, may seem understandable if not yet inevitable. These American citizens, however, appear not to have asked each other—and certainly not answered—why the richest of nations has such a poor record of health care among its citizens, when compared to other peoples. They have not explored what changes would necessarily be made if the provision of health care were to become, for Americans, *a right*.

Like the forums on abortion, those in 2008 on health care were conducted with energy and sustained with interest. Experiences had been presented with feeling and listened to patiently; some opinions had been explored, some alternatives contributed, and some potential trade-offs, if not carefully weighed, were at least implied or acknowledged. But the outcomes—in that the value of public deliberation is to reflect movement, or absence of movement, toward a shared public understanding and democratic decision making—were yet different from what one might typically expect from public deliberation, as we have explored it in the preceding chapter.

The Political Import of Public Thought

The deliberative public sessions on the issue of abortion, as we noted, had left participants with an implied, although not formulated, *recognition of differences* among them. That recognition, obviously, left people variously disappointed and in some instances, perhaps, piqued. There was no doubt, however, about the quality of conversation, nor the *civility* of the kind of understanding that, as citizens, the participants shared, despite some infrequent but powerful, persistent, and deeply rooted differences in belief and behavior. The health-care deliberations, in contrast, while reflecting an occasional disagreement in principle or dogma, made increasingly clear, as each forum progressed, an inescapable and seemingly universal dissatisfaction with a system that effectively denies appropriate health care to large numbers of its citizens in need. Therefore, there remained a shared or collective sense of urgency in participants' commitment to change. These two sets of public deliberations, then—on abortion and health care—each of them repeated countless times in communities throughout the nation, may suggest or illuminate for us some of the subtly different uses that deliberative public forums may serve on issues whose potential impacts may be differently valued, yet always need be broadly understood—by citizens as well as governments—if democracy is to work as it should. The abortion forums revealed an astonishing broad sympathy for a human situation that many believe categorically unacceptable, while the health-care forums reveal an overwhelming desire for a system that many are not, as a public, able to describe in detail or practice. It is also a desire that is determinedly opposed, with or without principled convictions, by some interests among us.

The ancient Greeks, who gave us the democratic idea, appear not to have labored much over it; and the Romans, although also exquisitely literate and familiar with the politics of the *agora*, seem sometimes to have been not far removed from 20th-century versions of the military dictatorship (despite the imagined throw-away of Shakespeare's Mark Antony to his "friends, Romans, countrymen"). Still, thanks perhaps to a rebellion of the peers against the king in 13th-century Britain, and of its serfs 100 years later, the *idea* of a government of, for, and by the people seems to have grown steadily enough, over time, for Lincoln to encapsulate it succinctly in the United States of the 19th century.

Yet in fact, the actual capturing and effecting of a *public will* remains more elusive. Here in the United States of the 21st century, government by representatives—elected at enormous cost with the help of a relatively small number of interests (who are prepared to pay those costs in order to secure the interest that they depend upon and cherish)—is only metaphorically "of, for, and by" the people. That is of course why it is critical that we devise and extend practices like those of the National Issues Forums, which enable people, generally and quite readily, to distinguish outcomes, policies, and actions that they would *like*, from those that they could *put up with*; and to distinguish those they must *continue to work on* from those that they find *morally or literally intolerable*. Public deliberation has revealed, pretty well anywhere a public meeting is held, that a similar range of attitudes and concerns will be expressed, sooner or later compellingly, by numbers of people in society's response to any issue that will affect them all, as a people. And granted that we remain consciously open and tolerant as a civil society, an inherent feeling for humanity tends to make a carefully disciplined tolerance of individual choice at least *provisionally* possible, although not necessarily approved or recommended by those with profoundly differing personal convictions or significant personal investment at stake.

The deliberations on what should be our attitude, as a people, toward the abortion dilemma offered one case in point. Those among us who are firm in our conviction, and who represent an interest that we believe works for the public good, can nonetheless embrace with a common sympathy even a practice that remains forbidden amongst us and against which we shall continue to work. There are still many among our fellow citizens who devoutly believe that our society should not—except under quite extraordinary and precisely specified circumstances—permit abortion to be performed; and they work openly and fervently toward that end. But momentarily at least, in public dialogue, they were able to share in sympathetic conversation with fellow citizens who accept what they themselves cannot condone. During the Cold War, citizens held radically different senses of what should be our attitude toward the use of nuclear weapons—and those who did not discuss the issue deliberatively sometimes protested their contrary points of view with passion, even violence; but we have seen (in our second chapter, above) how, as fellow citizens, we slowly adjusted our sense of what attitudes might prove most useful in our relationship with other nations, some of whom were similarly weighing their options and the potential outcomes. Even in the past few years we have observed that, while attitudes toward undocumented aliens may be radically different in different parts of the country, a recognition that we *need*, even *depend upon* the services of some such aliens leaves the way open for continuing policy dialogue among citizens concerned in quite different ways about what we—in this "nation of immigrants"—still have to face in the near future.

In this sense, then, deliberative dialogue among citizens may not be an instrument that will dictate policies to be quickly enforced; but it does make a way toward understanding as the key to fruitful dialogue, even between citizens whose attitudes seem to be rooted in differing concerns.

The situation is significantly different, however, with respect to health-care policy at the present time, since what is at stake here are apparently conflicting *interests*, quite literally. In one sense, individual lives may be at stake; in another, corporate wealth. A given individual life may turn out to need unaffordable care, or to be salvageable only at the cost of individual bankruptcy; the said "corporate wealth" may also translate into individual wealth, of course, at least among officers, shareholders, and employees of relevant health-related interests, but it may facilitate, also useful investment in all of our citizens' future health.

Yet the insurance company's investments must bring returns greater than the immediate costs of patients' treatment and their own administration. The pharmaceutical industry and many indispensable professional services similarly find themselves stakeholders in a complex of services that are undergoing change. Here then, we do not have merely a public, trying to hammer out (or deliberate over) what it is prepared to accept as a way to an improved public good, a fundamental good, a collective good to all parties. The public deliberations about health care in 2008 and 2009 reveal that citizens are indeed prepared to accept—actually know that they already do, to a degree, accept—triage: that is to say, the provision of medical care that gives some patients priority treatment, while other patients, whose condition is either less critical or virtually irreversible, might nonetheless accept postponed ameliorative treatment. We also know, from media stories tied to the preparation of congressional legislation, that some among the insurance industry are prepared, at least as a bargaining point, to forgo their present patterns of raising the rate of, or cancelling outright, individuals' policies on the basis of age or changing physical condition; and that pharmaceutical companies are prepared, in some ways as yet unspecified, to curtail the extraordinary profit they could make, apparently, if the government were to absorb in some not-yet-clearly specified way the cost to the public of getting well. We are given to understand, too, that a patient's right to choose his or her physician or hospital, and to accept or deny given treatment, will not be impaired. The underlying public issue, then, remains whether or not we, as a people, should and will provide the health care that may prove necessary for all of our citizens, or just that for ourselves (and our families) alone, or just what we can pay for, ourselves, in the always-feared moment of crisis. And we must understand what such services might cost and how that cost could be met.

What is in fact at issue, then, is whether, or to what degree, we should treat health care as a national obligation—in a sense, as we do children's education, national defense, the community's protection from fire and crime, our supplies of drinking water, control of the airways, the right to vote (wherever we reside), and so on—and how we might best cover the cost of such practice, if we incline toward it. All of such privileges that our culture appears to take for granted are accepted and paid for in carefully and appropriately prescribed ways. What has been *argued* between legislators and those representing the interests of the health-care industry, however, are the ways in which health *insurance* might be modified to ensure broader and more economical treatment for a significantly larger number of citizens than are currently insured. What is being argued among professionals and legislators is how close we should come to care, and by what means, and at what cost, to which segments of the citizenry—granted the perpetuation of a system of health-care insurance. What is being argued in Washington—as was the case a few years ago, when pharmaceutical costs became integrated with the Medicare program—is a case for enhancing the profit of certain industries (primarily insurance and pharmaceutical industries) at the public's (that is to say, the taxpayer's) expense, by means, apparently, of subsidies from *other* citizens to *some* citizens who are unable to afford such insurance by themselves. What has *not* been at issue in Washington, apparently, is what seems to be the public's concern that health care, like education and security, be *assured*. In all likelihood, this concern cannot be adequately responded to unless the concerns of others are also; and the interests of the health-care industries are, to elected officials, as valuable, almost literally, as the interests of those upon whose votes at election time they depend. The industries and the voters, however, do not always hear (or care for) each other's language. Or they may not understand it.

It is, of course, never a simple matter to determine three or four carefully articulated options for action to provide basis for discussion in a deliberative forum. Such options might, up front, in themselves do no more than invite argument, or at best debate. Obviously, in the Cold War discussions of nuclear arms policy, the three "choices" over which deliberation was reported in our second chapter were somewhat simplistic versions of complex policy positions, the difference between which might have been life and death on a massive scale. Historically, both the National Issues Forums and a number of other successful convenors of deliberative forums have assumed that participants would pretty much understand the problem, as well as the values they share in their concerns, and therefore would treat seriously the three or four policy options toward which they might take somewhat different approaches in their search for actionable conclusions. We make such assumptions with confidence because we will have used highly competent focus group analyses to complete extensive studies of the initial thinking among a broad range of citizens when questioned about the topic at issue, in order to identify—or frame—the broad options that we know will include or imply a significant number of principles and interests, or goals and actions that will reveal the tensions between concerns of individual participants as a group's deliberations progress. This works in group, face-to-face deliberations because it is a way of conveying understandably the complexity of the issues we face when we are talking of a recognized community interest, with people responding at will to trains of thought that others seem to be wrestling with around us. It presumes, however, the active presence of a large enough variety of recognizable "fellow citizens" to ensure initial response and reservation toward a range of specific aspects of the problem. Experience tells us—and those who lead focus groups know this—that this sense of *sharing* differences among a recognizably acceptable group is the place to begin public deliberation—usually with tentative inquiry about the nature of the problem itself, as a matter of experience in people's own lives. To get people thinking and talking among strangers, it is necessary to say, in effect, "what do you think about health care/immigration/Wall Street?" and so on. Their responses will eventually constitute a framework of actions that *might* be undertaken, aspects of the problem that are at "issue"—and with which different participants will most easily start as their points of departure.

Just a few years ago, in the 25th-anniversary year of the National Issues Forums, David Mathews wrote what may be the most distinguished of the many ". . . afterthoughts" essays with which he has customarily sealed each issue of the occasional magazine, *Kettering Review*, over the years. In it he distinguishes most clearly, one from another, the concepts of what we think of as traditional institutional politics—the politics practiced by democratic governments and institutions—and public politics, practiced by democratic peoples, in their place as communities. Importantly, the ultimate focus, responsibility, and concern of the two should differ hardly at all; yet one is driven by numbers and command, the other by understanding and agreement. Each accordingly tends to—or pretends to—value the aid of the other; yet they share very little at all, much of the time. The value of public deliberation, however, is the shared *understanding* that it seeks, rather than the narrower *interests* that we each instinctively react to protect. Ideally, public deliberation about health care, for example, will consider the significance of investment industries, the energies of pharmaceutical industries, and tax privileges of wealthier citizens, even as it responds to the fears of families in crisis and individuals in pain. In our contemporary world, institutional politics can close its eyes and ears to strangers more readily than to those able to pay the costs and circulate the stories upon which electoral success may too often depend. That is why public politics must be central to the contemporary democracy.

Deliberation about our common life is, on the one hand, appealing in itself to significant numbers of good citizens who welcome slightly more structured and perhaps slightly more serious conversation about current challenges in their collective life than are offered by familiar daily conversations or often-conflicting news reports. (Were that not so, none of us would have gotten into the game, to begin with!) But among us, on the other hand, we do find tendencies that lead some of us sometimes to want to *persuade* others—including not only our deliberative friends but also elected political representatives—of the ease and satisfaction likely to attend one particular course of action, or the achievement of a specific goal, not yet accepted by a number of interested parties known to our elected representatives better than to us.

What should be the outcome, then, of public deliberation? This deliberative monster, "democracy," has many pairs of hands, alas, still. For some, a goal discovered to be widely shared should have the effect of *command*, and—such being the nature of our open, political life in America—this means for some of us that public deliberation ought to be persuasively presentable to our elected representatives or to interests in conflict. That, of course, presumes a magical potency; it begins to sound like the making of a "popular front." So, too, does a quite different expectation: that citizens who have deliberated thoughtfully together will determine what *they, themselves, collectively* must do, what coordinated actions they will actually take, together, personally, to gain entry to the promised land, regardless of what their no-longer-trusted representatives may do or other public groups plead for.

Quite evidently some of the public conversation of the past 30 years that this book's casual "history" has referenced are patterns of public thinking by which Americans have sought to accommodate themselves—and some of the conflicted interests that they represent—to courses of action, or direction, that encourage hope rather than despair, or that awaken the glimmer of possibility, if not always a promise of universal satisfaction. Some of those deliberations have been reported directly to legislators, as though that in itself were the goal at the end of the road of public deliberation. Others of them have reflected clearly the tensions that exercise the public mind in America—and where we have recorded a succession of deliberative events and national concerns over periods of several years, much indeed can be learned therefrom. Some of them, however, report only profound dissatisfactions or desiderata, yet resist any weighing of alternative responses that profess to *deal with* specified discomforts. And some are merely—or justly—

recapitulations of the frustrations of living together, a people with disparate aspirations and unequal resources.

As such, these deliberations that we have described may sometimes seem far, far away from the ideal of public deliberation as the means toward democratic self-government. And perhaps they are! Still, if the practice of public deliberative politics is to be carefully analyzed—and the outcome of that analysis to be reported broadly and considered wisely—we must first, surely, be able to explain clearly what it is we are reporting, to whom it should be of interest, and what, therefore, we should expect to follow from our report.

Yet despite all the years over which Americans have engaged designedly in public deliberation, and despite all the good advice about naming and framing and moderating public issues in deliberative forums that has been published, we've not extensively explained to ourselves *the kind of politics* we imagine being practiced. Rather, it seems, we have consistent indications from the past quarter-century that the outcomes of public deliberation are of little value to elected legislators in the pursuit of their goals, except to the degree that they suggest some endorsement of efforts (however slender) already under use in the political arena. Intermittent congressional interviews over the past half dozen years bear this out consistently; and we should also remember that the 16 years of public television's *A Public Voice* were designed, consistently, to use the outcomes of public deliberations (in the context of contemporary press stories and legislative gestures) as a means toward engaging primarily the *public interest itself* in such current, and popular, political deliberation. Those nationally broadcast programs were not crafted to enhance politicians' interest in the "public voice"; the aim was to make the public voice more accessible *in the public sphere*, thereby to encourage more deliberative public habits. (We were contributing, after all, to *public* television!) Meanwhile, we live, perhaps, with the very different kind of politics that Sheldon Wolin, the distinguished professor emeritus of politics at Princeton, describes in his recent book *Democracy Incorporated,* as a political condition of "inverted totalitarianism," a democracy by way of an elected oligarchy

> furthered by power-holders and citizens who often seem unaware of the deeper consequences of their actions or inactions. There is a certain heedlessness, an inability to take seriously the extent to which a pattern of consequences may take shape without having been preconceived.

It can be argued that the first and profoundly influential success of the first effort of the National Issues Forums—called, at the time, readers will remember, the "Domestic Policy Association"—at the Gerald Ford Library in 1983 (with Presidents Ford and Carter presiding and David Mathews and Daniel Yankelovich as masters of ceremony) was a significant, potentially meaningful, kind of political event because, although attended by noticeable alumnae of the White House and federal agencies, it was not trapped in congressional politics. Similarly, the subsequent NIF presentations, to congressional and executive branch staff in specially hosted meetings in Washington, DC, have proved more rewarding than have presentations closely tied to highly politicized legislative issues and made directly to congressional and executive branch leaders. Of a different order of significance, although complementary in import, we will note that some of the most valued outcomes from public deliberation have been localized in communities, either because—as we shall discover when we turn, in our next chapter, to Cincinnati and Grand Rapids—those communities themselves framed the problem or—as in West Virginia and in Alabama—the work was carefully tailored toward action by, within, and for local citizens themselves.

In this growing movement of a "public politics," reflective of different as well as common experiences and cultures, we, moment by moment, tend to cast different shadows, utilize different language, reveal differing values. And when it comes to explaining how a public *will* is found, sized, and transfigured to occupy appropriate space in the scenario of current *legislative* politics, we know that we risk asking for the impossible or perverting sound patterns of movement toward premature expressions of sentiment and judgment. As both a practitioner of deliberative public politics and an analyst of that practice, this writer is sympathetic to both Yankelovich's concept of a "public judgment" and to Mathews' commitment to a concept of "public work" as desirable outcomes from a deliberative public—and to a dozen other expositions of what is important in what we call "popular democracy." Still, we need be cautious of the confusion or chaos that can ensue if public politics is prompted by no more than the misleading intention of getting more people to feel as though they are involved in "talk radio"—even if today's version of that turns out to be a blog site or Facebook. We first must ask for simplicity and clarity in the expression of what is proposed by the phrase *public deliberative politics*. What does this public deliberative politics seek? How will that goal be shown to have been reached? And where, noticeably, does the impulse tend to fall short of its aspirations?

V.

Deliberative Communities . . . The Persistence of Popular Will

IN JOHN MILTON'S extraordinary epic, *Paradise Lost,* when Adam recognizes that he and Eve are to be exiled forever from the Garden of Eden, he first denies any hope:

> All otherwise my thoughts to me portend:
> That this day's death denounced will prove no sudden
> But a slow-paced evil, a long day's dying
> To augment our pain. . . .

Yet a few hundred lines later, the long poem ends, describing Adam and Eve, our human forebears, leaving Paradise in this way:

> Some gentle tears they dropped, yet wiped them soon
> The world was all before them, where to choose
> Their place of rest, and Providence their guide.
> They, hand in hand, with wand'ring steps and slow,
> Through Eden took their solitary way.

That was the entry of our first parents into this "brave new world" in which we live. And while it may be a somewhat grandiose and overly theological way of approaching public deliberation, Milton's image of two people—somewhat uncertain, and knowing all too little of what the outcome may be, with still slow and "wandering steps," yet "hand in hand," moving into a not quite familiar world, choosing together—is a poetic image akin to that climactic moment in, for example, the forum on abortion, referred to many times above: people understanding, and sharing their understanding, in a world of uncertainty and difference, and often disappointment.

Sharing life together, as a community, is not always easy and requires inevitably that we deliberate together, from time to time, as problems arise between us. The needs and fortunes of families and individuals change; nor do we all share comparable talents or similar tastes. And when inequality begins to merge into inequity, only well-designed policies can shape for us the security that we need for community to continue. It is then, however, that deliberation among us may have to prove a means to this end. For a peculiar quality of deliberation is that, unlike argument, which posits acceptance or denial, deliberation assumes *possibility*.

This sense of movement toward a recognized hope, despite sometimes the voicing of what seem to be unalterably opposing principles, is characteristic, we have found, when people deliberate upon the patterns of their community life together. Community issues were not at the forefront in the first decade of the consistent practice of deliberative forums, despite the initial identity ascribed to the National Issues Forums—the "Domestic Policy Association," as the National Issues Forums network had first called itself, in the early 1980s. When the association began its work, the expectation was that what Washington, DC, and the national media think of as policy questions would be its subject matter; and certainly, in that first decade, primarily issues relating to the Cold War, the economy, Social Security, race, and so on were carefully presented for public deliberation. Yet the thousands of citizens who found it potentially useful to discuss these issues openly and thoughtfully together were, they discovered, "citizens" in a classical sense: that is, they were members of a community that was *civic* in that it was defined not merely by its history but by its *continuing* history, which the community's members themselves would make, through their thoughts, their works, and their actions, collectively. "Communities," in our familiar usage, are the product and the instruments of *learning*; their deliberations represent a *learning culture*.

National problems and policies are, ultimately, reflections of, or are molded by, what citizens in their own communities are troubled by, and have had ideas about, and responded to. So issues of nationwide importance have turned out, often, also to be citizens' own issues, known because of their experience and their practice in their own communities and their own families. AIDS in 1988 was such an issue; alcoholism in 1999; the public school, again and again and again, over the years—these turn out to be *community* issues, *nationwide*. About all three of them—and these are just three among many—decisions have had to be made and actions of a remedial nature have had to be undertaken. (Or sometimes were not!) And in all three, as in the earlier example of the abortion issue, apparently incompatible positions were presented and clearly held the commitment of some of the participants, while others resisted. Since our sources, for the purpose of this study, are recordings and writings that reflect only the deliberative process itself, we cannot offer subsequent evidence of practical outcomes in given communities; still, the approach to these issues as they arose, in what were always, by definition, community-based National Issues Forums over the past quarter-century or so, may themselves provide some intriguing insights into the practice of democratic self-government in the setting of the democratic community.

In the late 1980s, AIDS, not a widely familiar disease until that time, became quite extensively reported; with the deaths of distinguished and widely respected stars of Hollywood and Broadway, what was soon to become broadly referred to as "the gay community" became in itself a topic of news and reflection, publicly. At issue, to a degree and perhaps fundamentally, was the legitimacy of homosexual practice, having been considered for so long "the love that dare not speak its name"; but the topic in open and widespread *public* discussion had quickly become the challenge to prevent, or at least control and alleviate, the spreading epidemic of AIDS. Granted the development of popular interest in this topic, and a recognition of the uncertainty and ignorance, as well as intense conflict, that was associated with it, the National Issues Forums network prepared a careful issue guide that, in its time, was widely used among the growing network of National Issues Forums.

In 1988 a memorable forum occurred in Chattanooga, Tennessee, where a group whose leaders were associated with the university there convened a public deliberation on this challenge at a beautiful public facility in the heart of the city. Among the large number of participants that turned out, some represented the staff of local health-care facilities, most of them experienced professionals, directly and deeply concerned with the care of those who were or might become victims of an epidemic. On the other hand, however, there was also present one citizen described by the local convenors as a well-known "street-corner preacher"—perhaps to imply both his disassociation from some formal religious institutions and possibly to suggest also his vigorously outspoken awareness of the wrath of God! Around them, individuals and families apparently had come with social and personal interests. To a small group who were visiting a number of deliberative public forums nationwide to assess their impact (a group that included the present writer), all this was taken as a caution to us that there might turn out to be more passion than deliberation in the evening event.

And so indeed it began. The said "preacher" was energetic, articulate, and never short of breath; clearly, he had assumed that this was to be *his* congregation for the evening. Perhaps fortunately for the assembled company, however, the issue guide that had been offered to all of the participants had noted (from interviews, focus groups, and quite thorough research in the literature) that public concerns included not only the value of moral reprimand and reform (which may indeed be appropriate business of the preacher) but also medical care in hospital and hospice, and disciplined education as means toward prevention. So, after the preacher's eloquent opening salvo, the moderator was able to call on other, no-less-articulate citizens who saw the problem in different light and with no less feeling, if somewhat more modest vocal intensity. The forum proved both lively and good humored as the evening progressed, and while one cannot presume that the preacher felt any less sure of his concept of sin or damnation, there was clearly a deep sense of concern for the care of human suffering among the whole company as the deliberation progressed. Opinions, even commitments, had already been expressed differently, but questions were asked, too; and, surprisingly, some expressions of obligation and acceptance were shared, one sensed, in the room. The meeting adjourned, finally, with continuing conversation. Indeed, we out-of-town auditors sensed that many of the participants had more to talk about together, as they left, than they had thought at the start.

Of course, one seldom knows how a given deliberation will affect the lives and behaviors of individual participants, for the public forum itself is "an event," merely. Afterwards, the participating citizens return to different experiences (as we assume had been also the case with participants in the forums about abortion); and, guided by different priorities, in different social contexts, they will doubtless act in ways that their trusted intimates consider appropriate, while some of their partners in the forum might or might not approve.

While the Chattanooga forum on how to cope with the apparently growing threat of AIDS did not produce such dramatically intense moments of shared human recognition as we have recorded from the Mississippi forum on abortion, there was here, however, a nonetheless shared and felt recognition of a serious problem that we must address, all of us—and that we should also address as a community, for communities can be confronted by problems collectively (as our preacher well knew). Differences about what matters, what must be achieved, obviously persist, and if what was at issue had been matters essentially of *policy*—as the more recent concerns about the cost of health care, and of providing it more broadly to Americans, fundamentally are—then differences of priority and interest might quickly have matured into the kinds of angry antagonisms that had been first feared as the Chattanooga forum began. Yet through the forums of the past quarter century, we have come to recognize that people who fundamentally disagree may discover, if they deliberate together on the reasons for and the outcomes of certain sets of values (and species of action appropriate to those values), that they share an appreciation of the values themselves. In the case of the Chattanooga forum, the preacher, it seems, respected the "Good Samaritan" work of both professional and volunteer nursing aids and teachers; they in turn, no doubt, recognized a potential value in his moral and disciplinary, principled concern, if not in his judgmental intensity of style. In this sense, it is not merely the *outcome* of deliberation—that is to say, the resulting political action—that matters, but that the process of deliberation is itself a means of making community. *That* matters . . . because the human community must encompass disagreement.

Other AIDS forums proceeded, as it turned out, amicably—and with patience, even humor, at differing parties' expense. This may not represent a close step toward what we think of as public judgment; nor are such forums as this precisely an example of popular democracy at its self-governing work. Yet they do represent a kind of awareness—a kind of learning—that permits us all to continue on what we believe is the task we are challenged to perform for and with our fellow citizens—which we sometimes must do without much support from others, or even despite particular burdens that we'd prefer not to endure and differences that we'd prefer to put out of mind. And it may be that this is at least a kind of pre-democratic condition of democratic public progress.

Deliberative Learning, Common Trust and Individual Need

The awareness and learning we noted in the deliberative forums on AIDS are, in fact, a general feature of public deliberation. If we think of public deliberation as a means by which the public may move toward a shared—or better, *collective*—judgment, it is apparent that the process is designedly educative, albeit in a non-academic way. Indeed, as a fashion of human discourse, deliberation is inevitably educative in that it weighs one option for action against another, in light of their likely outcomes. This is a process that is necessarily informative although it may not always be decisive; and might be assumed, even, as morally indifferent except insofar as it is taken as a means toward social betterment. "Deliberation," after all, suggests etymologically the weighing of pros and cons in order to decide among competing outcomes, each of which may be still far short of perfection.

Public deliberation, however, is peculiarly democratic in that each of the options presented for consideration as policy is argued (which means both presented and opposed, or qualified) on the basis of a value, or set of values, that are (1) commonly recognized by all other participants, but (2) have not necessarily been yet consciously associated by all of them with the problem at issue. Thus, the personal experience of a given participant may become meaningful insofar as others recognize the impulse for his or her tentative (and maybe provisional, up to this moment) attitude, even if they had not themselves earlier thought of the issue in quite that way. Such a process of discovery is meaningful to the degree that emotions associated with the telling of the personal experience are consciously shared as the telling occurs. The quiet moment of revelatory self-discovery that became *shared* in the Mississippi deliberations about abortion is a rarely affecting example of that. The young mother at the abortion forum affected her fellow citizens, momentarily, because they shared her pain. We do not necessarily think of pain as "a value," yet in that moment it had become the value that united all of the participants in a shared understanding of a human predicament. Such a sympathetic outcome was not apparent in the Chattanooga forum about AIDS; yet there too, participants and observers obviously enlarged their understanding of the world in which they felt they needed to act, one way or another.

That is perhaps the most common experience of *learning* in deliberative forums; and it is very different from the process of rational reasoning, as Noëlle McAfee, a political philosopher with a special interest in democratic theory and practice, has carefully explained in her classic essay, "Three Models of Public Deliberation," written originally as a reflection upon the 2003 National Issues Convention on "Americans' Role in the World" (the weekend of public deliberation described above, in Chapter 2). McAfee calls the first of her three models of deliberation a "preference-based" model, resulting from "the political scientists' adoption of the language and theoretical structures of economics"—which, she explains, is limited by the difficulties of "aggregating a set of individual preferences into a social preference order." (This of course is what the poll or survey does.) A second she calls the "rational proceduralist model"—represented most famously by Jürgen Habermas and John Rawls—in which the assumption is that the better argument will prevail, so that "participants should ultimately agree on which proposal is most rational and right." Each of these first two approaches, of course, has an illusionary appeal in the practice of modern democratic politics; but a third model, which McAfee thinks of as "quasi-Deweyan," and calls the " integrative model," so well captures the patterns of public deliberation we are tracing here that it is worth presenting at some length.

> In keeping with Dewey's insight, actual public deliberations usually spend a great deal of time developing a public picture of what a problem is and how it affects those in the room and others throughout the political community. As deliberators develop a public understanding of the nature and the many aspects of the problem at hand, they also begin to see themselves as a public.
>
> This view distinguishes itself by aiming for the *integration* of multiple, heterogeneous views. Unlike the second model, which expects deliberators to act according to the Enlightenment universalizing ideal, this model accepts and makes use of citizens' particular perspectives. Because each starts out with a limited picture of how a policy under consideration might affect others, participants deliberate in order to learn. They seek information, not so much about facts but about the con-

> sequences of various policies. In this model, citizens' partial perspectives can be *integrated* into a viable, sound policy choice, but one that is always provisional and subject to change.
>
> When people come together to deliberate on matters that affect their policies, they seem to transform personal concerns and interests into public ones. . . . It is not that public deliberations turn participants into altruists. Rather, public deliberations help forge an immediate interest in matters public, conjuring up the history of the term "interest" itself: *inter-esse*, a way of being between and with others. Participants develop an interest in the welfare of their political communities.
>
> Moreover, this model attends to the problem over . . . how to set policy direction when there is not full, or even much, agreement. Participants use their disagreements as productive constraints, helping them identify in which, albeit few, possible directions the polity might move. Following the many deliberations that my colleagues at the Kettering Foundation and I have observed, participants leave saying that even when they did not agree with other participants, they did come to see why the others held the views they did. They came to change their views of others' views. Even in the face of the trenchant disagreement, participants would focus on coming up with a direction that would accommodate the plural concerns in the room.

As we have seen—in the forum on abortion and in the forum on AIDS, as examples—there are times when the outcome is not an action but a change in awareness and an acceptance of those who continue to disagree with us on what is acceptable. Those of us who have analyzed deliberative forums carefully and consistently know this. Yet we continue to look for more—for a *pattern* in deliberative public thinking about an issue because we find public deliberation a means of approaching public judgment precisely to the degree that, on reflection—or retrospectively, upon analysis—we discern movement in the general or collective thinking *toward one end rather than others*; or toward a smaller concentration of outstanding questions than seemed present initially because, initially, different groups of participants had routinely discarded or unconsciously skipped over other arguments than their own.

To ensure that such discussion among heterogeneous groups of citizens moves in the general or collective thinking *toward one end more clearly than others* does require that, if public deliberation is formally to begin and proceed coherently, the subject issue must necessarily have been "defined" (in a manner of speaking) by a generally arguable sense of its importance, then presented in terms of three or four clearly distinctive approaches that *could* be followed, and *if* followed would likely point toward conclusions, each of which would imply particular and different kinds of actions, while perhaps also rejecting some others. In theory, such a "framing" task might engage the beginning of a public deliberative gathering—or the first of a series perhaps, in any community—even though in itself this is less a deliberative process than one of analysis and synthesis.

In practice, in fact, it has generally proved more satisfying if a framework of possible approaches is developed by those who have already made themselves familiar with the challenge, on the basis of interviews (or informal focus groups) held in appropriately varied locations. The outcome of such pre-deliberative research is, of course, reflected in the dozens of issue guides that have been produced, over the past 28 years, through the Kettering Foundation, for the National Issues Forums. Yet, flipping through them now, and through the annual reports of what happened in the forums that used them, it is indeed surprising to find how often the three or four popular *concerns* about an issue—that is, the three or four presumably distinctive points of departure around which the issue is framed for public deliberation—turn out to be complementary, rather than in conflict. In other words, the approaches, on whose comparative utility or persuasiveness the deliberation is focused, do not lead toward the choice of one end rather than another but, instead, all turn out to be in themselves compelling, up to a point, and to a degree, then, surprisingly—even, sometimes, paradoxically—*interdependent*.

A discussion guide to an issue explored in 1999, for example, was titled, perhaps not felicitously, *Alcohol: Controlling the Toxic Spill*. The guide suggested deliberation weighing three seemingly sensible approaches to dealing with the problem of alcoholism, which itself was described thus:

> Alcohol abuse can wreck the lives of drinkers and their families. . . . Excessive drinking creates countless personal disasters, including job losses, bankruptcies, suicides, divorces, crimes, lost friendships, and ruined family life. Nearly one-in-ten adults meets criteria for chronic alcohol abuse or alcohol addiction. How can a democratic society safely control the drug, alcohol?

Sensibly enough, it would seem, the courses of action suggested as worth some deliberation in response to that question were (1) to "demand citizen responsibility"—essentially a more severe enforcement of existing laws to stress the importance of deterring alcohol abuse; (2) to treat this as a "public health epidemic"—an approach looking toward "prevention, early detection, counseling, and treatment"; and (3) calling for "society-wide educational efforts to dispel falsehoods and ignorance . . . and generate popular social norms and public policies for responsible behavior."

The published report that Paul Werth Associates subsequently presented from these forums, nationwide, reflected very clearly a broad public agreement with *each one* of these goals. Thus, as is sometimes the case in public deliberation, "all of the above" solutions seems to be the outcome of the deliberations on alcohol abuse. Further, apart from a general recognition that we should "make the consequences and personal costs of illegal behavior clear," there emerged from these forums on alcohol abuse no vital sense of a collective action—or a collection of actions—that we, as a public, should make. Yet the issue has continued to be widely deliberated, and the issue guide extensively used by both volunteers and professionals who have found deliberations on these lines popular and apparently helpful to their purposes.

Now it should be noted that this topic was one generally and quite readily confronted on the personal, or community, or institutional level. Except for occasional reference to law and the "management" of public opinion, the public dialogue on alcohol abuse had a great deal to do with cultural, social, and individual behavior and *little* to do with politics, as generally understood, although it did reveal a great deal about collective observation and popular will. In this sense, it is, for our purposes, readily comparable with the public deliberations on AIDS (although in none of the alcohol abuse forums we have examined was there a distinctively directed *individual* voice, like that of the Chattanooga preacher, noted on that topic), or with those on abortion (although there was no marked question of spiritual belief at stake here). It is apparently the case—and it can be noted increasingly, through materials from the past three decades—that when forums are *not* specifically associated with conflicts between ideologies and interests but are more immediately concerned with community life, they tend to move toward (though do not necessarily reach) judgment in a cumulative way. Within our communities, in effect, we tend to recognize that we are *social* animals. That is to say, participants tend to include, on their way to decisions about handling a civic problem, "all of the above" options—perhaps because at least they share a deeply felt understanding of the importance of the given *problem*, despite their sometimes seemingly irreconcilable and irreversible commitments of faith or principle.

There are some things, after all, that some people will *not* accept, personally, as in the response to the issue of abortion. A similar resistance of some people to an "all of the above" outcome was apparent, too, when, in 1997, NIF addressed issues that surround the deeply moral and professional medical questions that are raised by the treatment afforded (or treatments that *might be* afforded) patients suffering from an acknowledgedly terminal illness or virtually fatal accident. Reflecting increased public interest (and a president's personal inclinations), that issue of "assisted dying" emerged for deliberation again eight years later, in 2005, revealing values virtually unchanged and a similar "all of the above" outcome, still with individual reservations, nationwide.

That issue, incidentally, *as an issue*, turns out not to be peculiar to the United States. In Britain, too, the law, forbids "aiding, abetting, procuring or counseling" suicide—all of which actions are punishable (but are not therefore necessarily punished) by serious jail time. Apparently, an "all of the above" response has been accepted in Britain in this context, although it is profoundly unacceptable to many—at least to the degree that legal judgments may need to be freed from the task of interfering in matters that to many citizens are matters of conviction. In response to a recent ruling by Britain's highest court, the Senior Prosecutor promised a list of circumstances that, according to reports in the *New York Times*, "could influence the authorities *not* to prosecute." They include, apparently, the motivation being compassion, the deceased clearly wanting to die, and the deceased being terminally ill. On the other hand, it seems that the prosecutor *could be* influenced to prosecute if the deceased were under the age of 18, mentally handicapped, or not sure about his or her wishes, or not in fact seriously disabled, terminally ill, or suffering from a degenerative disease. (At the time of writing, these provisional guidelines, apparently, are in Britain open to public comment for a limited time, presumably to be taken into consideration by the prosecutor.)

Granted the interest in assisted dying remains as intense (and the tensions as strong) in these United States, it may be that deliberations on this subject have had a critical if seldom noticed function in our own, perhaps more heterogeneous democratic society, whereby we learn not only what to do to *solve* a problem that affects us, collectively, but also, perhaps more important, how to acknowledge and even placate the continued differences among us that may have proved, and may continue to prove, valuable to our multiple achievements as a people of common trust, if sometimes seemingly irreconcilable individual needs. It is a form of learning that helps us live together.

Public Education . . . the Problems We Live With

Oddly, then, for all that the National Issues Forums and the practice of public deliberation, now widespread nationally, were initially established to encourage a more effective public voice in conventional political practices associated with policy and legislation, they have become particularly useful in addressing community questions whose moral and social import precedes—or is dependent only in a limited way on—politically agreed action or policy. This is not because community questions are geographically smaller in scale—indeed, as has been noted, they are often experienced nationwide, in effect—but because they are locally present in an immediately recognizable and accessible form. The problems of abortion, alcoholism, death and dying, and so on, are significant, not because they necessarily must be corrected (or "answered") by policy and law, but *because we live with them*; what we do in the context of such concerns will *define* us as a community. The community may change as the people within it change, but it is the people who *are* the community. The community is not, as a community, dependent on politicians and professionals who may be subject to interests that are not ours and contests in which we are not all of us players. Rather, the community defines itself and redefines itself, deliberatively, over time—*or it is not a community at all.*

Serious national policy decisions, like those about the energy and health-care crises, are intensely realized community by community. Yet although there is, to be sure, a difference between the politics of the community and the politics of nations, there is also a relationship, even a resemblance. Each will both influence and become influenced by the other; but like many other useful experiences, public politics begins at home. Looking through the records of broadly nationwide deliberation on close to a hundred issues over the past quarter-century or so, it is intriguing to see how many of them are talked about as *community* issues, even though only a relative few of the accompanying discussion guides were actually designed and written by a local or regional group with a specific community in mind.

Now, a session or two of public deliberation does not *solve* the community problems we face, as a people; nor do records suggest that they prompt actions that, undertaken together, correct the abuse or aberration that stimulated deliberative meetings to begin with. This is quickly apparent when we notice how often, during the almost 30 years of this practice—under the various leadership of National Issues Forums, America*Speaks*, or the many other groups that now engage thousands of participants to deliberate, nationwide—a given problem has been time and again readdressed, and how insistently communities present themselves as wrestling with the same continuing dilemmas!

It is not that nothing has been done, no efforts to change been made; and it is not merely that "public" or "outsider" efforts are ill-organized, amateurish, inappropriate, or (this least of all) misguided. For one thing, it may be that governments, and even non-governmental organizations, are shaped by institutional imperatives that satisfy their own wants and therefore frame their purposes and narrow their outcomes differently than would a genuine community sense of the public will or a vision of the public good. As the discussion of health care in the preceding chapter has suggested, we should do well to consider that, in many *public* matters, *private* interests are more profoundly influential than a public choice. For the moment, however, to see how public deliberation on a given problem may take effect over time *within a community*, let us look at some of the attempts that have been made to rethink, as a public, the purpose and nature of public education, the role of the public school. Like foregoing glimpses of repeated deliberation on continuing problems, such repeated efforts may themselves serve as a fundamental reminder that democracy remains, at its roots, of, for, by, and *among* the people, who are themselves continuously creating, consciously or unconsciously, the community wherein their problems dwell.

Let us note first, however, an important difference between, on the one hand, AIDS and alcoholism, and, on the other, public schools. AIDS and alcoholism are matters of behavior, in which some of us, as a community, inevitably sense a reason—maybe "a right"—to be heard. The schools are a public *institution*, however, designed specifically for the education of young citizens. What goes on there is implicitly a matter of public choice. Nonetheless, as we shall see, the many forums on public schools mostly come to the same outcome as the forums on AIDS and alcoholism—a general recognition of need but no specific judgments on what is to be done or not to be done.

The first NIF issue guide produced to assist people in deliberations about the schools, in 1992, was titled, *Education: How Do We Get the Results We Want?* It was prefaced by its writer with this observation:

> Of all the challenges facing America today, improving education is among the most urgent. Although community after community has talked about reform, Americans, on the whole, still aren't getting the results they want from education. Committees have often become mixed in "solution wars," in which citizens spend their energy debating which of a number of predetermined solutions is best, when, in fact, no one has even agreed on what the problem is.

The response of these 1992 forums, guided by the detail presented in the NIF issue guide, was clearly that the community—meaning parents, shopkeepers, leaders, teachers, and so on—should set and monitor the goals and practices of the public's schools. That this is already, supposedly, theoretically and historically the case, seems to have put the forum participants in fact into the more challenging (and it seems less appealing) position of considering creatively whether schools should be run for profit, like businesses, or by professional experts in education, or, in familiar capitalist style, by allowing parents (and kids) to compete for admission to the best school they could find or afford (as is presumably the fashion of other markets). The outcome was simply that members of the community apparently wanted control of what and how its young people were taught, without participants becoming any clearer about how, by whom, or to what ends that control might be exercised. As in the health-care discussions nationally, the conversation became essentially a means whereby each participant might present his or her own interest, informed (occasionally) by gripes!

When NIF forums addressed the issue again at the end of the decade, it was gratifying to find a little more specificity emerging from the dialogue—to the effect that adequate public funds should be provided for schools; that schools be responsive to the community's own sense of its needs; that standards, especially in what are now thought of as "basics" (assuming there is agreement on those aspects of the curriculum), be firmly established and maintained by a *professional* staff; and that parents should have their choice among schools. A forum participant in New Hampshire remarked:

> One common theme I heard [in our forum] is that the problem with our public schools is a problem of what's happening in our society. We're talking about democracy; we're talking about equality. The fact that we talk about public schools as being critical for democracy (small 'd') and the idea that we need a common experience show how important this is to all of us.

The deliberation seems to reach a recognition that decisions have to be made and acted upon by the people. Yet reports from participants at the forums that year did not suggest that participants arrived at any collective sense of how that common experience, deemed so critical by the New Hampshire participant, might best be achieved. Participants apparently did share a sense of purpose for the schools, but not of a policy or policies that might best secure such ends. Rather, the reports of these deliberations tell us essentially that citizens everywhere may have ample fuel for griping at the public schools, perhaps much as they do about the nation's provisions for health care; in either case they may not know what they need, or how to set about achieving it.

Now public griping is not public deliberation, especially if the gripes are (and they are!) many. But it may be where the seeds for deliberation are sown. The schools seem not to care. A man in Pennsylvania said:

> When I was in seventh and eighth grades, I'd get Fs. I didn't learn a thing. But I got promoted anyway, because my teachers didn't care.

A man in another forum said:

> "Educators" are, professionally, not adequately trained for specific tasks. I'm a big supporter of the public schools. Our first two children went to public school. Then we adopted our daughter, who had been abused and who has emotional problems. She didn't do well in public school and so we put her into private school where she is doing great. But I'm still a strong supporter of public schools. They just didn't work well for her.

John Doble's report on the forums as a whole that year, commissioned by the Kettering Foundation, explains further:

> Many said there is not enough discipline in the schools. "They don't enforce the rules," said a woman from Bangor, Maine. A Denver woman said, "Teachers are discouraged from sending disruptive kids to the principal's office." A man from Milwaukee said, "There's no discipline in schools today. And when there's no discipline, there's no learning."

Schools were inadequate because of some fundamental failure in our society, concluded Doble's report. Doble tells us that a man at a state prison forum in Chester, Pennsylvania, said,

> A lot of teachers feel threatened, afraid they'll get robbed or killed. Even in the classroom, where they're supposed to be the authority, they can't teach well because they're afraid.

Now if the task of these forums were to generate a solution or solutions to the given problem, these deliberations in themselves would not take us far. There is, indeed, no real evidence of working through—at least, not if it entails working through the trade-offs, the downsides to be anticipated with any course of action set to address these complaints. Courses of action are not in themselves examined: only goals, or intentions, or perhaps merely a listing of the characteristics of desirable outcomes, in contrast with the present, *un*desirable outcomes. The substance of the discussion, as reported, is (heavily) gripe, while the wished-for outcome may usually remain "pie in the sky." While participants in these forums were consistently discussing problems in the schools, they were *not* deliberating about purpose nor alternative actions.

This does not, in itself, seem to do much toward solving the acknowledged problems of the nation's schools, and, taken at face value, experience with this "public school" issue since the turn of the century would not suggest that much political power will attach itself to public deliberation about a community's problem with its schools. Yet the issue has continued to command attention, and more and more communities have reframed the issue to meet what they consider effective local reference. The forums staged through the good offices of local institutions and organizations have not lacked for participants.

Just a few years ago, the West Virginia Center for Civic Life (associated from its very early years with NIF), led by two of its members, Betty Knighton and Julie Pratt (who are longtime NIF leaders), prepared an issue guide titled, bluntly, *What Is the 21st Century Mission for Our Public Schools?* And that straightforward question, in itself preliminary to any course of action that citizens might develop, does in its own way reveal what *has* been worked through and what citizens, genuinely committed to probing the seriousness of the problems that beset young citizens in our schools, may usefully tackle in deliberation together.

At almost the same time as this work was going on in West Virginia, another long-time associate of the Kettering Foundation, Bob McKenzie, was gently orchestrating an effort at the David Mathews Center for Civic Life, in Alabama, to tackle, publicly, the question, "What Should Our Community Do?"—in the context, specifically, of "preparing today's kids for tomorrow's jobs." Both this question and the question asked in West Virginia, turn out to have "all of the above" answers; for as we have observed earlier in this chapter, people may sometimes discover that there is more than one desirable—nay, necessary—outcome that they must reconcile, if they are satisfactorily to re-create their community in the face of unmistakable divisions created by complex family, social, and community problems in modern times.

Yet the emphasis is on *purpose* in the titles of both efforts, and "purpose" is instructive as we explore the outcome of these forums. One of West Virginia's approaches—referring conscientiously to the relative efficacy of different styles of teaching, associated with Rudolph Steiner, Howard Gardner, and Maria Montessori—may tend to look, in lay parents' eyes, a little too professionally toward educational theory; we may suspect that relatively few of the parents of public school children share this kind of professional and academic concern. Nonetheless, in these locally organized forums, the tension between, on the one hand, a sense that our rock-bottom goal for the schools should be students' success in the workplace and, on the other, a sense that becoming active and responsible citizens is ultimately why our nation early established the school in each community, is inescapable. In these locally originated forums, the problem of purpose is being taken seriously. So, too, as other forums indicate, is the sense that helping children discover and develop their own individual talents might be what matters.

Several such themes have proved to be admirable means of engaging a community in refining its own undeniably real but complex sense of purpose for the schools' future. Such a progressive and commanding exchange of concerns might be a reason to think of public deliberation as in itself both an educative process and a shared experience, the essential core of a modern democracy in practice.

But—and here's the rub—that may improve neither the public school nor the quality of the students it prepares for their role in the world. In the long run—although these few years are not a very long run!—we have not found, or heard, that deliberation built around these "What should we do with the schools" guides has directly changed, or helped measurably to correct, specific problems associated with public schools in the United States. Yet if clarity of intent and the willingness publicly to address serious goals that remain generally beyond reach are meaningful, then we *can* say that the American public—taking forum participants to be, in a general sense, a "tasting of" or a "dipping into" the American public—could be slowly working its way through the complex and troubling circumstances that do leave too many American children at a disadvantage. It may be that eventually those disadvantages will appear neither inherent nor inevitable. But since the public schools have often been the subjects of similar public discussions in American communities that are economically, politically, and culturally relatively distinct from one another, we must, inevitably, sometimes ask ourselves why the outcomes of these deliberations seem to have had so little effect on practice. Why have they, despite sustained participation in dialogues that substantially address similar complaints, led to so little public, professional, or legislative change?

A Community's Problem . . . Leaving People Behind

These continuing discussions of schools in America, of what parents hope for, expect, or fear in their children's lives when they are assisted (or sometimes apparently hindered) by the schools and their teachers, may not in themselves have been peculiarly revealing, for by and large, it turns out that parents reflect values and express concerns that have changed little over time. Parents want their children to learn not only what they need for a decent living (preferably a slightly better one than their parents'), but also what they need to live *decently*, as participants in a community that is tolerably organized and acceptably humane. That shouldn't be such a tall order—except that any handful of educators and any handful of parents will invariably see these desiderata as best pursued by distinctly different means, each requiring support (which does include financial support), and each, at least to a degree, reducing the possibility of alternative desiderata being adequately satisfied. It is, again, the "wearisome condition of humanity" that has plagued humankind since long before the Baron Fulke Greville labeled it so in the 17th century:

> Oh, wearisome condition of humanity!
> Born under one law, to another bound;
> Vainly begot, and yet forbidden vanity;
> Created sick, commanded to be sound.

We apparently can't have everything! But that brings us to a new theme, rarely raised in the issue books about improving our public schools. The *collective* decision is about what to have, what not to have, and how to pay for it—or *who* is to pay *what* for it. And that is politics!

The real achievement of recent public forums on the schools may have been to produce a kind of increasing awareness that public judgment, rather than school board policy, is to be the critical instrument at play in the improving of public education. And the ultimate design is to expand the culture of learning, by which every human community, it seems, has to determine its future.

Here the writer must draw, for a moment, on his own experiences again—this time as a child growing up in the United Kingdom, where all children, in those now distant years, were required to attend school from age 5 until age 15 or 16. Schools were run by local metropolitan or county governments, although some children—albeit a very small minority—attended private schools, for reasons of ambition, religion, snobbery, traditionalism, or a serious parental concern about their children's need for authority. Between the ages 11 and 12, the public school children who were deemed exceptionally bright by their teachers could sit for a two-day, written "scholarship" examination, offered by the metropolitan or county school authority; if they were successful, they would then be transferred for the next five years to what in effect was a university preparatory school—either private or run by the metropolitan or county authority (which, in either case, paid the fees for these "scholarship" children). From there, such students "graduated" at age 16, upon completing a week-long series of written examinations; or at 18, when more demanding examinations, in only four academic subjects, could theoretically qualify them for matriculation into a university, although not guarantee it.

In my time, however, merely the top 250 such students over age 18, nationwide, would have their university costs and a modest allowance paid by the British government each year, although most university students in those days were family supported, as they had been throughout their teens, when most of the university preparatory schools, or "grammar schools," even those run by local governments, accepted appropriate numbers of fee-paying students. Meanwhile, the overwhelming majority of children—those who hadn't won a "scholarship" at age 11 or 12, or weren't among the very "best and brightest" at the university prep schools—had to look for work at age 16.

From this piece of ancient history, it may be apparent—as it was to this writer, barely a teenager, at the time—that a critical function of the school system was social, and that it both catered to and consistently modified a class system, to the obvious benefit of some people, while mollifying others whose destinies had been carved out, somewhat variously, over untold generations. It was apparent, in that now distant British childhood—as it is to me as a citizen of the United States today—that schools, and school children, and their families, while sharing some common limits and common needs, were not all thought or expected to be the same, as their lives were unfolding in the continuous creation of an historical although inevitably ephemeral society. School was an instrument of change, as well as learning. We Brits of the past century learned to think, and to write paragraphs, and to read Shakespearean soliloquies as examples of deliberation. Or we became scientists. Or soccer players. But the schools we attended were—though they would not have liked to admit it—instruments of politics; their response, in the long run, had to be to the will of the people. And that will, in the long run, is multifoliate.

Unlike the concerns about AIDS, abortion, the abuse of alcohol, or "assisted dying," all of which relate to personal behavior that may affect our confidence in the community, the public school, as we observed earlier, is a public institution established and financed by law to provide for certain requirements of our collective good. At risk of simplifying history, let us acknowledge that here in the United States, as among other peoples around the world, the value of children, long ago, in unsophisticated settlements, was their eventual contribution to the income of the family. The collective training of the young—"schooling," in effect—was then inescapably helpful to parents only until their children attained strength and knowledge appropriate to the anticipated tasks to be performed for the family. As in other cultures, education outside the province of the family itself was the privilege—as it was the necessity—for those born to exercise obligations to a larger society (and a larger economy) than their own domestic life commanded. Times more sophisticated—and occasionally more "democratic"—slowly have come to suggest the usefulness of intellectual disciplines of different kinds, and eventually labors of different kinds, all of which have led to schools of different kinds. Here in America, as elsewhere, they led to a *public* school that would ensure a generally accepted level of skill and knowledge throughout the nation, collectively, and at public expense, thus making provision ultimately for children who could outstrip their family's own treasury of useful knowledge. In the United States of the 19th century, with its interest in rights and freedom to citizens of all faiths—not to mention progress and prosperity—such an idea should have been a "slam-dunk" to effect. And indeed, the United States did, in short order, create an education establishment that included public colleges and professional schools that might become the envy of the world.

Over time, however, it also has created an underclass and a working class and an upper class and a leisure class, all with need of particular skills and the support of particular communities through purposefully designed institutions that themselves offer opportunity and demand skills that larger and increasingly various "publics" may find need for. To the question, "is there a public for the public school?" the answer continues to be, "Yes." But "*what* public school?" is the question that still follows. Each of us is "born equal," as that phrase is understood; but we are different in myriad ways, including both our potential and privilege.

The significant number of issue books on the schools that NIF has circulated remind us that "the school problem" is not simply the unresponsive school board, nor the inadequate teacher, nor the child left behind, nor teaching to (or failing to teach to) the tests, nor the percentage of irresponsible parents and children, nor guns (or sex) on the streets. And not the media or Facebook! Each of these may be—no! is—a problem for us as a people, and they are problems to varying degrees in different places. Yet we do not all learn the same things, nor need to learn them in the same ways—nor even, in many instances, at the same pace. The necessary relationships between child and school and skill and parent and public are highly personal and vary within broad social, economic, and geographic spectra. So what we, as citizens, want our young citizens to become is perhaps more significantly a *civil* matter than are the matters of management and pedagogy, of syllabi and test, with which NIF issue books on schools have often been surfeited. Conscious of educational institutions *as essential democratic instruments*, we might well remember to place them in their instrumental context as builders of deliberative democratic life; we might recognize that effectively changing them for the better involves deliberation about outcomes and costs that is as controversial as issues of war and peace, health and abortion, and energy and immigration.

The *New York Times* tells us that in 2010:

> Among students in the city's third through eighth grades, 40 percent of black students and 46 percent of Hispanic students met state standards in math, compared with 75 percent of white students and 82 percent of Asian students. In English, 33 percent of black students and 34 percent of Hispanic students are now proficient, compared with 64 percent among whites and Asians.

Now New Yorkers probably do not really assume that either the public or its legislators and lawyers can devise enforceable actions that will suddenly end the various educational difficulties that are awkwardly human and socially divisive. However, another recent NIF issue book to encourage public deliberation about the schools, developed for community use nationwide in 2007, did take this particular bull by the horns. It put an immediately recognizable problem into one phrase, in a direct question: *Too Many Children Left Behind: How Can We Close the Achievement Gap?* was the title designed to bring more citizens to work at this as a *political* issue in a targeted fashion.

In her preface, the executive editor of this new guide to addressing the problems of our communities' schools, Carolyn Farrow-Garland, writes:

> This policy guide for citizens describes how the academic performance of many African American, Hispanic, and Native American students lags behind that of their Asian American and white counterparts. The problem occurs in virtually every type of school system in the United States and is often exacerbated by socioeconomic factors, such as poverty. There is a widespread disagreement about what causes this problem and what to do about it.

The blunt directness of that initial paragraph may have been surprising to some readers, as they opened the slender issue guide. Perhaps it was the first guide about public schools so clearly to indicate its intent to explore what is a continuing problem for a democracy. Or it may even, possibly, have been a surprise for some to learn that "the achievement gap" (a phrase that has become already quite familiar in this 21st century) might be attributed to, or exacerbated by, both poverty and race. Only twice since its beginnings, 25 years earlier, had the National Issues Forums directly addressed the issue of race. Those early dialogues about race in the United States had generated both sympathy and promise, and even new glimmers of understanding in the years 1990 and 2000; but they had evidently stopped short of identifying broadly recognizable, collective action *in the schools* that might be undertaken to effect change with all possible speed.

Now, in 2007, citizens were to be invited directly to confront the challenge that there be "no child left behind" because of demonstrated unfairness and inadequacy in our expectations of different (minority) groups of students in public schools. In President Bush's phrase, a "bigotry of low expectations" was the essential culprit: our inadequate provision of labs, computers, up-to-date textbooks, and indeed qualified teachers, for the "left behind" students—as well, posited the issue guide, as underlying causes, "such as unresolved health problems, poor nutrition, stressful living conditions, and lack of parental support, which are likely to be sources of these deficits!" Thus ventured the introduction to public conversation in 2007.

In the practice of public deliberation on the problems of the schools over two decades, then, there had been evidenced both repetition *and* change, tendencies toward recommendation *and* reassessment. Each time, the spur to deliberation had been a dissatisfaction with what the schools were producing, and the substance of the deliberation referred to or looked for options for change. Thus, the deliberations were inevitably informative, yet seemed not until 2007 to have moved beyond the exchange of ideas for ideal outcomes, and few kinds of actions that *might* help effect some of them. In a real sense, most of these "how to improve" or "what's wrong with our schools" deliberations ended up, as we have discussed earlier, with "all of the above" responses—not because this in itself represents a conclusion upon which people had decided to *act* collectively (as may have been the case in deliberations on alcohol abuse and AIDS), but because each participant (or most of them, evidently) had come to recognize how futile the particular gripes with which they invariably began might prove if alternative gripes (or options) were not also themselves addressed and evaluated.

In 1992, the relatively unexceptionable sense of the issue had been, reportedly, that citizens spent their energy debating which of a number of predetermined solutions might be best, when in fact no one had even agreed on what the problem was. A decade later, the gripe was clearly still that "children are not learning enough in public schools," and the various remedies suggested were to let parents pick the individual public school they preferred (and presumably thought the best); to stress "the basics"—being, in this instance, a coupling of the academic basics and moral and social (civic) training; to engage the community, with all its skills and facilities, more fully in the work of the schools (or vice-versa, to engage students more often in "out of the classroom" learning experiences); and to provide more funds, evenly distributed among the public schools in each region. It is hard—and it proved neither possible nor to most participants desirable—to deny any of these as problems to be addressed. Yet they had remained, apparently, still "problems to be addressed."

Inevitably, there has been in the past a slight sense of *déjà vu* each time public forums have revisited public deliberations about the schools and what they should do. That sense is disguised by the accompanying hint of mildly hopeful promise in the titles NIF has given its guides for discussions of this problem, over the years: *Priorities for the Nation's Schools* (1983); *Education: How Do We Get the Results We Want?* (1992); *Public Schools: Are They Making the Grade?* (1999); *What Is the 21st Century Mission for Our Public Schools?* (2007); *Preparing Today's Kids for Tomorrow's Jobs: What Should Our Community Do?* (2008). The issue books raise serious questions, but thoughtful and serious responses to such challenges entail *political* decisions: agreements must be made to alleviate disagreement and enable action. The expression of a need, a complaint, or even an ideal goal, is merely *prelude* to the kind of public deliberation that is itself the real *doing* of politics in a democratic community.

The effort made with the school issue as framed in 2007 in *Too Many Children Left Behind* was itself a thorough exercise in research, carefully documented in a significant number of large urban and rural areas, nationwide. Early draft reports from observers at introductory forums had indicated that many school districts formally accepted and encouraged the framing of the issue in a variety of ways:

- by acting as "clients" and convening the forums;
- by rejecting the overall structure but accepting a program targeted at a specific "at-risk" youth;
- by acting as supportive observers;
- by supporting the process with space and resources in anticipation of a set of recommendations;
- by excluding school district leadership while including teachers and some staff in what were community and student processes.

The draft report from the Collaborative Communications Group, who monitored the project from 2007 to 2009 in six communities, makes it clear that there had been included, and could be heard, even a *student* voice.

> The conversation took an interesting turn as students discussed how they could be more motivated and engaged. One Bridgeport student asked, "If we are going to hold ourselves to a higher standard in terms of being motivated and engaged, can't we hold our parents and the schools to the same high standards?"

> In responding to this question, the group of young people made a series of piercing observations and outlined a set of actions necessary for change. They rated only about one in ten of their teachers highly. Their teachers should not be their friends, the students said. But the students did need the teachers to understand them, champion their dreams, and push them to perform. . . . When prodded, students said that only a few teachers managed to encourage most students to work hard. . . . While the society at large is rightfully demanding higher levels of performance, it is not providing the support to engage or motivate students in ways that will lead to higher student achievement.

The effort of the forums had not been seen by the monitors as an exercise in wishful thinking but as an exercise in making choices that school districts saw as an "action" agenda. More important, perhaps, the range of key findings drawn from this elaborate public deliberative effort included frank appraisals of the values and the difficulties of deliberations that engage simultaneously individuals and institutions, teachers and pupils, and elected leaders. The draft report tells us:

> The deliberative process generated dialogue, but faces some important challenges in converting dialogue to action. . . . Are we generators of creativity or agents of change? Do we feel responsible for closing the achievement gap, or responsible for generating the possibility of closing the achievement gap? . . .

> The deliberative process, in effect, in this sustained national exploration of the schools, revealed itself not as a means of "making a judgment," but as an instrument of community learning itself. *Who* is responsible for the nation's schools seems to remain an open question. Unless, perhaps, it is us, as members merely, of the democratic community.

Certainly, in this context of what we might call "extended" deliberation about the persistence of a public issue that affects us broadly in communities throughout the nation, we can begin to sense what public deliberation *might* accomplish. It can make the complex accessible; it can give us to understand that what is *most* important to us may be dependent on something else that is not our top priority; it may suggest that, whether or not we are ready to *work collectively*, various goals may be *defined collaboratively*. And it may help us, in the long run, to recognize the mutuality of our desires, although their objects be disparate and their expression typically self-concerned. Beyond the clamor of competing leaders and self-aggrandizing interests—even with an only obscurely representative government like that of our own heterogeneous democracy of competing interests—it suggests what democratic *self*-government is ultimately about.

Or could be!

The Community, Practicing Politics

The remarkable national exploration initiated by President George W. Bush, that began to explore public will about the "child left behind," has not yet generated a new public pride, and certainly not satisfaction, in the achievement of our public schools. But it does suggest interests that might be open to change: the role of the teacher; the functioning of the test; the budgeting of the school; the expectations of parents, professionals, and the community; the sources of "standards"; the factors of discipline; the influence—or the roles of—beliefs, values, and judgments. These are all interests at issue when we deliberate seriously on the future of our schools. The making and implementing of relevant decisions in a community, about the community's public schools, is properly, in a democracy, a *political* process; the deliberative public forums described in this chapter all had been designed as instruments *toward* that end, for the health of the communities that ventured them. It may still remain persistently difficult for us to see somewhat superficial deliberation, heavy on complaint, as being helpful in the improvement of communities' public schools, but the forums may at least have suggested that extensively shared deliberation can prove a positive learning instrument in the development of the democratic community itself.

How such collective community learning may take place is glimpsed in an illuminating and touching report prepared for the Kettering Foundation by Vaughn Grisham, director of the McLean Institute for Community Development. It describes how citizens in a selected handful of small communities came together, with virtually no outside help or nominal leadership, to deal with specific, local, "wicked problems that could potentially destroy them." Grisham writes:

> This report tells the story of the processes by which communities seek to deal with persistent problems that threaten their very existence. . . . This is a never-ending process, and there is no "happy ever after" in these stories. . . . This is a story of discovery.
>
> None of the places had major resources that would make it easier to address tough issues. In the beginning, they all agreed that their primary asset was their people. Most of the places would have parroted the phrase that "people are their greatest assets," but it seems doubtful that they actually understood the full importance and necessity of becoming a community of active citizens. Even if they had been told about the importance of engaging one another and becoming what the Kettering Foundation calls "a public," they probably would have missed the deeper understanding of a public. Each place had to discover the power of community by becoming and behaving like one.

These were all, then, very small communities; and the projects they undertook apparently were meant to improve the local environment—

and its value—at a time when the communities were "losing ground noticeably." The instigators, it seems, in every instance cared about the community but focused on a single problem area *within* it: "I care about the schools," or "the children," or "people having good health and access to good medical treatment." But in this study, Grisham further found that "only when local citizens took the 'ownership' of their own issues did they make meaningful progress." Then other individuals and groups "came on board at their own pace." For "although they wanted improvement for their community, they all feared change . . . and laughed at the irony!"

Some of the experiences that Grisham recounts are merely affecting to the reader. Some are dramatic in their outcome and productiveness; some are encouragingly civic in impact; some of them became even impressively corporate. Yet none of the actors initially refer to them as "political." Typical of the citizens whose civic work Grisham describes is a woman, the initiator of an arts festival, who says, "I don't know anything about politics; I leave that to those who do. But I do know how to make things pretty and that's what I like to do."

This denial of political interest on the part of an active citizen may seem initially puzzling. Or it may, of course, be taken as merely an expression of what is nowadays quite typical cynicism toward the professional political class, or as a serious extension of that to the point of a conviction that what matters is what we do ourselves—that politically "special interests" (as we have referred to them in preceding chapters) are necessarily at odds with what "we" as a community, a *public*, must arrange for ourselves. Yet each democratic community cannot thus be a law unto itself, without regard to a neighboring democratic community down the road; nor can a community of wealth refuse to bear any part of the burden of the community of need. At least, neither of these suggests what one would like to think of as prevailing circumstances of the democratic state. We noticed with respect to the issue of health care that citizens have many reasons for complaint; thus, they have a case for attention. Admirable health care is available, but costs more than many—if not most—can afford at the critical time of need. Similarly, good education is available, but unevenly, and beyond the reach of many who might profit from it. Yet to complain of such predicaments, to draw attention to them and to flaws in the practice of government, should surely not be the only business of a citizens' politics. Nor is politics merely concerned with the election of one rather than another candidate for government office. "Politics" infers responsive action to the needs of democratic citizens, the democratic community, with both purpose and risk in mind.

So, of his selected community leaders, or "catalysts," as he sometimes called them, despite their claim to be beyond politics, Grisham concludes:

> One of the common and vital characteristics of the "right people" is their deep understanding of both the culture and the intensely held values of the population. The catalysts may not share the values held by a majority of the citizens. In the words of one such leader, "I do not share all the values that are held by many local people, but I do understand them and respect their right to hold values and beliefs different from my own."

Let us be clear, Grisham writes, "these catalysts are not knights on white horses, come to save the community. They do not seek to save the citizens; *they seek to engage them in addressing difficult issues that face the greater community.*" It is this "engagement in addressing difficult issues" that is the core of what we think of as *public* politics in the democratic community.

In a recent and instructive note on this same topic, David Mathews explains:

> When looking for civic learning in everyday life, we have found it (or a need for it) in two places. One is as a necessary skill to be developed in the political education of future citizens.... Are students learning how to extract meaning from the world around them—and then decide how they should act? Deliberation is a means of collective learning: the exact meaning is to determine, with others, what is valuable in what is happening.
>
> The other place we have found civic learning is in high achieving communities . . . [where] the definition of civic learning is the same and the use of deliberation is the same: to determine how various options for action might affect what is valuable when what is most valuable is itself in dispute. The Greeks understood the role of deliberation in learning when they called it "the talk we use to teach ourselves *before* we act."

In the Kettering Foundation's 2009 annual commentary on its research, the magazine called *Connections,* Mathews writes:

> Communities that are continually learning as a community are usually able to bounce back from failure. This kind of learning is collective, and it involves more than acquiring information from what others are doing or from expert sources. It draws on people's experiences and the insights those experiences offer about the nature of the problems at hand, as well as the community itself—how it works, and what its assets are. This learning results in discoveries, and it requires a political environment open to experiments and not restricted to doing only those things that are likely to show immediate, measurable results.

Earlier in this chapter, we have observed that, as a means whereby the public may come to a shared or collective judgment, the process of deliberation is inevitably educative; this weighing of options, in the light of differing experience and anticipated outcomes, is not only *educative* in the context of a community's development, but it is also *political* in the context of democratic decision making. The actual doing of what Grisham describes in his small towns, or what the scattered but sizable communities are still pursuing in the "Too Many Children Left Behind" effort—or what brought the health-care workers, the evangelical preacher, and the gay community to the forum on AIDS in Chattanooga in 1988—these, in effect, constitute the practice of public politics itself.

Such a politics requires, certainly, what Grisham calls local "instigators" or "catalysts" who are hard-working citizens rather than "knights on white horses." And if their focus is the schools, then they will command also the engagement of citizens who are also professional educators, political and corporate leaders, and those whose social concern is their own or other's families and the actual contribution *they* should make to the communities in which they live. These, after all, represent the real "interests" that will have to be shared, as distinct from the individual or corporate or sectarian interests that all too often sway decisions of elective government, even in democracies.

A most striking story of this kind of deliberative and democratic community development over the past quarter-century is to be found in Grand Rapids, the little "city of churches," in Michigan. A booklet entitled *The [Im]possible Goal,* anonymously written and published, just a few years ago, by apparently 19 local institutions, begins with this assertion:

> In this city, leadership, opportunity, deep commitments to volunteerism, a plan of work, and a long history of ongoing civic dialogue, combine to make anything—even the most seemingly impossible of goals—possible.
>
> Today, this city—Grand Rapids, Michigan—teeters on the cusp of real systemic and cultural change.
>
> But it wasn't always this way.

In the summer of 1967, the booklet reminds us, "race riots burst out in 40 US cities." On July 25 of that year, tensions exploded on the streets of "quiet little Grand Rapids."

> It ended two days later. The main city thoroughfare, Division Avenue, which held many of the nightclubs and best restaurants, and many long-time businesses and shops, had been virtually destroyed. Store owners erected metal gates to protect their wares and conceal broken windows from passersby; but for most of the businesses future attempts to rebuild proved futile. The restaurants along Division Avenue moved, closed, or changed hands and fare. The stores and outlets followed suit—emptying out and leaving behind shells that sometimes became fast-food outlets or pawn shops, but often simply went dark and slowly decayed.

But now, some 40 or so years later, the brief, anonymous glance at history ends on this note:

> Grand Rapids is a community that, because of the National Issues Forums, has developed a strong foundation of civic dialogue. It is one of only a few communities in the US that has sustained the NIF, even during difficult economic times, because people have learned to value the safe forum provided in facilitated discussion, to listen and hear the other, and to modify sometimes strong opinions when they are provided additional information. Greater Grand Rapids is, in many ways, a learning community and its relationship with NIF is both the result and the cause of much of its learning.

Grand Rapids is not unique in this kind of experience. In a report written in 2003, Dorothy Battle tells us that in Cincinnati, Study Circles had begun, as early as 2001, to focus on action themes "particularly aimed at improving police-community relationships," looking toward reform of police procedures as well as community initiatives. The *Cincinnati Enquirer* "took an unusual step of reaching out and working with citizens to find solutions to the community's racial problems," she says, and editors at the *Enquirer* "became particularly interested in deliberative dialogue because it focused upon the participation of ordinary citizens in dealing with community problems." Critical in Cincinnati was the recognition that

> deliberative conversations would not necessarily bring about immediate and specific solutions, but they would allow citizens to figure out what was important and meaningful to them; and that once this took place citizens would see what could be done; and if they chose to, they could proceed to act.

Although, no doubt, some gave up right then, deciding not to proceed, that understanding proves to have been essential in Cincinnati and elsewhere, as Vaughn Grisham's report shows, for active success in citizen-driven politics—indeed, in democracy itself. Not always do we move quickly to collective action. First, of necessity, come shared understandings of the complex nature of given problems; then, perhaps, come similar understandings of potential actions, some of which may be more broadly tolerable than others; while, perhaps more slowly, given reservations are put to further test. So the practice of a public politics actually does continue, these decades later, in cities like Grand Rapids and Cincinnati—sometimes, over the long haul, more usefully than institutional politics where laws need be passed, reputations staked, interests beggared, and oxen gored.

The process of deliberative politics is ongoing and shared, for it is a continuing arrangement through which citizens determine *how* they may live together—and neither president nor prelate nor party has veto or is privileged with respect to it. Public deliberation is the source—indeed the only source—of what we have called sometimes "the public voice," but it is not what we call "a public voice" itself. That is arrived at through—and, indeed, drawn from—careful study of the *narratives* of public deliberations, like those to which we have referred in snippets on these pages. Public deliberation is multifoliate in its narratives of individual experience, opinion, and expectation. What we find and cherish as the "public voice" is not that whole public conversation, but sometimes just the collectively coherent narrative that is left in the basket or sieve *after* the winds of ego, passion, and interest have made their way across the deliberative room.

The relationship of that public narrative to *action*—which may or may not entail legislation or the formulation of policy—may follow therefrom, although in the democracies of today we can't any longer be quite sure of that! Particularly in America, where despite our historic sacrifices and vociferous praise for a government that is of and for and by the people, we seem, often, to refer to ourselves as though governed by fools, if not by the enemy, or by untrustworthy minions of alien interests. So let us look, finally, at how we, as citizens, do still or might yet aspire to govern our republic.

VI.
Reclaiming the Public Role

IN 1992, JUST A DECADE AFTER the National Issues Forums had published their first issue guide, the editor of a new guide prefaced it as follows:

> For just over a decade . . . the forums have encouraged Americans to sort through difficult choices that face the nation, issues that range from the deficit, AIDS, and drugs, to abortion, racial inequality, and health care. . . . This issue book asks readers to struggle with a different sort of problem . . . an exploration of the health of our political system itself.

A solution to *that* problem—"the health of our political system itself"—has regrettably not yet been reached. Once before, and twice again during the ensuing 15 years, this issue of our own government, and the effectiveness of the citizenry in it, had been or was to be raised; and what had evidenced a characteristic uncertainty and cross-directions in the many deliberations about the kinds of schools we need for our children was to become apparent, too, when we turned to problems of our democratic government—or at least, to the complaints we make about it. Even though in the titles of the issue guides for these forums we can sense the responsibility for self-government that democracy implies, participants have remained apparently unsure of actions that we, the people, might take to bring that about.

In 1992, the Cold War threat had passed; the threat of terrorism was not yet immediate and domestic. It was an election year in which economic projections were to be "read" from candidates' "lips" ("no new taxes!"); and the voter turnout, especially by the young, was not expected to be high. Perhaps therefore, public deliberation in 1992 and 1993 would focus on the funding of election campaigns—and on the apparent lethargy, with respect to political matters, of the American people, especially younger voters.

The title of the 1992 NIF issue guide on the health of our political system was *People and Politics: Who Should Govern?* Quite clearly the universal concern in the forums on this issue—and in the research that preceded them—was that the people *should* govern but that the government (or the election that routinely reestablishes it) was in the grip of moneyed special interests. Further, the power of those interests was clearly thought to be complemented by a reluctance among the electorate to get out and vote. Ours appeared to be a sadly undemocratic citizenry that had not experienced any effectively kinetic teaching of civic responsibility in its schools and was discouraged from voting, anyway, by inadequate, complex, or perhaps sometimes even deceptive, registration requirements; and by candidates who could not be relied upon to deliver what was promised—if, indeed, promises were made and could be understood.

So the conversations went.

In these deliberations, citizens' tentatively suggested responses to the predicament they themselves described did include increased citizen engagement. They cited real examples of attempts toward that end—including study circles, Ernesto Cortes' "Communities Organized for

Public Service," and others—as well as a demand for more help from the media. Yet no pattern emerged to outline a kind of *citizen* leadership, without which the hope of democratically addressing national threats like the deficit, urban decay, the depletion of natural resources, and so on, might be likely to fail. Participants in these forums, however, apparently saw the failures of government not as merely reflecting the diminution of an active public interest, but as being in some obscurely Machiavellian way the very *cause* of it. The ensuing and subsequent public deliberation on the topic no more than marginally changed the sense that "leaders" do not lead because no one demands it of them—reflected perversely in the comment of a man in a forum who said *people* didn't act because *leaders* didn't demand it of them.

This notion that people did not ask of leaders that they lead should surely, anyway, have seemed a distinctly odd reflection from a proudly democratic society. The French literary historian, Émile Legouis, once suggested that the first historic document of modern democracy, the British *Magna Carta*, was forced on King John by his nobles, in reaction to the presence of people who, overall, were beginning to frame a public voice, beginning, perhaps, to imagine even that there might be, one day, "no taxation without representation." Legouis wrote:

> In tones that are harsh and often coarse, which must have been echoed by common men up and down the country, the vices of the nobles, the state, and the clergy were denounced. Some sided with the people against their governors . . . even against the king.

Yet after several more centuries of democracy's growth, at the end of the 20th century, now, in America, Richard Harwood, responding to the implied question, "what is wrong with politics?" had argued in his relentless commentary, *Citizens and Politics: A View from Main Street America* (published a year before the "People and Politics: Who Shall Govern?" forums were convened):

> We do not face simply a problem of citizen apathy. Instead, we find ourselves confronting a pervasive sense of *political impotence* among the American people. This impotence grows out of a politics of disconnection—where citizens find little access to the process of politics; where they feel overwhelmed by a political system that seems to be running beyond their control; where citizens believe their relationship with public officials is perilously near to being severed; where citizens believe there is only a muffled "public voice."

Harwood does acknowledge that "there are pockets of public life" acting to improve their communities; indeed, from research reported in his own book, we find that Americans "hold a keen desire to act in the public arena."

Americans are both frustrated and downright angry about the state of the current political system. They argue that politics has been taken away from them—that they have been *pushed out of* the political process. They want to participate, but they believe that there is no room for them in the political process they now know. This sense of impotence differs greatly from the so-called "citizen apathy" we read about in weekly magazines and hear on nightly news programs. . . . Apathy suggests the making of a voluntary, intentional choice; most Americans feel, instead, that today's political situation has been thrust upon them. It is not something that they have—nor would have—chosen for themselves.

So the challenge becomes, for Harwood, "how can we reconcile people's sense of political impotence with their desire to act?" That is surely a challenge that a deliberative people ought to meet.

Five years later, however, John Doble Research Associates, who, in 1997-1998, covered extensively a further set of forums on this same topic of a recognized alienation of citizens from government, reported the deliberations as revealing that people still felt alienated and disaffected. Doble evidences that people apparently wanted to limit campaign spending and curb the influence of money in campaigns; they wanted government to be closer to the people; but they found it "hard to imagine how citizenship could be rediscovered." The "obstacles," they thought, nowadays would include apathy, mistrust of government by "the people," and, in Doble's words, "an inability to imagine what a public is or what it would do."

Strikingly, one man who had moderated forums on this problem, in Portland, Oregon, confessed:

> I've had almost every person come up to me [after the forum] and say, "Okay, so now what do we do?" And I'm not sure what to tell them.

And Doble observes that

> A number of participants maintained that civic involvement would be meaningful and effective only if it were connected to government action; and that officials would have to show people what to do and how their efforts connect to solving the larger problem. A woman from Atlanta said: "If the government could set up an agency and charge it with the purpose of mobilizing citizens, rallying them, showing them how they could contribute, then I think a lot of us would get involved."

Whether or not the irony of this fanciful notion registered on any of the forum participants—in Atlanta or elsewhere—we cannot say, having only oral records, often quite casual, from most places, although we are told that many nodded approval to the Atlanta remark. Events closer to the publication of this present book, however, may caution us of a tendency among nondeliberative voters to find themselves caught in a web of self-serving interests, not necessarily their own.

When the issue was first revisited again in this century, however, in 2006, the focus of the entire deliberation was on "reclaiming the public's role"—an interest that clearly evoked, if it did not actually reflect, a US tradition of the public's own democratic sovereignty. Instead of the timorous, "officials will have to show people what to do," this "reclaiming" had itself become our democracy's challenge—as the discussion guide title makes plain; *Democracy's Challenge: Reclaiming the Public's Role*. It seems as though the National Issues Forums, whose mission itself is to affirm and enrich the public's responsibilities in democratic self-government, were taking on the public! Appropriately, the naming of the issue thus, and the competing approaches whose putative merits would frame the "choicework" that public deliberation embodies, were drawn in clear lines from citizen complaints about the diminution of their role that had repeatedly emerged during the preceding decade.

In a stimulating little study, *Sustaining Public Engagement*, published in 2009 by the Kettering Foundation and Everyday Democracy, Elena Fagotto and Archon Fung distinguish between what they call "embedded public reflection" and "embedded public action." They describe the first this way:

> When a community uses deliberation with some regularity to address problems of weak social fabric, to transform individuals, or to inform public judgment, we say they have embedded public reflection.

And the second as follows:

> When a community translates public reflection into action to provide public input, to mobilize communities and resources to solve local problems, or to achieve collaborative gover-

> nance, we say they have embedded public action . . . intimately connected to institutions and organizations that possess the resources and authority to address the social problems at issue.

Now it is difficult, over the nearly 30 years we have been analyzing deliberations, in fact to identify more than a sample of communities in which we might confidently observe public deliberation as an "embedded" means of acting to change longer-embedded societal disorders. We would have little evidence from our nearly three decades of analysis of public deliberations in the National Issues Forums to suggest that deliberations have resulted in public action, routinely.

But in the half dozen chapters of this present study, repeated and related examples suggest that a pattern of public deliberation, even in a culture of such diversity as the United States of America, can and does consistently secure meaningful public reflection that may, given appropriate energy in leadership and institutional facility, be translated into effective political action of the kind that democracy aspires to. There are repeated and quite consistent indications that a deliberative public politics may transform individuals, inform public judgment, and address problems associated with a given social fabric.

As we have seen, the slowly shaping changes, over half a century of citizens' reflection on their appropriate role in the world, paint this development on a large canvas; so do the slow first steps toward a 21st-century sense of "the energy crisis" and "the immigration crisis." The possibilities of a shared tolerance glimmer even through dilemmas like those presented by matters reflecting differences of ideology and faith or cultural differences—like abortion, immigration, and AIDs. And even in a culture where paddling one's own canoe is an ideal, some alternative means of providing care to those most in need will nonetheless eventually be accepted.

Voice and Judgment

Looking toward the ideal deliberative community sometimes leads to glib talk that seems to imply that the *ideal* democracy is in the United States today as it was in Greece, BC. There, it seems to be inferred, the practice of public action was based on the *outcome* of public deliberations. Not that there isn't presumed to have been a governing order, but insofar as there was, then it was merely responsive to the predetermined and fully enunciated public will. The paradoxical history of that idea is not our business now, in this volume. It is important to note, however, that this ideal (or "routine") relationship between public will and its formal (or "official") enactment is difficult to evidence historically, and unlikely within contemporary structures of democracy, whose electoral systems have been traditionally unenthusiastic about shared authority, whose major nongovernmental organizations have become increasingly thought of by the public as instruments of government, and whose popular voting constituency tends always to be wooed by divided but sophisticated ideological oligarchies.

Certainly Yankelovich has always seen the deliberative "working through" process of the public as the ultimate guide to legislators—directions for policymakers, in effect; and Mathews has always argued it as the essential means through which the community comes to know itself—a necessary preface to public action. But the long movement toward a public coping more readily in a situation with international obligations (noted in our Chapter 2), and the misunderstanding of (or reluctance to cope with) shared obligations (as in our Chapter 4), and the persistent or repeated ease of complaint against government by a people who supposedly govern themselves (in this final chapter), suggest that what we, as a people, might best keep tackling is our reluctance, as citizens, to accept the responsibility of deliberating together.

The continuing *practice* of public deliberation itself reveals the slow-paced movement that translates the idea of change into the conceptualizing of public *action*. The forums of 2006 on reclaiming the public's role were instructive in the way in which they revealed citizens addressing the same old *problem*, but with an unmistakable difference of *tone* from that of a decade before. It may be like seeing a child after the first year of college, or a grandchild after a first term at nursery school, or a daughter, after marriage: what one knew before is still there, and recognizable, but there is an added confidence, a genuine spark of awareness, and the hope of achievement. "Democracy," wrote Harwood, now, "is based on people talking to one another"—what might be called "public talk." Indeed, democratic living is the antithesis of the monastic: we *become* ourselves as citizens only in the practice of *community-making conversation*. We learn as we weigh one choice against another, and we sometimes accept what we may individually forego as the price of what we may collectively achieve.

The democratic state is inescapably "ours" and inevitably "us"; the slow-paced movement that all of these sessions of public talk have reported reveals its unique choreography. What *first* happens when people gather to deliberate over ways in which to cope with a complex problem is probably little more than a kind of griping, even hand wringing, about the overwhelming fact of the problem's existence. That is perhaps inevitable and little more than a social affirmation of the agreement to talk. And we are not all likely to welcome reports of a familiar and pathetic gripe with banner headlines, as though it were a "finding" from public deliberation. We don't meet in deliberation merely to vent known frustrations or to advertise our confusion. Those are no doubt among our *reasons* for deliberating, but we meet to learn together something that we cannot know or have not been able to accept, *alone*.

In the early 1990s, when John Doble produced the first of his welcomed and subsequently widely recognized annual print reports of outcomes from the National Issues Forums—it was on foreign policy—the reason for its enthusiastic reception was that the skillful analysis of the patterns of thought expressed in the forums enabled him to present outcomes (with the accompaniment of supporting, but not determining, data collected from questionnaires) that reflect the clarity, if not quite the mathematical authority that we associate with a survey analysis that reflects polling data. Obviously, as all of us were always careful to point out whenever we presented the outcomes of public deliberation to professionals in government and media, these were merely descriptive and qualitative studies of the thinking among self-selected groups. We eagerly chose other ways—noting the nature of the groups, their diversity and geographic range, the clearly nonpartisan nature of support materials, and the inferred sense of "judgments" *in a formative stage*—to underscore what we sensed to be their potential *political* importance, hoping that might lead toward some professional political *acceptance*. And we took to employing the useful phrases "public thinking" and "a public voice" to distinguish what is unique in this work.

Yet from the start, such reports of public deliberation were almost inevitably hitched to the survey analysts' quasi-scientific credo, to the quantitative values of politics-as-usual. The reports were assumed to be persuasive only in so far as they recorded *widely shared* attitudes, if not technically majority opinions. What was sought in the professional establishments of politics and government—and certainly of commerce—was the *size* of opinion, the *mass* of discernible change, the *currency* of a specific concern. It is in the nature of reporting for political ends—as it would be, also, for marketing purposes—to record observations in this way; and in a democracy like ours, where both majority and minority opinions are only theoretically of importance to suit particular occasions, it is as appropriate as it is thoroughly regrettable.

In this respect, the nationally televised *A Public Voice* program had a somewhat easier task than print reporting in that it had real citizens to show, on film, as if in extended dialogue. It could offer visuals of a train of thinking, over time; and by editing, by juxtaposing individual responses of concern or uncertainty, it could more simply present an offered thought *in the process of change* as it came into contact with thought and experience from others. In effect, in the televised programs we had the advantage of real-life characters, and actually sometimes used recognizably the same people in different sequences to make what are genuinely human and individual changes in perception "real" to a video audience. Yet even though we had the interest and expectation of "characters," as in theater, rather than the baggage of science and numbers that is anticipated among professional social scientists, anyone who looks carefully at the video archives of *A Public Voice* can see that they are essentially collections of opinions, expressed in real time, juxtaposed in such a way as to reveal the patterns in the progression of public thoughts. The weight or breadth of approval collectively given to those thoughts is suggested by the number of approving or contradictory or qualifying perceptions that surround it—before a peculiarly succinct summation (or dismissal) by one or two on-camera participants opens the way for transition to a "next step" in the deliberative process. In other words, the original hours of film have been edited down to the familiar "television hour" in a way that reveals the *process* or *pattern* of public thinking, as it was found from an aggregate of many more deliberative hours, filmed in different sites over a few weeks of the year. (Shakespeare, we tell ourselves, and Euripides, set the pattern, albeit with more interesting subjects and more consummate grace, as well as their own gifts for language!)

Inevitably, then, we were sometimes obliged to show the value of a public *judgment* much as politicians and pollsters measure the import of public *opinion,* although we argue that public opinion, unlike the narrative of deliberation, is a fictive construct, implicitly defining possibility in terms of predetermined questions that relate to a preestablished agenda. We know, however—at least in our wiser if more theoretical moments—that public deliberation is valuable precisely because it is *not* so restricted by prior assumption. People's opinions are merely instrumental in public deliberation; they are refracted or enlarged as they accommodate newly reported experience, evolving into subtly different views, shared from others talking with them. Our own opinions may not, in the end, change for each of us as individuals; but our understanding of their implications will; our understanding of their costs will; our understanding of their limits and of the possible continuing usefulness of the opinions of others will—all this will change. And it is the nature of these changes, and the circumstances of these changes in the course of deliberation, that represent the real, the *political* usefulness of what we call "public thinking." Opinion is a fuel of public thinking; but public thinking should not be mistaken for a measure or demonstration of public opinion. Rather it tells us *what* concerns drive people, and *why* such concerns drive them. In a democracy, wise policy and satisfying practice may emerge from this, as it does not from opinions measured in contest, one with another. From deliberation, we learn not how to write laws, but what kind of community we want to be. We do not deliberate to *govern* ourselves, but in order to *learn* . . . that we might be governable!

Reflection . . . and Experience

When considering *opinion,* context is everything; a public in deliberation together builds its own complex context; that is why *deliberation* matters. "A spade," the poet Christopher Fry once remarked, "is never so merely a spade as the word 'spade' would imply." He might have said the same of opinion—and that is why deliberation matters. Some of what our fellow citizens say in the course of giving their opinions about this or that will strike us as potentially negative; we may be adversely critical of some attitudes as perhaps ill-informed, self-indulgent, even willfully self-deceptive. Fair enough, no doubt! One does hear such attitudes expressed, widely, among the public, and spottily, even within carefully moderated deliberative public forums. But somehow the traditional tone of public deliberative thought, once we move beyond mere complaint, is one of assurance and hope; of direction, and therefore inevitably progress *beyond* opinion. That is why deliberation matters.

We value public judgment because it exists as a *celebration* of the public's critical importance to the polity, rather than as an instrument by means of which to *judge* the public's adequacy or inadequacy. For us, as a democratic people, the concept is a means of fixing our position, as a people on a journey, so that we might more readily know and more effectively accomplish what needs yet to be done on the public's course toward the satisfactory resolution of the problems by which it is, for the time being, overtly preoccupied and profoundly worried.

Any rhetoric or experimental design that suggests making a judgment *about* the public, as though it was "wrong," or "guilty," or merely "inadequate" at any one of the stages on the journey toward judgment, is contrary to what this thesis suggests. For us, then, the question, importantly, has long been *not* about whether the public is (or isn't) thumping along at appropriate speed, but about what, in our national or institutional life, is causing movement in this stage to be anything less than with "all deliberate speed" in the public's progress toward what it seems to be thinking might ultimately be a desirable outcome for our collective life. The goal, so to speak, or destiny at the end of the road, is a clarity of purpose: *what should be done*. "Granted where the public seems now to be, what should be done, *next?*"

At a recent public meeting to estimate, from filmed interviews, how the public is doing on its path toward a judgment about both the energy crisis and health-care costs, this writer noticed that among the panelists who made the most glowing estimation about the public's progress were Jean Johnson, vice president of Public Agenda, and Richard Harwood, president of the Harwood Institute—both of whom were genuinely involved during the years when Yankelovich was formulating his concept of public judgment—and Carolyn Lukensmeyer, who had established America*Speaks* to link the "citizen voice" to the governance of the nation. All three defended strongly what appeared to be public attitudes on the energy problem presented in the face of what appeared to be contrary responses (or lack of response) from political and governmental leaders. They also remarked upon the extraordinary progress that "the man on the street," in interviews that had been captured on film, was making (like some of the experts we had also interviewed) toward a judgment about how to cope with health-care costs, when compared to where they had been a dozen or so years earlier, in the early 1990s, when—as we have noted in Chapter 4—health care had dominated the conversations of the public and the press mostly as a source of gripes.

Those filmed interviews, it should be explained, were not of a *deliberative* public forum but of people in unorganized casual conversation, a few at a time. The public approaches a "judgment" by means of deliberation, but that deliberation is a product of exchanged reflective experience, rather than necessarily of the public organized in a deliberative forum. The latter (*pacé* NIF) is merely an artifice toward the end of *shared* reflection. The steps that need to be worked through on the way toward a shared public judgment represent, each of them, the achievement of a milestone. Not good or bad in themselves, their achievement is revealed in the kind of public deliberation that enables us better to consider what should *now* be done, granted where we, the public, have revealed ourselves to be on our journey *toward* judgment, how ready we are to acknowledge the cost that a given course might put upon us.

It is true that the kinds of analyses of motive and intent that we have learned to undertake may be abused—and too often are—in the corporate sector and (increasingly, now) the political. Personal taste or individual interest are too often offered as factors in argument, as though a public good could be determined by the sheer mass or power of those to whom one course of action seems initially appealing—as though a judgment may be made without evidence being weighed. But at Kettering and Public Agenda, and in other institutions that sponsor public deliberation, participants' analyses of motive and intent have been consistently used to reveal how the public interest, *as expressed by the public*, might better be served. It is not and surely could not be our business to certify a judgmental verdict on the acceptability of the current thinking of a public that is sovereign; we can, however, isolate aspects of that thinking, characterize them, and suggest what impedes or might drive them on toward a still more broadly satisfying judgment.

Individual assessments of common problematic situations—unlike analytical judgments—may of course vary, according to experience, perspective, and focus. We know that when heterogeneous groups of citizens are asked together to consider what they think should be done in the context of a given civic or social problem that affects them all variously, they will each start with what is essentially an opinion that reflects how near the "feel" of the given problem is to their personal and anticipated experience. Granted that the problem is not "theirs" uniquely, nor responsive readily to their own personal efforts, their understanding of its complexity and of the usefulness of various courses of action will grow as they encounter others' responses from different experiences and with different anticipations. Since the "end" of their deliberation (and the goal of public policy) is to make "the problem" go away or be contained, we can—like "judges" of a dancing or a figure-skating contest, up to a point—comment on the degree to which they have coped or yet need to cope with obstacles known to be of the kind inevitably to be found on the way to the goal. Those are "stages" in moving toward public judgment. Thus the goal is known; it is public judgment. The obstacles are known; they mark, for example, the Yankelovich "stages," and each represents a hill to climb, a demonstrable drawback to what might, in other respects, be an appealing course of action. All any of us can do, ultimately—be we analysts, or commercial entrepreneurs, or political leaders—is act as essentially commentators on the progress (or lack of progress) in relation to the goal and the stages.

Lest this sound too much like John McEnroe commenting, play-by-play from Wimbledon, or someone "calling the field" as horses approach the first turn at Belmont, let's put it another way. Our interest is in learning where people are on their road toward public judgment. Some of us, periodically, like to *show* where people are. Knowledgeable readers or viewers *might*—although in fact they almost never *do*—question the reliability of the evidence we offer. But all we can invite them to judge are the factors that hold people at various "stages" in the progression, and what might be needed to *release* them to go onward in their journey toward what we will think of (when it emerges) as a "public judgment." What matters, politically, is that we understand the problems encountered on *their* journey to a judgment, rather than measure that progress toward a judgment we as individuals may have already inexpertly, privately, and self-interestedly made. The essence of democracy is in the practice, not the vote; in the journey, not the election; in the public dialogue, not the policy decision.

The public deliberations on energy, for example, through the past few years, have been extraordinarily revealing and consistent from the outset of the first NIF forums on the topic in December 2006. They have presented, frankly, not only the present public uncertainties but also the kinds of actions that may be expected to give people the confidence and the energy (no pun intended) that may be needed to effect changes of behavior. A public will, in other words, is neither arbitrary nor artfully created; it depends upon circumstance, promise, and a collective sense of possibility. The reports offered in evidence make clear what those expectations have been. (The only other "judgment" anyone may offer has to do with the likelihood of these expectations being realized—and one could anticipate an extraordinary range of responses to a request for that!)

Those who in the past few years have shared the reports from Dan Yankelovich's Viewpoint Learning group, which designs and conducts dialogues about public policy, will recognize how thoroughly and cleanly he still toes the line that he originally drew, those many years ago. Nowadays, in a more sustained and concentrated deliberative experience—reflecting, in some ways, the Fishkin style of "a convention," but on a regional basis—he scrutinizes a sustained "working through" process to the point where he, as an extraordinarily careful and experienced analyst, can himself describe where people are in the movement toward judgment, what is impeding their progress, and why it should be so—with implications, of course, about what *should be done* to relieve whatever blockage there currently may be. Research organizations like Kettering and Public Agenda and Viewpoint Learning are clearly in the business of learning about the public, of encouraging a way of incorporating public engagement in the genuine political life of a democratic people, and illuminating the various confusions and obstructions that impair what is taken to be desirable progress toward that end. All of these are appropriate (and indeed, intended) ways of using the concept of a public deliberative journey toward judgment—which exists ultimately and only in relation to what deliberation will have revealed as a desired eventual outcome.

No jury and no individual expert, however thorough in research, is empowered with authority to preempt the public, who alone ultimately will determine what the judgment is to be. The value of analytic work is that it enables public work to go forward by isolating and clarifying the points at which it is currently obstructed or has been misrouted: the task is to identify that, making it clear *where* and—if we can discover it—*why* it has happened. But we cannot identify what the "judgment" *should* be, or is destined to become. We can consider only how effectively the public is dealing with the specific stages that it considers as *preconditions* of judgment. People might learn what is to be done through their experience of the "grief reaction"—anger, grief, blame, self-pity, all of which are learning experiences—and from their confrontation with tensions and trade-offs, certain suppressed or hitherto inadequately recognized disadvantages and possibilities, or information of relevance . . . and so on.

The challenge for "experts" here, then, is essentially to investigate what is discovered about where people move forward and where they are stalled. Historically, organizations like the Kettering Foundation have encouraged public deliberation, and from time to time have briefed other interested parties about outcomes or about how they might go about organizing such research among "publics" themselves. Sometimes, as we have noted, organizations have staged and circulated televised sessions of politicians and experts confronting the evidence of citizens in their movement toward understanding (or in the throes of dilemma), to help discover what is going wrong, why it has been going wrong, and what has been done, can be done, or should be done, now, in order to move matters forward. That is, in its own way, perhaps, moving toward a judgment of the most valuable kind, because it provides not an *end* to an affair, but a way of *going forward, through it,* as an obstacle.

Clearly, a continuing personal, citizen-to-citizen exchange is the *sine qua non* of public deliberation that needs to be sustained and responsive, over time, with the intent of reaching, over time, shared and actionable decisions. This may require a pattern of dialogic exchange that involves a continuously evolving sequence of three elements—an introductory segment to establish the shared nature of the given problem; a deliberative, substantive segment of "choicework"; and a segment, ultimately, that gathers or outlines the nature of the understanding, apparently shared—and what appear to be the tensions that public judgment has accepted. "How nearly has anyone come to this core issue?" The imagining of this triple sequence—within institutions, the media, and perhaps even online—requires careful thought, as well as imagination. Essentially, these are continually overlapping "find out" assignments, not to be completed without a great deal of sensitivity. We, individually and institutionally, need to be clear of the differences between public deliberation and sundry *opinion* pieces delivered electronically or personally, even from our valued friends. And sooner or later (when we know what really concerns us), we'll need the occasional expert. And we shall need to recognize voice, judgment, and action as distinct but essential components of the popular democracy.

Coming to Knowing

"Every government that does not act on the principle of a *republic,* or in other words that does not make the *res publica* its whole and sole object," says Thomas Paine, "is not a good government." And Paine thinks republican government "most naturally associates with the representative form."

> Republican government is no other than government established and conducted for the interest of the public, as well individually as collectively.

Granted the apparently irreconcilable interests that elected representatives often seem individually to represent, and the sometimes mischievous distortions adopted in the service of those interests—as well as the gullibility and selfishness of all of us, as individuals—it does not always turn out (as Paine ultimately argues) that "in the representative system, the reason for everything must appear." The ultimate virtue of our elective form of democratic government may rest only in that it offers citizens the assurance that it can be changed, if push comes to shove.

So when Winston Churchill observed that while democracy may not be the perfect form of government, it is nonetheless the best we've found, he may have been right! Yet kings and oligarchs have not always governed badly; nor, especially in recent times, have elective and apparently popular governments always ruled wisely, or fairly, or for the indisputable welfare of all of their peoples. All governments exercise power. Their instruments are promises, reported achievements, and the force of law. They require support, if their rule is to be sustained, and "supporters" expect, to a degree, recognition and satisfaction, if not reward! Democratically elected governments, like others, must retain the faith of those over whom they rule—and faith is variously secured.

For a democracy, that thought may be as disturbing as it is promising. When this writer first had the privilege of working with Daniel Yankelovich, many years ago, I remember how, after looking at two or three seemingly contradictory or irreconcilable responses to questions on a survey, he would reflectively comment, "What they are really saying is . . . " and there would follow a thoroughly persuasive, imagined sentence that, in the context of those two or three questions, made perfect sense—and also made sense of the two or three seemingly irreconcilable answers! I was reminded then of a theater director, who, when I was teaching Shakespeare, many, many years before, had perfected a wonderful way of stopping rehearsal at a critical moment, striding up to the actor concerned and, waving the script at him, saying, "Don't you understand, he's saying?" And there would follow a paraphrase, delivered with passionate intensity, in colloquial (but colloquially unShakespearian) language, of what the author had originally written. Both Yankelovich and that director understood that *meaning* is in the *context*. The function of a deliberative forum is to provide that context for what is otherwise merely ephemeral opinion—or a prejudice that has not yet been allowed the mercy of fading.

In a popular television soap opera, some time back, an elderly man, learning that he is in the early stages of Alzheimer's, quietly, poignantly, expresses the wish that "the darkness would come faster." A few minutes later (representing a few days in screenplay time), he asks that a cherished watch be repaired because, he says, "time matters." These are both *opinions*; neither is "true" or "false." Nor is truth somewhere between them, as consensus and compromise are sought between two extreme points of a line of argument. They coexist equally, they are irreducible—like the unyielding tension of hope and despair in the one old man's diminishing life. In institutional political arrangements, it is more often the case that compromise and consensus are located on an *arc* between two points, nearer to one than the other, or at the apex of a triangle further from both than the midpoint between them. But in politics, as in other experiences of living, different truths really continue to coexist in tension: expectation and fear, hope and despair. Imagine a broad field of understanding from which opinions spring and where they will no doubt continue to seed. Such a field of partial understandings, so to speak, is where public deliberation comes into bloom.

Why, then, are political writers instinctively reluctant to report from deliberation the "geography" of this field and what in fact it can yield? Why do they masquerade so often in the ill-fitting costume of the social scientist? Yet we do! Uneasy about what a public voice might be saying, we look for the comfort that the social scientist typically finds in random and representative samples, in percentage differences and margins of error. Yet vaunted public opinion is *not* what we devotees of democracy—and deliberation—have to report; that is *not* the battle that we have to fight—although candidates for elective office, who live by the business of numbers, inevitably appear to. What we learn from deliberation is about the relationships between seeming contraries. As the poet John Donne noted, "to vex me, contraries meet in one!" Judgment depends less upon a triumph between them than upon the recognition of those contraries. And deliberation enables us to acknowledge that our lives are themselves energized and generous to the degree that we understand this paradox of mortality. Our business, as a democratic people, is to cope with it; for, left to themselves, institutional governments, even supposedly productive ones, tend inevitably to serve the rich and powerful, the oligarchies that sustain them—especially in contemporary elective governments, where the election may be brief but the campaign seemingly everlasting!

What uniquely we can present when we report from public deliberation is the *tension* that lies between seemingly irreconcilable views; and what we learn when it yields or is sustained; and how that knowledge affects people, our fellow citizens. What was absolutely astonishing about preparing the immigration issue for television a few years ago—and enormously gratifying in preparing the televised *A Public Voice*, year after year—was to find that underlying the conversation of the leaders and experts at the Press Club, in almost every single response (and certainly in every sequence of responses), were clear indications that participants in the circle of experts and politicians recognized and understood the value of precisely the kind of understanding—the kind of "coming to know together"—revealed in the videos of citizens in deliberation. Time and again, panelists pointed back to the expression of a conscious awareness of ambiguity by one or another of the forum participants; and in any given instance, what was at issue politically was not whether the citizens on the tapes offered an answer that was better or worse than any other, but whether it implied a course of action *in the context of the understood situation*—in effect, a means *toward* public *judgment,* in relation to an issue in tension.

There was, for example—and we have mentioned it, in passing, in Chapter 3—the interesting exchange during deliberation on immigration, when one of our Press Club gurus insisted that forum participants should have addressed the terrorism concern (on which they had been notably silent)—and all of the other panelists ganged up to explain to her, not that there wasn't a genuine reason to be concerned about terrorism in that context, but why that was *not* the concern of these members of the public in the context of deliberation about the immigration problem *as they experienced it.* The discussion in fact culminated in a remarkable exchange between Frank Sesno, the on-camera moderator of the event, and three members of the panel:

> Richard Harwood: I think there's a great example of where blanket labels don't work. You know, we want to apply a single label to every person who's coming over the border and assume that everyone is the same. What I heard people saying in this tape is: "Some of these folks are making my salad that I'm eating at a restaurant. They're helping mow our lawns. They're helping run the chicken factories"—whatever they're doing.
>
> Frank Sesno: But why wasn't I hearing, Richard, anybody saying: "Some of these folks may be plotting the next terrorist attack."
>
> Richard Harwood: Because I don't think they believe that some of those folks *are*. A lot of these folks are part and parcel of their daily lives. That is different than the folks that they may fear who are going to come into this country and do terrorist acts. There is a fundamental —
>
> Frank Sesno: That's a very fundamental difference from the debate that we have and hear a lot, right here in this town [Washington, DC].
>
> Doris Meissner: People know that these people are not the terrorists.
>
> Frank Sesno: Somebody may be . . .
>
> Doris Meissner: Well, somebody may be. But people do not associate the folks that are doing the chicken and the mushroom picking with terrorism. . . . Now it may well be that . . . the ways in which those people get to this country also create the circumstances that—that should make us worry about terrorism. But those two are not the same thing, I find, where the *people* are concerned.

> Mirta Ojito: I actually think that the reason they didn't bring it up, is that when people talk about undocumented immigrants in this country, they think Mexicans. And I don't think they "feel" Mexicans in that way. I think that they know that Mexicans are not by and large terrorists; and Mexicans happen to be the people who work in their gardens, and their nannies, and the people who work in the supermarkets. And we feel we know them. We may fear them for other reasons, but it has nothing to do with terrorism.

The same kind of difference was apparent, too, when another of the expert panelists complained, prematurely, that there was nobody advocating the building of a 20-foot wall at the border, and Frank Sesno responded, "They will." And they did! Not that there was any widespread, public sense that such a wall *should* be built. But there was a clear sense that *the problem* must be addressed in a way that considered the potential import and impact of a 20-foot wall. And of a work permit. And of a somewhat immoderate US appetite for goods. And of a welcome for aliens.

What public deliberation has to give us is not "what the opinion poll gives us, only more so." Nor does it seek a vote for one policy rather than another. Nor is it *merely* an exercise in the development of a rationally agreed judgment. In the brilliant essay (from which we have already quoted) that Noëlle McAfee contributed to *Public Thought and Foreign Policy,* the volume that Kettering published about the National Issues Convention in Philadelphia in 2003, McAfee carefully draws the distinction between that convention's use of the deliberative validation of public opinion—the Habermasian concept of a rational dialogue to find the most logically persuasive argument—and what we here call *public deliberation*. The latter model, she writes—and it is the model we are examining in this book

> aims at getting participants to arrive at a choice that takes into consideration other participants' concerns, aiming for a choice that reflects a considered, public judgment on the issue. Through their deliberations, deliberators come to see possible outlines for public action. And they come to see themselves as part of a public, as public actors with considered judgments and purposes who can help shape policy.

And McAfee points out that when people come together to deliberate on matters that affect their polities, they seem to transform what were personal concerns and interests into *public* ones.

Participants focus on solving public problems in ways that are consistent with their publicly formed understandings and ends. They do not separate political ends from the fact that they are living with other people who are also affected—sometimes quite differently—by these policy choices. Instead of seeing politics as a matter of bargaining about preferences, they see politics as a different matter—of deciding what kinds of communities they are making for themselves. Nor does public deliberation offer the triumph of reason (as does Habermas). It does, however, suggest to us when rhetorical gestures or half measures will fail; and it does tell us what minimal achievement will entail. The public voice seldom echoes exactly what the press has chosen for its headlines. And it is far too frank and complex for today's elected and appointed political leaders to cope with directly, because *they* may often function in more immediate relationship to a special interest than to a public good.

There can be a problem for the *public* interest in a special-interest society (as some have noted in past years in the health-care "arguments" on Capitol Hill). It is anomalous for political leaders to steer a course with quiet integrity through oceans of political icebergs, to juggle interest groups that, as it were, can't be met in the same room together. Exponents of given ideologies experience comparable difficulties when their political message does not meet at all points the practical concerns of the public-with-a-voice; or when, somewhere between the political establishment and the experts, they are caught in the "beltway" trap, where the agenda of "important" topics (which most often also infer accepted solutions) has been predetermined. That is why the National Issues Forums were able to present, for almost 20 years, through video extracts of the commentary of politicians and professionals, a useful opportunity—because of subject matter and personalities—to examine what the real aim of a distinctively *public* voice might be in a democracy, where the sovereign citizens may be revealed moving *toward* judgment about "what should be."

The public voice is seldom the voice that the establishment—the political, corporate, and press establishments—is anxious to hear. And unless we are prepared to present and explain the *dilemmas* that the public acknowledges and is preparing to cope with—rather than primarily the *opinions* that people in their uncertainty express—we might as well leave the public voice at home, or in its many homes. What that voice tells us is not what public opinion *is*, but *why* those opinions have been voiced and *what dilemmas* they lay before us. Insofar as choices *are* made, public deliberation will tell us what legs of fear and hope they rest on—and with what sacrifices they must expect to be bought.

When we began our study of public deliberation close to 30 years ago, we did not use the word *deliberation*. The phrase *working through* was our way of describing what people did in modest deliberative gatherings. The phrase was borrowed, as we have noted, from psychologists, who use the phrase sometimes to describe what is called a "grief reaction": the process by which people tend to work their way through the seemingly instinctively experienced emotional states that follow upon the sudden loss, for example, of a loved one—states including pain, anger, blame, guilt, depression, and despair—before they recover normal emotional stability. Similarly (the idea went), people get together to "work their way through" the concerns, attitudes, opinions, hopes, and fears that they form in response to problems in their shared life as a *polis*. It was a good metaphor, for it implied, perceptively, that the process entailed shared talk, thought, and *work*, in response to circumstances for the generation of which participants themselves might often bear no individual responsibility. It was a useful metaphor for public deliberative politics. This process of working through provides us with, in fact, a unique opportunity to present to legislators and to a broader public, by means of various reports, the understandings that some professionals and deliberative fellow citizens may have made from their experiences of public deliberations, issue by issue.

As we have seen, when people come to acknowledge a shared problem, they first identify it as it appears to them individually, in their many different ways. What is at issue first is, then, in a real sense, the naming of the problem, since each of us may have a slightly different sense of what is problematic about a given situation of uncertain import. But before we can deliberate and figure out together how best to approach whatever we decide the problem to be, we must first frame the issue in public terms. That is to say, we must (through careful research) sort out into manageable groups, or "sets," the different ways in which different people seem to see the problem, according to their individual concerns, fears, hopes, and values. If we do well that job of "framing up" what is genuinely at issue when we all face the shared problem, then we will see the astonishing process of deliberation unfold its truth. We agree on a general "name" for the *problem* that we share; but at *issue* are the differing ways in which we think of it—the differing ways in which we each seem to be naming and renaming it, according to our limited experiences that grow more extensive—less limited—as we come to share an understanding of the experiences of others.

In Daniel Yankelovich's *Coming to Public Judgment,* it seems, the critical word is *coming*. For it is in the process of *coming* to judgment that the public exercises its sovereignty. At the last, as thoughtful and scholarly critics, we must caution ourselves against any tendency to pass judgments on that deliberative public whose goals we are in fact attempting to identify. And assist in their pursuit! The stages in our movement toward a *public* judgment are not measures on a rule; nor are they regimental drills or strategies in a campaign. They are not always experienced in sequence, nor by every citizen at the same time. The real beauty is that they are the practice of democracy itself, the means by which democracy does "work as it should." They are the "tents" in which democracy lives, within which government can formulate the viable statute. The judgments themselves are never eternal—perhaps happily so—but the continuing processes of *coming* to public judgment are the life of democracy. As such, they are worth evaluation, from time to time, in relation to the public's problems, the recurring dilemmas of our passing years.

Acknowledgments . . . and a Note on the Sources

ALTHOUGH THE (LARGELY) ARCHIVAL materials from which this volume quotes (or that it refers to) are identified, those who have contributed to this book are too many to be named here. They include, for example, all of those people who, committed to the idea of our American democracy, have convened public forums, or moderated them, or taken advantage of the privilege of citizenship (or of being guests on our shores) to contribute in such meetings their current thinking—albeit sometimes tentative, sometimes a mite too assured. They include also the incredibly patient and eloquent interviewers and analysts who, in seemingly endless meetings with both fellow citizens and fellow professionals, have shaped what they had heard in interviews and focus groups into discussion guides that were balanced, fair, complete, yet eminently readable by those who hadn't the advantage of their own professional training. And they include other writers, too, some of them referred to in these pages, who had the courage and the will to present formal reports of these "citizen" events to members of Congress, as well as to several administrations in Washington, DC, and in a number of states.

Deep appreciation is offered similarly for the professional services of Milton Hoffman and his television crews, who captured almost every one of the public forums referred to here, from all over the country, at the rate of half-a-dozen or so each year, for 16 years, in broadcast-quality video form that could be edited down to critical minutes of conversation, usefully shared with members of Congress and the Washington press corps in *A Public Voice*, broadcast each year from the National Press Club in Washington, DC, through public television stations across the United States. This book includes, too, a number of thoughts, even sentences, that were first presented as parts of this writer's contribution to a short essay, "The Experience of the National Issues Forums," co-authored two years ago with Keith Melville, in *Toward Wiser Public Judgment*, edited by Daniel Yankelovich and Will Friedman, and published in 2011 by Vanderbilt University Press. The idea for this book took shape at the time of that writing; and the publisher's permission to include excerpts from that material in this book, without specific reference, is deeply appreciated.

Finally, the author's appreciation and gratitude must be expressed to long-time friends and associates John Dedrick, Harris Dienstfrey, John Doble, Richard Harwood, David Holwerk, Jean Johnson, Noëlle McAfee, and Keith Melville—and to Sarah Dahm, his guide and assistant, throughout this labor. They have not only shared, variously, many of the experiences observed in this book, but have contributed what might otherwise have been more valuable hours of their time, to exploring, extending, or correcting both the thoughts that inform it and the author's attempts to express them.

Occasional references to and quotations from other works are acknowledged in the text as they occur. Almost all of the sources for this exploration of the patterns of public thinking on political issues, however, are to be found in the archives of the Kettering Foundation. They include primarily the following materials:

1. Issue guides, prepared annually for participants in National Issues Forums, beginning in 1982, by, variously, Keith Melville, Michael de Courcy Hinds, Julie Pratt, Gloria Danziger, Richard Harwood, Tony Wharton, David Patton, Gerald Orr, Steven Mitchell, Brad Rourke, Julie Fisher, and Fanny Flono. Similar issue guides have been prepared for local use by various institutions, and produced for the National Issues Forums Institute, through the Kettering Foundation, by various publishers. Routinely, from 1982 until 2000, the Kettering Foundation encouraged and helped prepare for extensive public deliberation on three issues each year. Occasionally, and routinely of recent years, the foundation has produced fewer guides annually.
2. Narrative reports on the forums, nationally, for each given year from 1983 to 1990, written by Keith Melville and published by the Kettering Foundation.
3. During the first eight years of the National Issues Forums' work, a summer meeting of many of the organizers and participants was convened annually in Washington, DC, so that they might report to each other and to their congressional representatives, and to the White House, of their purposes and findings. No formal minutes or reports were issued from such meetings, although two one-hour video records were broadcast on The Learning Channel (in the years 1983 and 1984); and two televised "forum dialogues," in which some half dozen congressional participants and 50 or so NIF participants joined, were produced for the Kettering Foundation and circulated although not broadcast. Such records as these were reviewed as this book was written but are not specifically referenced within it.
4. Similarly, in each of the early years 1983-1987, outcomes of the preceding year were reviewed in formal conferences of two days at

the Presidential Libraries of Presidents Ford, Kennedy, Johnson, and Carter, then again Ford (in that sequence) over the five years. The first of these is referenced in the text because it is the most useful evidence we have of that first experiment in organized public deliberation, and its potential for government, formally. The complete five-year sequence, however, was invaluable in giving the experiment its legitimacy, and has led to a maintained if various continuance, including the sponsorship of such public forums by the Presidential Libraries and a continued willingness of the Federal Department of Archives to offer its generous hospitality to the Kettering Foundation and the National Issues Forums Institute at the National Archives in Washington, DC.

5. Analytic reports on the forums, nationally, written each year from 1993 to 2008, by John Doble, and published by the Kettering Foundation. (Comparable analytic reports were produced also on the specific issues of alcohol abuse, by Paul Werth Associates, in 2001, and by Maxine Thomas on Americans' attitudes toward China, in 2005.)
6. Complete unedited video recordings of NIF forums, on various issues and from various US communities (usually four to six different communities each year), from 1991 to 2007, produced by Milton Hoffman Productions (Robert J. Kingston, executive producer).
7. *A Public Voice*, a 60-minute television program produced by Milton Hoffman Productions (Robert J. Kingston, executive producer) for the Kettering Foundation, staged at the National Press Club in Washington, DC, and broadcast nationwide each year from 1991 to 2007, by PBS. Each program presents a panel of congressional representatives, DC journalists, and experts on the given topic, responding, in 3 progressive segments, each of

approximately 10 minutes, to the pattern of public thinking as edited down from the footage described in # 6, above, into 3 progressive segments of public deliberation, each of approximately 7 minutes in length. The first *A Public Voice* television presentations each included three annual issues, but subsequent broadcast programs presented only one, although in both 1993 and 1995, two National Press Club video programs were staged and broadcast nationally. The complete list follows.

Date	Subject and Location	Panel Members	Moderator
1991	The Battle Over Abortion Regaining the Competitive Edge Remedies for Racial Inequality	Paul Duke, *Wash. Week in Review* Ellen Goodman, *Boston Globe* Charlayne Hunter-Gault, *MacNeil-Lehrer NewsHour* Frank Sesno, CNN Rep. William H. Gray III, Pennsylvania Rep. James Leach, Iowa Rep. Mary Rose Oakar, Ohio Sen. Paul Wellstone, Minnesota Rev. Wendell Manuel, Trinity Presbyterian Church, Mississippi David Mathews, Kettering Foundation Maxine Thomas, Univ. of Georgia Law School Daniel Yankelovich, Public Agenda Foundation	Bob Kingston, Kettering Foundation

Date	Subject and Location	Panel Members	Moderator
1992	America's Role in the World Energy Options The Boundaries of Free Speech	David Gergen, *U.S. News & World Report* Ellen Goodman, *Boston Globe* Charlayne Hunter-Gault, *MacNeil-Lehrer NewsHour* Frank Sesno, CNN Sen. John H. Chafee, Rhode Island Rep. E. Thomas Coleman, Missouri Sen. Joseph I. Lieberman, Connecticut Rep. Louise M. Slaughter, New York Sen. Timothy E. Wirth, Colorado William H. Gray III, United Negro College Fund David Mathews, Kettering Foundation Daniel Yankelovich, Public Agenda Foundation	Bob Kingston, Kettering Foundation
1993	Governing America	David Gergen, *U.S. News & World Report* Ellen Goodman, *Boston Globe* Charlayne Hunter-Gault, *MacNeil-Lehrer NewsHour* Jack Nelson, *Los Angeles Times* William H. Gray III, United Negro College Fund David Mathews, Kettering Foundation Richard C. Harwood, The Harwood Group	Bob Kingston, Kettering Foundation

Date	Subject and Location	Panel Members	Moderator
1993	Governing America (cont.)	Sen. Pete V. Domenici, New Mexico Rep. Jane Harman, California Sen. John F. Kerry, Massachusetts Sen. Richard G. Lugar, Indiana Rep. Eleanor Holmes Norton, Dist. of Columbia	Bob Kingston, Kettering Foundation
1993	Prescription for Prosperity Health Care Crisis Criminal Violence	David Gergen, *U.S. News & World Report* Ellen Goodman, *Boston Globe* Charlayne Hunter-Gault, *MacNeil-Lehrer NewsHour* Frank Sesno, CNN Sen. Nancy Kassebaum, Kansas Sen. Robert J. Kerrey, Nebraska Rep. Jay C. Kim, California Sen. Patrick J. Leahy, Vermont Rep. Marjorie Margolies-Mezvinsky, Pennsylvania Rep. Craig A. Washington, Texas David Mathews, Kettering Foundation Daniel Yankelovich, Public Agenda Foundation	Bob Kingston, Kettering Foundation

Date	Subject and Location	Panel Members	Moderator
1994	Health Care Cost Explosion Poverty Puzzle The $4 Trillion Debt	Barbara Cochran, *CBS News* Sen. William Cohen, Maine Sen. Thomas Daschle, South Dakota E.J. Dionne, *Washington Post* David Gergen, Counselor to the President Sen. Patty Murray, Washington Rep. Nancy Johnson, Connecticut David Mathews, Kettering Foundation Michel McQueen, *ABC News* Frank Sesno, CNN Robin Toner, *New York Times* Daniel Yankelovich, Public Agenda	Bob Kingston, Kettering Foundation
NEH 1995	Contested Values	Sen. John Ashcroft, Missouri Sen. John Breaux, Louisiana Rep. Lee Hamilton, Indiana Rep. Connie Morella, Maryland Barbara Reynolds, *USA Today* Claudio Sanchez, National Public Radio	Bob Kingston, Kettering Foundation

Date	Subject and Location	Panel Members	Moderator
NEH 1995	Contested Values (cont.)	Frank Sesno, CNN Sheldon Hackney, National Endowment for the Humanities David Mathews, Kettering Foundation Jean Bethke Elshtain, University of Chicago James Davidson Hunter, University of Virginia Kevin Phillips, American Political Research Corporation Alvin Thornton, Howard University	Bob Kingston, Kettering Foundation
1995	Juvenile Violence Immigration	Sen. Bob Graham, Florida Sen. Harry Reid, Nevada Sen. Richard Shelby, Alabama Sen. Craig Thomas, Wyoming Suzanne Fields, *Los Angeles Times* Syndicate Georgie Anne Geyer, Universal Press Syndicate Robert Siegel, National Public Radio David Mathews, Kettering Foundation Roger Wilkins, George Mason University Daniel Yankelovich, Public Agenda	Bob Kingston, Kettering Foundation

Date	Subject and Location	Panel Members	Moderator
1996	The Troubled American Family	Sen. Dan Coats, Indiana E.J. Dionne, *Washington Post* Rep. Chaka Fattah, Pennsylvania Georgie Anne Geyer, Universal Press Syndicate Sheldon Hackney, National Endowment for the Humanities Richard Harwood, The Harwood Group Gwen Ifill, *NBC News* David Mathews, Kettering Foundation Lynn Neary, National Public Radio Rep. Marge Roukema, New Jersey	David Gergen, *U.S. News & World Report*
1997	The National Piggybank: Does Our Retirement System Need Fixing?	Jodie Allen, *Slate* Candy Crowley, CNN E.J. Dionne, *Washington Post* Jim Glassman, *US News, Washington Post* Sen. Kay Bailey Hutchison, Texas Rep. Barbara Kennelly, Connecticut Sen. Richard Lugar, Indiana David Mathews, Kettering Foundation Rep. Mark Sanford, South Carolina Roger Wilkins, George Mason University Dan Yankelovich, Public Agenda	David Gergen, *U.S. News & World Report*

Date	Subject and Location	Panel Members	Moderator
1998	Governing America: Our Choices, Our Challenge	E.J. Dionne, *Washington Post* Rep. Chaka Fattah, Pennsylvania Sen. Tim Johnson, South Dakota Sen. John F. Kerry, Massachusetts Sen. Frank Lautenberg, New Jersey David Mathews, Kettering Foundation Michel McQueen, ABC Rep. Sue Myrick, North Carolina Frank Sesno, CNN Sen. Gordon Smith, Oregon Ray Suarez, National Public Radio Dan Yankelovich, Public Agenda	David Gergen, *U.S. News & World Report*
1999	What Goes on the Internet?	Linda Chavez, Syndicated Columnist Rep. Chaka Fattah, Pennsylvania Sen. Bill Frist, Tennessee Sen. Kay Bailey Hutchison, Texas David Mathews, Kettering Foundation Michel McQueen, *ABC News* Lisa Napoli, *New York Times, Cybertimes* Soledad O'Brien, MSNBC Sen. Jack Reed, Rhode Island Frank Sesno, CNN	David Gergen, *U.S. News & World Report*

Date	Subject and Location	Panel Members	Moderator
2000	Public Schools: Are They Making the Grade?	Sen. Evan Bayh, Indiana Sen. Susan Collins, Maine E.J. Dionne, *Washington Post* W. Wilson Goode, Deputy Asst. Secretary, US Department of Education (former Mayor of Philadelphia) Sen. Chuck Hagel, Nebraska June Kronholz, *Wall Street Journal* David Mathews, Kettering Foundation Rep. Anne Northup, Kentucky Frank Sesno, CNN Roger Wilkins, George Mason University	David Gergen, *U.S. News & World Report*
2001	Money & Politics	Candy Crowley, CNN, Inc. Rep. Elijah Cummings, Maryland E. J. Dionne, *Washington Post* Richard Harwood, The Harwood Institute Gov. Mike Johanns, Nebraska Jill Lawrence, *USA Today* David Mathews, Kettering Foundation Rep. Christopher Shays, Connecticut Sen. Debbie Stabenow, Michigan	Frank Sesno, CNN America, Inc.

Date	Subject and Location	Panel Members	Moderator
2001	Money & Politics (cont.)	Sen. Craig Thomas, Wyoming Juan Williams, National Public Radio	Frank Sesno, CNN America, Inc.
2002	Racial and Ethnic Tensions	Ward Bushee, *Cincinnati Enquirer* Linda Chavez, Center for Equal Opportunity Hon. Elijah Cummings, Maryland E.J. Dionne, Brookings Institution Richard Harwood, The Harwood Institute Hon. Marc Racicot, Chairman, Republican National Comm. Barbara Reynolds, Reynolds News Service Hon. Kay Granger, Texas Roger Wilkins, George Mason University Hon. David Wu, Oregon Sumaiya Hamdani, George Mason University	Frank Sesno, CNN America, Inc.
2003	Terrorism	Alison Bethel, Washington Bureau Chief, *Detroit News* Charles Bierbauer, University of South Carolina, School of Journalism Rep. Marsha Blackburn, Tennessee E.J. Dionne, *Washington Post* Richard Harwood, The Harwood Institute	Frank Sesno, CNN America, Inc.

Date	Subject and Location	Panel Members	Moderator
2003	Terrorism (cont.)	David Mathews, Kettering Foundation Rep. Anne Northup, Kentucky Gen. Dennis Reimer (Ret.), Memorial Institute for the Prevention of Terrorism Sen. Jeff Sessions, Alabama Sen. Debbie Stabenow, Michigan Sen. John Sununu, New Hampshire	Frank Sesno, CNN America, Inc.
2004	Health Care	Georges Benjamin, MD Rep. Allen Boyd, Florida Marsha Lillie-Blanton, Henry J. Kaiser Family Foundation E. J. Dionne, *Washington Post* Richard Harwood, The Harwood Institute David Mathews, Kettering Foundation Rep. Tim Murphy, Pennsylvania Sen. Jeff Sessions, Alabama Joanne Silberner, National Public Radio Sen. Debbie Stabenow, Michigan	Frank Sesno, CNN America, Inc.
2005	Immigration	John Fund, *Wall Street Journal* Dan Griswold, Director, Center for Trade Policy Studies Cato Institute	Frank Sesno, CNN America, Inc.

Date	Subject and Location	Panel Members	Moderator
2005	Immigration (cont.)	Richard Hardwood, Harwood Institute Tamar Jacoby, The Manhattan Institute Rep. James Leach, Iowa Rep. Sheila Jackson-Lee, Texas Pat McGinnis, The Council for Excellence in Government Doris Meissner, Migration Policy Mirta Ojito, *New York Times* Rep. Silvestre Reyes, Texas	Frank Sesno, CNN America, Inc.
2006	Facing Democracy's Challenge	Rep. Allen Boyd, Florida Cole Campbell, Dean, Reynolds School of Journalism Rep. Elijah Cummings, Maryland E.J. Dionne, The Brookings Institution, and syndicated columnist, the *Washington Post* Richard Harwood, President, the Harwood Institute, and author, *Hope Unraveled* Michel Martin, Program Host, National Public Radio, and Contributing Correspondent, *ABC News* David Mathews, Kettering Foundation	Frank Sesno, CNN America, Inc.

Date	Subject and Location	Panel Members	Moderator
2006	Facing Democracy's Challenge (cont.)	Lynn Neary, Host and Correspondent, National Public Radio Sen.Jeff Sessions, Alabama Jill Zuckerman, Chief Congressional Correspondent, *Chicago Tribune*	Frank Sesno, CNN America, Inc.
2007	Energy	E.J. Dionne, *Washington Post* Betty Sue Flowers, Lyndon Baines Johnson Library and Museum Jay Hakes, Jimmy Carter Library Mike Johanns, US Secretary of Agriculture Sen. Mary Landrieu, Louisiana David Mathews, Kettering Foundation Rep. Charles Gonzalez, Texas Andrea Seabrook, National Public Radio Sen. Jeff Sessions, Alabama Jerry Taylor, CATO Institute Roger Wilkins, Author and Analyst	Frank Sesno, CNN America, Inc.

8. Analytic commentary on each A Public Voice program recording made annually at the National Press Club from 1991-1995, with additional transcribed excerpts from participating forums, by Robert J. Kingston and John Doble, and published by the Kettering Foundation.
9. Analytic Kettering Foundation memoranda by Robert J. Kingston on the patterns of public thinking, nationally, circulated (but not published) prior to the presentation and filming of A Public Voice, each year at the National Press Club, from 1995-2008.
10. Within the past 20 years, a number of institutions—primarily but not exclusively universities, community organizations, and libraries—have convened public forums in the National Issues Forums mode on issues (often of local importance) identified and framed locally. Some of these issues have also been presented nationally through, and encouraged by, the NIF Institute and the Kettering Foundation and with leadership or encouragement from other concerned sponsors who have, in many instances, prepared significant reports, some of which are referred to appropriately in their context in the foregoing pages of this book.

Bibliography

BECAUSE THIS BOOK was conceived as an extended, reflective essay, rather than as a contribution to scholarly knowledge, neither footnotes nor endnotes appear on its pages. Specific references to published works are documented within the text itself, but for those who may be interested in pursuing incidental quotations or occasionally more substantive references further, the following brief checklist may be helpful.

Ackerman, Bruce, and James S. Fishkin. *Deliberation Day*. New Haven, CT: Yale University Press, 2004.

Bachtiger, Andre, Simon J. Niemeyer, Michael Neblo, Marco R. Steenbergen, and Jurg Steiner. "Disentangling Diversity in Deliberative Democracy: Competing Theories, Their Blind Spots and Complementarities." *The Journal of Political Philosophy* 18 (1) (2010): 32-63.

Barber, Benjamin R. *Strong Democracy: Participatory Politics for a New Age*. Berkeley: University of California Press, 1984.

Barber, Benjamin R. "Civic Schizophrenia: The Free Consumer and the Free Citizen in a Free-Market Society." *Kettering Review* :10-21 (Spring 2006) 24 (1).

Bellah, Robert N., Richard Madsen, William M. Sullivan, and Ann Swidler. *Habits of the Heart: Individualism and Commitment in American Life*. Berkeley: University of California Press,1984.

Bellah, Robert N. *The Good Society*. New York: Alfred A. Knopf, 1991.

Benhabib, Seyla, ed. *Democracy and Difference: Contesting the Boundaries of the Political.* Princeton, NJ: Princeton University Press, 1996.

Benhabib, Seyla, Ian Shapiro, and Danilo Petranović, eds. *Identities, Affiliations, and Allegiances.* New York: Cambridge University Press, 2007.

Bessette, Joseph M. *The Mild Voice of Reason: Deliberative Democracy and American National Government.* Chicago: University of Chicago Press, 1997.

Bohman, James, and William Rehg, eds. *Deliberative Democracy: Essays on Reason and Politics.* Cambridge, MA: The MIT Press, 1997.

Boyte, Harry. *Everyday Politics.* Philadelphia: University of Pennsylvania Press, 2004.

Boyte, Harry. "Breaking the Silence." *Kettering Review* 24 (1) (Spring 2006): 33-45.

Burns, Nancy, Kay L. Schlozman, and Sydney Verba. *The Private Roots of Public Action: Gender, Equality, and Political Participation.* Cambridge, MA: Harvard University Press, 2001.

Button, Mark, and David M. Ryfe. "What Can We Learn from the Practice of Deliberative Democracy?" In *The Deliberative Democracy Handbook: Strategies for Effective Civic Engagement in the 21st Century,* edited by John Gastil and Peter Levine, 20-33. San Francisco: Jossey-Bass, 2005.

Campbell, Cole C. "Journalism and Public Knowledge." *Kettering Review* 25 (1) (Winter 2007): 39-49.

Chambers, Simone. "Deliberation and Mass Democracy: Counting Voices and Making Voices Count." Paper presented at the annual meeting for the American Political Science Association, Toronto, Canada, September 3-6, 2009.

Coelho, Vera Schattan P., Barbara Pozzoni, and Mariana Cifuentes Montoya. "Participation and Public Policies in Brazil." In *The Deliberative Democracy Handbook: Strategies for Effective Civic Engagement in the 21st Century,* edited by John Gastil and Peter Levine, 174-184. San Francisco: Jossey-Bass, 2005.

Cohen, Joshua. "Procedure and Substance in Deliberative Democracy." In *Democracy and Difference: Contesting the Boundaries of the Political,* edited by Seyla Benhabib, 95-119. Princeton: Princeton University Press, 1996.

Cohen, Joshua. "Deliberation and Democratic Legitimacy." In *Deliberative Democracy: Essays on Reason and Politics,* edited by James Bohman and William Rehg, 67-92. Cambridge, MA: The MIT Press, 1997.

Cohen, Joshua. "Deliberative Democracy." In *Democracy, Deliberation, and Participation: Can the People Govern?* edited by Shawn W. Rosenberg, 219-236. London: Palgrave Macmillan, 2007 .

Cohen, Joshua, and Archon Fung. "Radical Democracy." *Swiss Journal of Political Science* 10 (4) (2004): 23-34.

Colapietro, Vincent. "Democracy as a Moral Ideal." *Kettering Review* 24 (3)(Fall 2006): 21-31.

Cortes Jr., Ernesto. "Toward a Democractic Culture." *Kettering Review* 24 (1) (Spring 2006): 46-57.

Dahl, Robert A. *Democracy and its Critics.* New Haven, CT: Yale University Press, 1989.

DeBardeleben, Jon J.P. *Activating the Citizen: Dilemmas of Participation in Europe and Canada.* London: Palgrave MacMillan, 2009.

Delli Carpini, Michael X., Fay L. Cook, and Lawrence R. Jacobs. "Public Deliberation, Discursive Participation, and Citizen Engagement: A Review of the Empirical Literature." *Annual Review of Political Science* 7 (1) (2004): 315-344.

Delli Carpini, Michael X., Leonie Huddy, and Robert Y. Shapiro, eds. *Political Decision-Making, Deliberation and Participation*. Amsterdam: JAI, 2002.

Doble, John. "The Times, Are They a'Changin'?" *Kettering Review* 25 (1) (Winter 2007): 50-61.

Dryzek, John S. *Deliberative Democracy and Beyond: Liberals, Critics, Contestations*. Oxford: Oxford University Press, 2000.

Eliasoph, Nina. *Avoiding Politics: How Americans Produce Apathy in Everyday Life*. Cambridge: Cambridge University Press, 1998.

Estlund, David. "Beyond Fairness and Deliberation: The Epistemic Dimension of Democratic Authority." In *Deliberative Democracy: Essays on Reason in Politics*, edited by J. Bohman and W. Rehg, 173-204. Cambridge MA: The MIT Press, 1997.

Fagotto, Elena, and Archon Fung. *Sustaining Public Engagement: Embedded Deliberation in Local Communities*. Occasional research paper. East Hartford, CT: Everyday Democracy and Kettering Foundation, 2009.

Fishkin, James S. *Democracy and Deliberation*. New Haven, CT: Yale University Press, 1991.

Fishkin, James S. *When the People Speak: Deliberative Democracy and Public Consultation*. Oxford: Oxford University Press, 2009.

Fishkin, James S., and Cynthia Farrar. "Deliberative Polling: From Experiment to Community Resource." In *The Deliberative Democracy Handbook: Strategies for Effective Civic Engagement in the 21st Century*, edited by John Gastil and Peter Levine, 68-79. San Francisco: Jossey-Bass, 2005.

Fung, Archon. *Empowered Participation: Reinventing Urban Democracy*. Princeton, NJ: Princeton University Press, 2004.

Fung, Archon. "Deliberation before the Revolution: Toward an Ethics of Deliberation in an Unjust World." *Political Theory* 33 (2) (2005): 397-419.

Gastil, John. *By Popular Demand: Revitalizing Representative Democracy through Deliberative Elections*. Berkley, CA: University of California Press, 2000.

Gastil, John, and Peter Levine, eds. *The Deliberative Democracy Handbook: Strategies for Effective Civic Engagement in the 21st Century*. San Francisco: Jossey-Bass, 2005.

Goodin, Robert E. *Reflective Democracy*. Oxford: Oxford University Press, 2003.

Goodin, Robert E., and Simon J. Niemeyer. "When Does Deliberation Begin? Internal Reflection Versus Public Discussion in Deliberative Democracy." *Political Studies* 51 (2003): 627-649.

Grisham, Jr., Vaughn L. *Tupelo: The Evolution of a Community*. Dayton, OH: Kettering Foundation Press, 1999.

Guinier, Lani. "Sustaining Democracy." *Kettering Review* 24 (1) (Spring 2006): 22-32.

Gutmann, Amy, and Dennis F. Thompson. *Democracy and Disagreement*. Cambridge, MA: Harvard University Press, 1996.

Gutmann, Amy. *Why Deliberative Democracy?* Princeton: Princeton University Press, 2004.

Gutmann, Nurit. "Bringing the Mountain to the Public: Dilemmas and Contradictions in the Procedures of Public Deliberation Initiatives That Aim to Get 'Ordinary Citizens' to Deliberate Policy Issues." *Communication Theory* 17 (4) (2007): 411-438.

Habermas, Jürgen. *Moral consciousness and communicative action*. Translated by C. Lenhardt and S.W. Nicholson. Cambridge, MA: The MIT Press, 1990.

The Harwood Group. *Citizens and Politics: A View from Main Street America*. Dayton, OH: Report prepared for the Kettering Foundation, 1991.

Harwood, Richard C. *Hope Unraveled: The People's Retreat and Our Way Back*. Dayton, OH: Kettering Foundation Press, 2005.

Jacobs, Lawrence R., Fay Lomax Cook, and Michael X. Delli Carpini. *Talking Together: Public Deliberation and Political Participation in America*. Chicago: University of Chicago Press, 2009.

Kadlec, Allison, and Will Friedman. "Deliberative Democracy and the Problem of Power." *Journal of Public Deliberation* 3(1) (2007). http://services.bepress.com/jpd/vol3/iss1/art8.

Kemmis, Daniel. "Beyond National Democracy." *Kettering Review* 25(1) (Winter 2007):15-26.

Kingston, Robert J., ed. *Perestroika Papers: An Exercise in Supplemental Diplomacy*. Dubuque, IA: Kendall Hunt Publishing, 1988.

Kingston, Robert J., ed. *Public Thought and Foreign Policy*. Dayton, OH: Kettering Foundation Press, 2005.

Kymlicka, Will, and Bashir Bashir. *The Politics of Reconciliation in Multicultural Societies*. Oxford: Oxford University Press, 2008.

Levine, Peter, Archon Fung, and John Gastil. "Future Directions for Public Deliberation." In *The Deliberative Democracy Handbook: Strategies for Effective Civic Engagement in the 21st Century*, edited by John Gastil and Peter Levine, 271-288. San Francisco: Jossey-Bass, 2005.

Levine, Peter. "Learning and Democracy: Civic Education." *Kettering Review* 24 (3) (Fall 2006): 32-42.

Lippmann, Walter. *Essays in the Public Philosophy*. New York: Little, Brown & Co, 1955.

Lukensmeyer, Carolyn J., Joe Goldman, and Steven Brigham. "A Town Meeting for the Twenty-first Century." In *The Deliberative Democracy Handbook: Strategies for Effective Civic Engagement in the 21st Century*, edited by John Gastil and Peter Levine, 154-163. San Francisco: Jossey-Bass, 2005.

Luskin, Robert C., James S. Fishkin, and Roger Jowell. "Considered Opinions: Deliberative Polling in Britain." *British Journal of Political Science* 32 (2002): 455-487.

Macedo, Stephen, ed. 1999. *Deliberative Politics: Essays on Democracy and Disagreement*. New York: Oxford University Press.

Manin, Bernard, Elly Stein, and Jane Mansbridge. "On Legitimacy and Political Deliberation." *Political Theory* 15 (3) (1987): 338-368.

Mansbridge, Jane. *Beyond Adversary Democracy*. Chicago: University of Chicago Press, 1983.

Mansbridge, Jane. "Everyday Talk in the Deliberative System." In *Deliberative Politics*, edited by Stephen Macedo, 211-239. New York: Oxford University Press, 1999.

Mansbridge, Jane. "Self-Interest in Deliberation." *Kettering Review* 25 (1) (Winter 2007): 62-72.

Mansbridge, Jane, James Bohman, Simone Chambers, David Estlund, Andreas Follesdal, Archon Fung, Cristina Lafont, Bernard Manin, and Jose Luis Marti. "The Place of Self-interest and the Role of Power in Deliberative Democracy." *Journal of Political Philosophy* 18 (1) (2010): 64-100.

Mathews, David. *Is There a Public for Public Schools?* Dayton, OH: Kettering Foundation Press, 1997.

Mathews, David, and Noëlle McAfee. *Making Choices Together: The Power of Public Deliberation*. Dayton, OH: Kettering Foundation, 2003.

Mathews, David. *Politics for People*. Champaign: University of Illinois Press, 1994.

McAfee, Noëlle. "The Myth of Democracy and the Limits of Deliberation." *Kettering Review* 24 (1) (Spring 2006): 58-68.

McAfee, Noëlle. *Democracy and the Political Unconscious*. New York: Columbia University Press, 2008.

McCoy, Martha L., and Patrick L. Scully. "Deliberative Dialogue to Expand Civic Engagement: What Kind of Talk Does Democracy Need?" *National Civic Review* 91 (2) (2002): 117-135.

Neblo, Michael. "Thinking through Democracy: Between the Theory and Practice of Deliberative Politics." *Acta Politica* 40 (2005):169-181.

Neblo, Michael A., Kevin M. Esterling, Ryan P. Kennedy, David M.J. Lazer, and Anand E. Sokhey. "Who Wants to Deliberate—and Why?" *American Political Science Review* 104 (3) (2010): 566-583.

Nisbet, Robert A. *The Quest for Community: A Study in the Ethics of Order and Freedom*. Oxford University Press, 1953.

Sirianni, C. and L. Friedland. *Civic Innovation in America: Community Empowerment, Public Policy, and the Movement for Civic Renewal*. Berkeley: The University of California Press, 2001.

Slim, Randa. "Facing the Challenges of Emerging Democracies." In *Kettering Review* 25 (1) (Winter 2007): 27-38.

Stuhr, John J. "Neither Mission Impossible nor Mission Accomplished: Democracy as Public Experiment." *Kettering Review* 24 (3) (Fall 2006): 9-20.

Tocqueville, Alexisde. *Democracy in America*. Translated by Harvey C. Mansfield and Delba Winthrop. Chicago: University of Chicago Press, 2000.

Walzer, Michael. *On Toleration*. New Haven: Yale University Press, 1997.

Warren, Mark E. *Democracy and Association*. Princeton: Princeton University Press, 2001.

Wolfe, Alan. *Does American Democracy Still Work?* New Haven: Yale University Press, 2006.

Wolin, Sheldon S. *Democracy, Inc.: Managed Democracy and the Specter of Inverted Totalitarianism*. Princeton and Oxford: Princeton University Press, 2008.

Yankelovich, Daniel. *Coming to Public Judgment: Making Democracy Work in a Complex World*. New York: Syracuse University Press, 1991.

Yankelovich, Daniel. *The Magic of Dialogue: Tranforming Conflict into Cooperation*. New York: Simon & Schuster, 1999.

Yankelovich, Daniel, Steve Rosell, Heidi Gantwerk, and Will Friedman. "The Next Big Step in Deliberative Democracy." *Kettering Review* 24 (3) (Fall 2006): 54-66.

Yankelovich, Daniel, and Will Friedman. *Toward Wiser Public Judgment*. Nashville: Vanderbilt University Press, 2011.

Young, Iris Marion. *Inclusion and Democracy*. New York: Oxford University Press, 2000.

Young, Iris Marion. "Activist Challenges to Deliberative Democracy." In *Debating Deliberative Democracy*, edited by James S. Fishkin and Peter Laslett, 102-121. London: Wiley-Blackwell, 2003.

Young, Iris Marion. "De-centering Deliberative Democracy." *Kettering Review* 24 (3) (Fall 2006): 43-53.

Young, Iris Marion, and Jane Mansbridge. "Deliberation's Darker Side: Six Questions for Iris Marion Young and Jane Mansbridge." Interview by Archon Fung. *National Civic Review* 93 (4) (2004): 47-54.

About the Author . . .

Robert J. Kingston

BOB KINGSTON HAS BEEN a senior associate of the Kettering Foundation—a research organization—since 1981, when he was invited to join in shaping what were to become known as the National Issues Forums. Since that time, he has had a hand in virtually all of the foundation's programs, both nationally and internationally. He has been editor of the *Kettering Review* since its inception in 1982, and he served as executive producer of the television program, *A Public Voice*, annually distributed nationwide by PBS from the National Press Club in Washington DC, from 1991 through 2006.

Kingston was born and educated in England and served in the British Army of Occupation in Germany in the 1940s. He took a "first" at Oxford, then served as an assistant tutor at the University International Graduate Summer School in the 1950s, and contributed programs to the BBC's radio and foreign services before coming to the United States in 1954, to teach at the University of Michigan on a one-year, international faculty exchange. He stayed to serve in teaching and administrative positions at several US colleges over the next 15 years—and became a US citizen.

In 1969, Kingston was invited to join the National Endowment for the Humanities, a newly established US federal agency, where, as Deputy Chairman and Acting Chairman in the Nixon, Ford, and Carter administrations, he guided the development of fledgling programs—like the state-based councils on the humanities, international museum exchanges, and early public broadcasting efforts in the humanities, like the *Adams Family Chronicles* and *Sesame Street*. After leaving government service in the late 1970s, Kingston also served as president of the College Board and as executive director of Public Agenda in New York City.